CW00406432

# PALACES FOR PIGS

# PALACES FOR PIGS

## *Animal architecture*

## *and other*

## *beastly buildings*

### LUCINDA LAMBTON

ENGLISH HERITAGE

Published by English Heritage, The Engine House, Fire Fly Avenue, Swindon SN2 2EH
www.english-heritage.org.uk
English Heritage is the Government's statutory adviser on all aspects of the historic
environment.

© Lucinda Lambton 2011

The views expressed in this book are those of the author and not necessarily those of
English Heritage.

Images (except as otherwise shown) © Lucinda Lambton

Every effort has been made to trace other copyright holders and we apologise in
advance for any unintentional omissions, which we would be pleased to correct in any
subsequent edition of this book.

First published 2011

ISBN 978 185074 989 9

Product code 51197

*British Library Cataloguing in Publication data*
A CIP catalogue record for this book is available from the British Library.

**All rights reserved**
No part of this publication may be reproduced or transmitted in any form or by any
means, electronic or mechanical, including photocopying, recording, or any
information storage or retrieval system, without permission in writing from the
publisher.

Brought to publication by René Rodgers, Publishing, English Heritage.

Typeset in Scala 9pt

Edited by Susan Kelleher
Indexed by Chris Dance
Designed by George Hammond

Printed in England by Butler Tanner & Dennis.

*Frontispiece: The horse's head keystone atop the stable arch at Rendcomb in
Gloucestershire. The stable was designed by Philip Charles Hardwick for
Sir F H Goldsmid in 1867.*

*Dedication: Stained glass of some of my dogs, 1992,
by Graham Brant of Cuddington, Buckinghamshire.*

# CONTENTS

DEDICATED TO MY HUSBAND PERRY,

AND TO DOGS PAST AND PRESENT.

# ACKNOWLEDGEMENTS

I would like to thank the following for their great help, kindness, guidance and tolerance, always laced with good humour: Mr G Adams; Derek Adlam (Curator, Portland Collection); Clare Allen; Mr and Mrs L G Allgood; Ian Anstruther; Rene Baker; Lt-Colonel H H Barneby; the Duke and Duchess of Beaufort; the Duke and Duchess of Bedford; Steven Bee; Charles Beresford-Clark; Mr J Berkeley; Mrs Margaret Biggs; Jane Birt; Simon Blow; Mr H Bonfield; Sir William and Lady Boulton; Charlotte Bradbeer; Tony Brainsby; British Telecom (Wotton, Surrey); Mr and Mrs R Brooks; Andy Brown; John Bull; Mr and Mrs R Caffyn; Mr H R M Calder; Richard Carew-Pole; Caroline Carr-Whitworth (Brodsworth Hall, South Yorkshire); the Lady Anne Cavendish-Bentinck; the Dowager Marchioness Cholmondeley; Sir John and Lady Clerk of Penicuik; Timothy and Jane Clifford; the Hon L H L Cohen; Alan Collyer; Patrick Connor; M B Cook; Mrs B Cooke; Julian Cooksey; Roger and Caroline Coombe; Mr A Cooper; Mr A T P Cooper; Mr and Mrs C Cottrell-Dormer; Mr T Cottrell-Dormer; Mr J S Cox; Commander Crawford; Mrs Ann Crookshank; Mr D Crowden; Mr and Mrs Dalrymple; Debbie Dann (Longhorn Cattle Society); Gillian Darley; Sir Francis Dashwood; Mr M Davis; Warren Davis; Ivo Dawney; the Countess of Derby; Deborah, Duchess of Devonshire; Jill Dew; Miss Margaret Dickinson; Digital Doctor of Holt; Alan Dodd; Richard Downing; Captain Humphrey and the Hon Mrs Drummond; the Lady Dulverton; the Bishop of Durham; Mr R Earle; Jill Edwards; Lord Eliot; Mr N E Elliott; Dr A W Exell; Edmund Fairfax-Lucy; Peter Ferguson; Mr and Mrs B Feuding; Mr Roger Fleetwood-Hesketh and Lady Mary Hesketh; Mr and Mrs Fretwell; the Earl and Countess of Gainsborough; Lisa Gee (Director, Harley Foundation); Mr B J Gibbs; Mrs Pamela Gilbert; Mr Timothy Gilbert; Mark Girouard; the Knight of Glin and Madame Fitzgerald; Paul Golding; John Goode; Sir Charles Graham; Francis Graham; Miss R Griffin; Desmond and Penny Guinness; Mr I Hadgkiss; George Hammond; Andrew Hann; the Harpur Crewe Estate; John and Eileen Harris; David Harrison; Lady Harrod; Barnaby, Huckleberry, Alfie and Archie Harrod; the Hon Lady Hastings; Lord Hastings; Mr and Mrs J Hegarty; Jo Henwood (*Chester Chronicle*); Christian, Lady Hesketh; Lord and Lady Hesketh; Mr F Hetherington; Myles Hildyard; Mrs Jean Hill; Peter and Susan Hillmore; Mr and Mrs G Holbech; Mr and Mrs D W Houlston; Mr and Mrs J Howard; Dorothy Hubball; Neil Hynd; Edward Impey; Mary Innes; Ian Irvine; Gervase Jackson-Stops; Mr and Mrs S Jacques; Nicky and Suzannah Johnstone; Derek Keen; Susan Kelleher; Mr D Keyte; Bindie and Tony Lambton – my mother and father; Arabella Lennox-Boyd; John Lewis; the Earl and Countess of Lichfield; the Marquis of Londonderry; the London Library; Michael McGarvie; Mr P McKay; Deirdre Mackinnon; Mr and Mrs B Martin; Denis and Isabel Miles (Kings Langley Local History and Museum Society); Mr G Miller; Sir John Miller; Miss E Mills; Marie Claire Montgomery; The Hon Lady Morrison; Gina Murphy; Sir John Musker; Rose Musker; Mark Naylor; Philip and Isabella Naylor-Leyland; Jamie

Neidpath; Mr M Newman; Mrs D Norman; City of
Nottingham Museums; Lawrence Oates; Adrian
Palmer; Susan Palmer (Sir John Soane's Museum);
John Pearce; the Earl of Pembroke; PDQ Pro-Lab
(Watford, Hertfordshire); Mrs P M Price; David Rablin;
Jack Raynor; John Martin Robinson; Lucian Robinson;
René Rodgers; David Rowbotham; Royal Agricultural
College (Cirencester, Gloucestershire); Royal
Commission on the Ancient and Historical Monuments
of Scotland (RCAHMS); Alan and Lindsay Rusbridger;
the Duke and Duchess of Rutland; Ray Sandham; Mr R
Scott; Mr J T Sharp; Mrs P Sharratt; Mr and Mrs Slater;
Mr and Mrs Spenser; Stephen and Clare Squarey;
Staffordshire County Council; Mr and Mrs Freddie
Stockdale; Brenda Stone; Margaret Stone; the Duke of
Sutherland; Sir Tatton Sykes; Mr and Mrs Taylor;
Mr M Tebbutt; Mr and Mrs Thomson; David and
Bridget Trotter; Andrew Vines; Colonel R Waller; Major
A J Warre; Wendy Watt; Lavinia Wellecombe; the Duke
of Wellington; the Duke and Duchess of Westminster;
the Earl of Weymss; Mr and Mrs S C Whitbread; Ken
Wilde; Mrs June Williams; Jack Willoughby; Sir Marcus
and Lady Worsley; Mr R K Wynn; the Earl and Countess
of Yarborough; Mrs David Young; and Rory Young.

## CREDITS

Unless otherwise stated, all images are © Lucinda
Lambton. Other illustrations are reproduced as follows:
*The History of the Kingdom of Winnipeg, from the
Foundation to the Present Time BY ROYAL COMMAND*
(1823, never published) was loaned by Ian Anstruther
(p 185); © Country Life (back cover flap); by kind
permission of Dr Eva Crane (p 76); © Crown Copyright:
RCAHMS. Licensor www.rcahms.gov.uk (p 180b);
Reproduced by kind permission of His Grace the Duke
of Bedford and the Trustees of the Bedford Estate
(p 107); English Heritage (pp 157 and 232r (courtesy of
the Williams family)); English Heritage.NMR (p 120);
© English Heritage Photo Library (pp 26, 51, 195 and
197); Courtesy of the Kings Langley Local History and
Museum Society (pp 136–7 and 138); © NTPL/Andrew
Haslam (p 39); Private collection (p 66); RIBA Library
Drawings Collection (p 41); Courtesy of Alan Rusbridger
(p 205); By courtesy of the Trustees of Sir John Soane's
Museum (pp 68 and 115); and © The Trustees of the
British Museum (p 208). For permission to photograph,
I would like to thank Her Majesty the Queen (Windsor
Royal Dairy).

Kind permission was also given by Frederick
Whitridge for use of the verses from Matthew Arnold's
poem *Geist's Grave* on p 241 and Marcia Newbolt for
the verses from Henry Newbolt's poem *Fidele's Grassy
Tomb* on p 224.

Though I have tried to trace the sources for the
quotes in this text, this has not always been possible;
however, a great many of these unattributed quotes
add to the stories of the sites, and therefore I have
considered them worth including.

# Introduction

*J*OHN BUNYAN said that an Englishman would rather walk with a dog than with a fellow Christian. And so indeed say I, so CHEER I; but why? Why are we touched to tears of delight by such tales as a chicken's friendship with a horse, or a sparrow's morale-boosting card tricks in London's air-raid shelters? Why do we delight in a dog, a cat and a pigeon accompanying Vincent Lunardi on the first balloon flight over Britain in 1784? And why is it that even the most stoically unemotional find they possess an emotional streak and abandon what little is left of British reserve when faced with a horse, dog, cat or even a budgerigar? In spite of accusations of disproportionate sentimentality, our hearts pound on: as defiantly stirred, say, by Mary, Queen of Scots' dog – the one who after his mistress's execution refused to move from his mournful position between her severed head and shoulders – as by the fate of the poor queen herself. The tears well up, the heart is pierced and the soul is soothed, but by what in particular? It is, I believe, the artlessness of animals. With no ulterior motive and with an innocence that is unsullied by either cynicism or scepticism, they are a source of constant and consoling comfort in our often contorted lives. We may have fallen from grace but animals have not, and with them we are somehow tuned into a simpler and more innocent world. (The jungle, of course, is riddled through with ruthlessness, but the animals that charge through these pages have left the jungle behind.) In our ever-changing culture animals have remained constant and, whilst soothing as well as invigorating our lives, they have given us cheerful support throughout the ages.

There are those who question the devotion between man and beast. Lady Byron was one – according to Doris Langley Moore's book *Lord Byron: Accounts Rendered*, she was reputed to have said: 'The reason why some tyrannical characters have been fond of animals and humane to them, is because they have no exercise of reason and could not condemn the wickedness of their master.' A sneering solution for some, but one that I deny, having often used dogs as Geiger counters as to the character of callers. My fear is that we may well be using the untainted spirits of animals for our own ends. For example, the pleasure given to us, most particularly by dogs, may be largely the pleasure of having our vanity preened. Many's the time that I have shrieked 'Mirror mirror on the wall' to my canine companions, and never once has the pleasing reply not been 'Fairest of them all'.

There is no question that animals give me profound pleasure, in one way or another, every day. It is a pleasure that is matched, also every day, only by architecture and it has been my great good fortune to put these two whoppingly powerful forces behind the production of this book. Fortunately for this endeavour it is the love of animals raging within the British breast that, over the last seven centuries, has produced an array of animal buildings which are second to none in the world. In what other country can you find an extravagant building to house poultry or a pink sandstone castle that was created for salmon? Where else would you come upon a 30ft-high stone obelisk honouring a pig or a tombstone to a cow? The answer is nowhere.

How well I remember the genesis of this book. I was walking through the village of Ford in Northumberland when suddenly there before me was a sight that had it all. A horse was being shod in front of the blacksmith's forge of 1863 – a building with a great stone horseshoe, including 'nails' of stone, that was then 'framing' the horse as it stood there that day. What a building, what a horse, what a picture – what a book there could be!

Eureka! It was a defining moment that years later resulted in *Beastly Buildings: The National Trust Book of Architecture for Animals*, published in 1985.

Today, more than 25 years on, great and good fortune is mine once again for English Heritage has suggested that the book be updated, with yet more extraordinary examples of Britain's buildings for animals; hence the publication of *Palaces for Pigs*. Although the geographical remit for this book is primarily focused on England, occasionally this restriction had to be defied. It would have been impossible to leave out such treasures as the 18th-century 'Chinese' pagoda for monkeys at Culzean in Ayrshire (now rip-roaringly restored with balustrades of wrought-iron monkeys' tails from the ruin that it was when I first saw it); the battlemented castle for goats at Larchill in County Kildare, built, if you please, around the end of the 20th century; or the lofty tower of an 18th-century dovecote that doubles up as a privy in Abercamlais, Wales (*see* p 13).

There have, of course, been other and excellent reasons – over and above the honouring of animals – to build ever more adventurously. The mid-17th to well into the 18th century was, after all, 'The Age of Improvement', when both technology and taste were driving the agriculturalist and the aesthete to ever-greater heights, and animals supplied a good excuse for architectural experiment. For example, John Claudius Loudon – the compiler of weighty tomes on architecture, and agricultural and arboreal culture – proposed in his *Encyclopaedia of Cottage, Farm and Villa Architecture and Furniture* of 1833 that all stables should be circular as, '[t]he domestic quadrupeds ... are all more or less wedge-shaped'. So it was that on the foundations of English eccentricity, extravagance, fashion and entertainment, remarkable buildings for creatures rose up all over the British Isles. The animal inhabitants

could never complain, however idiosyncratic their dwelling. 'TO PLEASE THE PIGS' incised in stone on a tiny pyramid sty in Tong, Shropshire, was a misleading inscription if ever there was one – at any rate for its scrunched-up occupants. As for the combined cow house and greenhouse illustrated in the *Gardener's Magazine* in 1831, I doubt whether that was of great benefit to the beasts. Under the headline 'Heating Hothouses by the breath of Cattle', it judiciously placed openings in the party wall shared with the greenhouse, through which the cows would breathe warm air over the blooms. At Exton in Rutland, the 18th-century cattle shelter was combined with a dovecote so as to give the house across the park an eye-catching view – again not exactly much help to the doves or the cattle (*see* pp 10–11).

When building for animals, the builders' imaginations could flourish unbridled – often with scant regard for architectural convention. Thus we find that a temple for terrapins was built at Wotton House in Surrey, a Tuscan-columned arch was a cockpit at West Wycombe in Buckinghamshire and a bear made his home in an exuberantly Victorian game larder at Shadwell in Norfolk (*opposite*). The 19th-century 'Bear Hut' at Killerton in Devon is thatched and 'rustic' – with its exterior laid with logs in patterns and one floor made from the knucklebones of deer. Castles were also built throughout Britain for bears, as well as bees, deer, hounds, doves, cows and even guinea pigs – all indulgences of the wildest flights of architectural fancy.

Nor was it just the amateur architect who applied himself. All the big boys such as Robert Adam, Henry Holland, Humphry Repton and John Nash did too. None of them thought it beneath their dignity to create architecture for animals. There could be no better example of this than Sir John Soane, who – already architect of the Bank of England – also seriously applied himself to the design of timber nesting-boxes for poultry. And very fine nesting-boxes they were too, with a 16ft-long façade of symmetrical classicism and nine arches for the hens to come and go through. Soane's great draughtsman Joseph Gandy proposed pyramids for pigs and for poultry in his pattern book *The Rural Architect* of 1805, and William Adam, father of Robert, created Chatelherault (*below*), the most ennobling animal building of the lot, in 1731–43. Illustrated in Adam's *Vitruvius Scoticus* and described as the 'Dogg Kennells', it was in fact designed as a hunting lodge for the Duke of Hamilton. It had a 280ft-long façade with two pavilions – each with a pair of pedimented towers – which were linked by an arched and decorative wall. The duke and duchess had apartments and an ornate banqueting room on the right, and the kennel man, the hounds and the horses lived on the left. These have recently been magnificently restored.

My book is a trumpet voluntary to such an astonishing assembly of architecture and to the delight that the British took, and still take, in their animals. Nevertheless some order had to be imposed on such a multitude of oddities. A top-notch monument to a cat that circumnavigated the globe between 1740 and 1744 would be surprised to find itself in the company of kangaroos surrounded by Gothic grotesquery of 1820. The book, therefore, has been divided into four chapters: 'Sport & Speed', which soars to such supreme architectural heights as stables – so often built with the same scholarship as the house that they were to serve. No sport in fact was exempt from serious architectural consideration; fishing temples alone could handsomely represent the whole pantheon of Britain's building styles. So too can dovecotes and with 'Plate & Palate' there are buildings showing that the eye could be every bit as well satisfied as the stomach when building for animals who are destined for the table. What surprise could be greater,

I ask you, than to come upon an early 19th-century Grecian temple for pigs in a field in Yorkshire; what pleasure finer than to find, standing on a wall in Cheshire, a beehive in the form of a red sandstone castle on the back of a red sandstone elephant? 'Adored & Adornment' cheers the sheer joy of architectural extravagance with such flamboyance as the baroque aviary at Waddesdon in Buckinghamshire, now restored to its original splendour with pure gold leaf. As for menageries, created so as to show off exotic creatures throughout the 17th, 18th and 19th centuries, they were buildings that induced every bit as much wonder as did the occupants themselves. 'Death & Decoration' is the grand finale commemorating animals in all manner of materials and forms. Stone obelisks and pyramids, temples and tombstones, they are all to be found honouring our animal pals. In Gloucestershire there is a tombstone to a trout and in Dorset a gilded wall painting honouring two robins glows forth from church walls.

While it used to be taken for granted that animals had been put on earth solely to serve humans, today there is an ever-growing school of thought that believes in the genuineness of animal rights – the right of a fox, for example, not to be torn apart by hounds and the growing clamour, although not yet nearly loud enough, against factory farming, as well as questions about the fate of animals undergoing laboratory experiments. Science, too, is extending a helpful hand by attributing a degree of intelligence to dogs, for example, which makes their traditional description of 'dumb animals' or 'mere animals' start to sound out of kilter with our age and somewhat patronising, unsympathetic – even discriminatory! In other words, all those so called 'eccentrics' who have seen fit to glorify their relationship with animals with exuberant architecture may yet be proved to have blazed a trail which the rest of us will soon be proud to follow. Indeed, if the 20th century was the century of the common man, it could just be that the 21st will prove to be the century of 'the common animal'. Is this wishful thinking? Let us hope not. A land fit for animals to live in, that is my hope and prayer.

> For that which befalleth the sons of men befalleth beasts; even one thing befalleth them: as the one dieth, so dieth the other; yea, they have all one breath; so that a man hath no pre-eminence above a beast: for all is vanity.
> *Ecclesiastes 3:19*

*nue a mile. Diftant from, & Frenting the Palace*

*Left: Chatelherault, the 18th-century hunting lodge for the Duke of Hamilton.*

# Sport & Speed

*Previous page: The stables at Seaton Delaval in Northumberland.*

*Right: The painted ceiling of the fishing temple on Monkey Island at Bray, Berkshire.*

*S*PORT PRODUCED the grandest architecture of all, although herein seeps poison. For all too often the crueller the sport, the more beautiful the building. Nothing short of stately homes were designed for relishing bear-baiting, bull-baiting and cockfighting, as well as shooting and coursing.

Bear- and bull-baiting were sports that it is almost too painful to write of, with dogs biting and baiting chained and tethered creatures to the death. The bear or bull would usually be secured to a rope or chain in the middle of an enclosure that had quarters for spectators as at Swarkestone in Derbyshire. Bets were placed on which dog could bring down the wretched creature and, fuelled by ghoulish goading, the sports were a great success. Elizabeth I particularly enjoyed such activity; she even overruled the House of Commons when it tried to introduce a ban on bear-baiting on a Sunday. All the animals suffered immensely – to try and reduce the deaths and injuries to dogs, special breeds were developed with short noses and broader heads, such as the bulldog and bull terrier. No one, though, seemed to care a jot about the bear or the bull – in fact in some places it was a legal requirement for butchers to bait all bulls as it was believed that the exercise and agitation made the meat tender; a view incidentally – at least as far as tenderising meat goes – that was enthusiastically endorsed by my butcher in Buckinghamshire today.

Cockfighting is an ancient sport and it was one that was once relished by all levels of society in Britain. Betting was the key element and winning birds changed hands for big money. They were specially bred to be as aggressive as possible and they had their beaks filed, wings clipped and sharp spurs attached to their legs to ensure they could inflict the maximum amount of damage on their opponent.

In 1762 James Boswell wrote of the horrors of cockfighting in his *London Journal*, where the birds

> armed with silver heels ... fight with amazing bitterness and resolution ... One pair fought three quarters of an hour ... I was sorry for the poor cocks. I looked around to see if any of the spectators pitied them when mangled and torn in a most cruel manner, but I could not observe the smallest relenting sign in any countenance ... thus I did complete my true English day ... and came home pretty much confounded at the strange turn of this people.

In 1822 the Cruel Treatment of Cattle Act was passed, later amended in 1835 to include cockfighting as well as bull- and bear-baiting. In 1849 this was repealed and replaced by the Cruelty to Animals Act of 1849.

Fishing, by comparison, seems the most gentle and agreeable of pastimes. 'Never yet have I met an angler who was not a genial man', wrote James John Hissey in *Across England in a Dog-Cart in 1891*, 'and I wish all the fraternity a light heart and a heavy creel.' In 1676 Charles Cotton built a fishing house for his friend Izaak Walton, author of the famed *The Compleat Angler*; Cotton wrote that nobody was happier than he

> Who with his angle and his books,
> Can think the longest day well spent,
> And praises God when back he looks,
> And finds that all was innocent.

Many fishing temples – also known as houses or pavilions – belied this simplicity when grandees went the whole decorative hog, most particularly with the oriental style which was seen as a suitably exotic addition to their parkscapes. In the early 1800s George IV commissioned a fantastical Chinese fishing pavilion at

Virginia Water in Berkshire: with its finials and spirals, its banners, lanterns and hanging bells, as well as dragons' heads and birds, it could not have been more extraordinary. In the mid-1700s the 3rd Duke of Marlborough had commissioned Andien de Clermont – whose speciality was *singerie* (paintings of monkeys enjoying human pastimes) – to cover the ceiling of his little temple on Monkey Island at Bray, Berkshire, with monkeys indulging in sport (*above*). They shoot – one cruelly killing a kingfisher – and they punt, angle and net fish. One is harpooning a dolphin while two more carry a basket full of eels and fish; two are 'beaters' putting up a snipe. In the central panel three monkeys ride along in a shell drawn by dolphins – two of them embrace while the third serenades them by blowing a conch – and a tiny Cupid monkey flies overhead.

As for hunting, there have been palatial buildings for the sport since the earliest Tudor hunting lodges. This was the golden age when art and sport were in happiest harmony. My old pal Mark Girouard – in his 1963 *Country Life* article 'Arcadian retreats for the chase' – tells us that: 'Civilisation was still rural rather than industrial; and society was dominated by the concept of the "complete gentleman," who went hunting with Virgil in his pocket, and was able to draw the Five Orders as well as a covert.' Such an all-round approach was much admired: 'The average gentleman of the day was able to give – or get others to give – convincing artistic expression to his sporting pleasures... Hence ... the Tudor and Stuart hunting-lodges. A peculiar poetry exudes from these buildings... .' However, there was a peculiar lack of poetry exuding from the hunt itself.

Richard Blome in the *Gentleman's Recreation* of 1686 wrote of

> [t]he Death of the Stag with the Ceremonies to be observed therein: He that give the falling blow, aught of righte to ... assemble together the rest of the company ... the Huntsman presents the person that took the Essay with a drawn Hanger to have a Chop of his head, and after him everyone hath a chop if it is not cut off; and generally the Huntsman ... is provided with such a hanger that is not over sharp, that here may be more chops for gaining more fees, every one giving him a shilling at least.

Deer hunting had been a favourite sport for the royals and grandees for hundreds of years. Throughout the 15th and 16th centuries every monarch – save Edward VI and Queen Mary – relished the chase. 'To read the history of Kings', wrote Thomas Paine, leading light of the American Revolution, 'a man would be almost inclined to suppose that government consisted of stag hunting.' Never mind Paine's *Rights of Man*, what about the rights of deer? They were slender indeed with this so-called sport. For example, it was common practice to drive deer into an enclosure, where the terrified creature would then be shot at close range by a longbow (capable of 10–12 arrows a minute), a crossbow (at 2 bolts a minute) or a bow and arrow. Known as 'bow and stable' hunting, this was particularly denounced by James I as a 'theevish' form of the sport.

In John Nichols' *The Progresses and Public Processions of Queen Elizabeth* of 1823, there is an account of 'Fortune's Empresse' indulging in such monstrous practices – laced through with finery – at Cowdray in Sussex in 1591:

> On Munday, at eight of the clock in the morning, her Hignes took horse, with all her traine, and rode into the parke: where was a delicate bowre prepared, under the which were her Highnesse musicians placed, and a crossbowe by a Nymph, with a sweet song, delivered to her hands, to shoote at the deere, about some thirtie in number, put into a paddock, of which number she killed three or four, and the Countess of Kildare one.
>
> Then rode hir Grace to Cowdrey to dinner, and about six of the clocke in the evening, from a turret, sawe sixteene buckes ... pulled downe with greyhoundes...

Deer coursing was another popular pastime enjoyed by the swells. At Ravensdale in Derbyshire there are the remains of a deer course dating from the 12th century; the one at Windsor Little Park dates from the mid-1400s; and in 1537 Henry VIII built one at Hampton Court. By the early 1600s deer coursing had taken the place of the even more detestable drive hunts when quantities of deer were driven to a 'sporting' death by crossbow or bow. The hunts were losing too many valuable beasts and killing one deer was seen as more economical.

The hunting of deer encouraged the building of houses, folds and shelters for them – buildings that did justice to the beauty of the creatures themselves. With such graceful inhabitants, no other animal buildings could so successfully perform the all-important role of enhancing the landscape. At Bishop Auckland in County Durham deer could shelter in a castle, while at Sudbury

Hall in Derbyshire the deer house of 1723 had corner towers with ogee domes and was plastered and painted white – then, as if that was not enough, it was thatched in 1750. At the same period, the parkland of Sledmere in East Yorkshire was improved by a whopping great eye-catcher of a neoclassical temple for deer that was built entirely out of brick – and very bright brick at that (*opposite*). As the deer became ever more admired as ornaments, so hunting them became ever more condemned. However, practices of abominable cruelty were still commonplace. For example, the 'carted' stag after having its hips dislocated or broken, or even a foot cut off, was then borne off in a cart to the spot of 'release' where the dogs would be ready and waiting. Fortunately enlightened help was on the way. 'Where is the unnatural, base, groveling, grinning, pimping scoundrel who can put his unfeeling claws to this act of grinding dislocation?' – so spat Humanitas in *The Sporting Magazine* of 1800. The clamour grew louder, with giants such as William Wordsworth, Samuel Taylor Coleridge, Lord Byron and Percy Bysshe Shelley, as well as William Wilberforce and Jeremy Bentham – to name but a few – vituperatively scratching away at their illustrious pens. All to great effect, for in 1824 the Society for the Prevention of Cruelty to Animals was founded; it was given the Royal Warrant by Queen Victoria in 1840, and in her Jubilee address of 1887 she said that 'among other marks of the spread of enlightenment' amongst her subjects, she had observed 'with real pleasure, the growth of more humane feeling towards the lower animals'.

By the late 18th century the fox had superceded the deer as the huntsmen's preferred prey and by various and dexterous management still looks like remaining so today. The enthusiasm with which the British pursued the fox was a source of some amusement to foreigners.

The German Prince Pückler-Muskau, who toured the British Isles in 1827, recorded an idiosyncratic example in his *Tour in England, Ireland and France*:

> The most striking thing to German eyes is the sight of the black-coated parsons, flying over hedge and ditch. I am told they often go to the church, ready booted and spurred, with the hunting whip in their hands, throw on a surplice, marry, christen or bury, with all con-ceivable velocity, jump on their horses at the church door, and off – tally-ho! They told me of a famous clerical fox-hunter, who always carried a tame fox in his pocket, that if they did not happen to find one they might be sure of a run. The animal was so well trained that he amused the hounds for a time; and when he was tired of running, took refuge in his inviolable retreat – which was no other than the altar of the Parish Church. There was a hole broken for him in the church wall, and a comfortable bed under the steps. This is right English religion.

The sports of hunting and racing have spawned real beauties of buildings for horses. Externally at least, the architecture of their stables was often as handsome as the houses they were built to serve – and in the case of Hovingham Hall in North Yorkshire they were all created as one. Between 1751 and 1778 Sir Thomas Worsley built Hovingham Hall and realised his grand equine plan of building quarters for his horses on the ground floor of his own house. The hall stands in the middle of the village with a rusticated entrance door overlooking the green. Suspecting nothing you would walk through the front door into a tunnel-vaulted passage and then, Abracadabra! – all about you was an arched and columned riding school of immense size. On straight through, so you thought, into the house. But then again, Abracadabra! – you were in stables and

ones of serene beauty at that (*opposite*). With a stone-vaulted ceiling and two rows of stone Tuscan columns standing on a floor of hexagonal oak blocks laid down for carriages, here was a strange state of affairs. Arthur Young, the agricultural critic and diarist, went to Hovingham in 1769 and in *A Six Months' Tour Through the North of England*, he wrote with alarm of the arrangements that he found. While admitting that '[n]othing should be condemned because uncommon', he nonetheless disapproved of the design of the *piano nobile*, with its Ionic reception leading into a ballroom, which in turn led out onto a balcony overlooking the riding school. 'I should suppose that when they are well stocked with horses in hot weather, it would be easy enough to *smell* without being *told* these two rooms (the best in the house) are built over the apartments of the "Houyhnhnms".' Over 200 years later his criticisms have been addressed with both the riding school and stables having been converted into elegant reception rooms for the house.

Horses had not always been so luxuriously appointed and until the late 1500s cruelty had been all too commonplace, with such alarming practices as, say, tying a live hedgehog beneath their tails for extra speed or, as a punishment, strapping a live cat tied to a pole beneath their stomachs. (I fear to say that in Romania, live hedgehogs are still tied beneath horses' tails to this day.) Such horrors were first written of in 1550 in Frederico Grisone's *Gli Ordini di Cavalcare* – The Orders of Riding. Horses were ridden into the ground and discarded in their thousands; but by the end of the century their lot was to change. Gervase Markham was one of those who led the way. In his 1607 *Cavelarice, or the English Horseman: Contayning all the Arte of Horsemanshippe*, all was set fair. Subtitled *As Much as is Necessary for any Man to Understand, Whether he be Horse-*

the condemned men was proving too heavy for the
horses: 'Come Gentlemen', said Holmes, 'don't let the
poor creatures suffer on our account. I have often led
you in the field. Let me lead you on our way to heaven.'
It was therefore not surprising that stables became
far more than farm buildings and were given the
architectural attention due to a building second only in
status to the house itself, as can be seen with the elegant
stables of 1825–7 at Marble Hill House in London,
built for Captain Jonathan Peel, brother of the Prime
Minister, Sir Robert Peel, and a successful racehorse
breeder (*see* pp 26–7). Some stables by John Claudius
Loudon, designed for a Colonel Mytton of Garth in
Montgomeryshire and shown off in his *Encyclopaedia of
Cottage, Farm and Villa Architecture and Furniture* of 1833,
rivalled the most splendid of stately homes, and as a
bonus, they were round. 'The domestic quadrupeds', he
wrote, '...are chiefly the horse, the cow, the sheep, and
the swine ... taken in the plan, or vertical profile, they are
all more or less wedge-shaped; the head being placed at
the narrow end of the wedge.' Eureka! A round equine
palace was the answer! He offered two – one classical,
the other Gothic, and both of them fantastically
elaborate, surrounded by arcades '...for exercising horses
and for riding and driving in bad weather'. Both had
soaring central bell towers.

It was not only the exterior that was considered
important; care was also taken over the horses' comfort
and welfare inside the stables. In the 16th and 17th
century stone was considered too cold for horses and so
wooden planks were used to make the walls and floors
of the stalls. Objections were rife; with seeping mires of
manure and 'with the evill savour of horse pisse',
wooden floors had stopped being laid by the mid-17th
century with stone coming back into fashion as can be
seen at Seaton Delaval (*see* pp 18–19). Efficient drainage

breeder, Horse-ryder, Horse-hunter, Horse-runner, Horse-
ambler, Horse-farrier, Horse-keeper, Coachman, Smith or
Sadler. Together with the Discovery of the Subtill Trade or
Mistery of Horse-coursers, and an Explanation of the
Excellency of a Horses Understanding*, it was one of the
first English books to suggest that training 'bee done
with all the gentleness and quiet means that may be'.

When horses started to cost more than a human
servant, so they became more sumptuously housed. By
the late 16th century stables became important buildings
in their own right to provide suitably splendid settings
for the ever more highly prized horse. Essential for so
many aspects of everyday life, horses also developed the
reputation of being an ennobling adjunct of their owner.
A Colonel Holmes, supporter of Monmouth, summed it
up, when, on his way to be executed in 1685, the cart for

systems were developed and other improvements in
equine care included the upright hay rack. It was
invented by Christopher Clifford and first described in
*The School of Horsemanship* of 1585 – another leading
work of the day. An example of this somewhat box-like
arrangement can still be seen at Peover in Cheshire –
it was a great improvement on the sloping kind as it
prevented hay and dust getting into the horse's eyes.
And it wasn't only the practicalities that were dealt
with – stables were also often embellished on the inside.

Even modestly sized stables such as those at Peover were
richly encrusted with plaster decoration. Sadly, Peover is
a rare survival of such decoration. What a tremendous
sadness it is to think of how many stables have been lost;
almost an entire chapter in the history of British
architecture.

The special relationship we have with dogs has been
celebrated with some splendid kennels. In 1788 John
Soane designed one disguised as a Roman temple, while
the 18th-century kennels for the Fitzwilliam Hunt at

Left: The elegant stables at Marble Hill House in London.

architects designing these country buildings – today's developers take note! – should 'take hints for the general forms and disposition of the masses, from the ground on which they are and from the surrounding scenery'. Even the humblest building, he wrote, should seem as if it had grown out of the ground 'instead of appearing to have been brought there from town or village'. The poet William Somervile thought that such canine extravaganzas were ridiculous. In *The Chace* of 1735 he wrote:

> First let the Kennel be the Huntsman's Care
> Upon some little Eminence erect,
> And fronting to the ruddy Dawn; its Courts
> On either Hand wide op'ning to receive
> The Sun's all-chearing Beams, when mild he shines,
> And gilds the Mountain Tops. For much the Pack
> (Rous'd from their dark Alcoves) delight to stretch
> And bask, in his invigorating Ray:
> Warn'd by the streaming Light, and merry Lark
> Forth rush the jolly Clan; with tuneful Throats
> They carol loud, and in grand Chorus join'd,
> Salute the new-born Day...
> ...
> Let no *Corinthian* Pillars prop the Dome, ...
> Better dispos'd...
> ...
> ...For Use, not State,
> Gracefully plain, let each Apartment rise.
> O'er all let Cleanliness preside...

Milton, near Peterborough, are in the shape of a medieval keep. Loudon showed in his *Encyclopaedia* of 1833 that he had cut no canine corners with two kennels designed for a Mr Lamb: one in the 'Italian' style with a circular tower faced with a semicircular colonnade; the other, 'Tudor Gothic', had a domed belfry, bastioned walls and an arched entrance courtyard. Both of them, he wrote, should have railings rather than walls, 'it being found that dogs are always quietest when their kennels command an extensive prospect'. He decreed too that

Loudon though was spot-on; it is thanks to him and the other architects and designers of the 17th, 18th and 19th centuries never considering it beneath them to create buildings associated with animals that we are able to revel in these architectural oddities throughout the British Isles. Nothing could be too ennobling when building for Sport & Speed.

## Swarkestone, Derbyshire

The Swarkestone Pavilion is a sombre yet majestic little building lording it over a walled enclosure. But what was it used for? There is evidence of payment for building it as a 'bowle alley house' in 1632 – to the tune of £111 12s 4d – but thereafter the possibilities are various. It was obviously a grandstand for viewing and it may well have also been a banqueting house with a fireplace to add to the comfort of spectators. The walled enclosure in front of it – according to Sir Nikolaus Pevsner in his *Buildings of England: Derbyshire* – was known as 'The Cuttle' and it has been suggested that this was used for bull- and bear-baiting, jousting or that it was an arena in which to slay deer.

Whatever went on in the enclosure, it was overseen by this little architectural masterpiece, built in Keuper sandstone – which had been quarried nearby – by local mason Richard Shepherd. Most interesting of all, this little building was designed by John Smythson, one of Britain's first 'architecters' – as architects were first called – and son of the great Robert, who created such marvellous buildings as Longleat and Hardwick Hall. Like father like son: among John's many triumphs was Bolsover Castle near Chesterfield, Derbyshire, as well as the miniature grandeur of the Swarkestone Grandstand – as it was also known – with its lead cupolas topped with ball finials, castellations and Gothic-arched loggia. It was commissioned by Sir John Harpur, whose coat of arms is carved on the grandstand. The ruins of his house – demolished in the mid-1700s – remain some 200yds away.

Strange to say, 113 years after it was built, this little beacon of Jacobean beauty would have witnessed some of the last gasps of the Jacobite Rebellions. Only yards

away stands Swarkestone Bridge (at three-quarters of a mile, the longest stone bridge in the country), where in 1745 Bonnie Prince Charlie turned back to Scotland – into the jaws of defeat at Culloden – during his last attempt to march south to regain the English crown.

The Swarkestone Pavilion was sold to the Landmark Trust in 1985. It was in a ruinous state with no roof, floors or windows and has undergone an exemplary restoration. Now joy of joys, it can be appreciated by one and all. In the Trust's handbook, we discover that the one disadvantage of staying there has been turned to a considerable advantage: 'the bathroom is in the top of one of the turrets ... and to reach it you must cross the open roof – an unlooked-for opportunity to study the sky at night'.

## West Wycombe, Buckinghamshire

The thundering Temple of Apollo, built to appear as a triumphal arch entrance, was also, incredibly, a cockpit. The pit was below the arch and the cages for the fighting birds were in a room above. It was built in 1761, it is thought by the architect John Donowell, for Sir Francis Dashwood – no doubt to encourage the ever more lustful pleasures and depravities enjoyed by the 'Brotherhood of the Friars of St Francis of Wycombe', also known as 'The Knights of St Francis' or 'The Friars' but who are known popularly today as the Hell-Fire Club. The inscription over the arch – 'LIBERTATI AMICITIAE Q SAC' – was their motto ('Dedicated to freedom and friendship'). Much too much has already been written about them, both true and false, but as it was Dashwood who built the Temple of Apollo and 'The Friars' who relished its role, here we go once again.

The members of the Hell-Fire Club, sometimes also known as 'Dashwood's Apostles', were an illustrious but rum bunch. Lord Sandwich, First Lord of the Admiralty

was one; John Wilkes, radical journalist and politician, another; and there were many poets and pamphleteers – all of them revelling in licentious and satanic rites. These took place in the semi-ruinous Medmenham Abbey nearby as well as in caves that Sir Francis had dug deep into the hills of West Wycombe. Each 'Friar', wearing a monk's habit, had a cell to retire to for 'private devotions' and there were regular black masses held beneath obscene frescoes. Horace Walpole said that their practices were 'rigorously pagan' and Dashwood in particular had 'the staying power of a stallion and the impetuosity of a bull'. Masked women dressed as nuns were also part of the extraordinary scenes, and the cockpit too was part of the fun – although his building of such a beauty demonstrated the more serious side of Sir Francis's character. He became Chancellor of the Exchequer – although, true to say, he was considered incapable of understanding even a bar bill of five figures, and had to resign when his tax on cider caused riots. He was the Postmaster General, a founder member of the Dilettanti Society – formed to promote the arts – and a knowledgeable connoisseur. He was also a pioneer neoclassicist, who practiced what he preached by commissioning the architect Nicholas Revett to exquisitely remodel his house. Nor is that all, since he also got John Donowell to classicise the medieval church high on the hill above West Wycombe. It was all somewhat mocked in *The Ghost* by the poet Charles Churchill, fellow member of the Hell-Fire Club:

> *Here* She [Fancy] made lordly temples rise
> Before the pious DASHWOOD'S eyes,
> Temples which built aloft in air,
> May serve for show, if not for pray'r.

And there was more: a huge and hexagonal open-to-the-skies mausoleum was paid for by his friend, the pleasingly named politician and fellow 'Friar', George Bubb Dodington.

Dashwood was also responsible for picturesquely placing some 20 buildings in the folds of West Wycombe's park – land which had been continuously and romantically landscaped from 1739. 'If not superfluous, at least profuse' was a local newspaper's polite description of them all picturesquely placed hither and thither. There were to be seven temples including the Temple of Apollo, and six years after that was finished, Nicholas Revett was employed to design the stables just behind giving them a flint wall to act as a screen. This has a niche to show off a statue of Apollo Belvedere and is arranged to be suitably framed by the arch of the Temple of Apollo. Built of flint with stucco dressings, the Tuscan-columned Temple of Apollo stands only yards from the house and there could have been no finer backdrop for the vile sport of cockfighting.

A very surprising footnote is that Benjamin Franklin often stayed at West Wycombe in the 1770s when he and Sir Francis Dashwood compiled a simplified version of the *Book of Common Prayer*, published in 1773. *The Buildings of England: Buckinghamshire* records that its purpose was 'to attract the young and lively and retrieve the well-disposed from the infliction of interminable prayres'.

## Beresford Dale, Derbyshire

The incomparable charms of Izaak Walton, author of *The Compleat Angler*, live on in the tiny stone fishing house on the River Dove that was built by Charles Cotton, writer, poet, translator and – most importantly for our purposes – fellow fisherman, friend of Walton and author of the second part of *The Compleat Angler*. Cotton was a gentleman with a large estate at Beresford Dale on the border of Derbyshire and Staffordshire – it was here that he built the fishing house for him and his friend Walton to enjoy; a sylvan spot from where they could enjoy fishing, strolling along the river bank, writing and talking together. Their entwined initials are carved onto the keystone over the door, beneath the words 'PISCATORIBUS SACRUM' (Sacred to fishermen) and the date 1676. Inside, there is a little fireplace with Cotton's crossed Cs on its surround. Topping the steep slate roof is a sundial beneath a stone ball.

*The Compleat Angler or the Contemplative Man's Recreation*, written in 1653, tells the story of three sportsmen friends: fisherman Piscator (Walton himself), huntsman Venator and fowler Auceps

travelling along the River Lea, with the thoughts they have and the sights they see. It is a very odd book indeed with a wealth of idiosyncratic and detailed instruction on angling, observations on natural history, festive songs, local and fishing lore, quotations from Francis Bacon and the Bible, as well as a good deal of poetry and even more contemplative thought – all with the background of intoxicating glimpses into 17th-century rural life. 'It was', as was written in the introduction, 'a peg on which to hang his ever-fragrant discourse of stream and meadow ... [with] that atmosphere of primitive innocence in which the childlike soul of Walton breathed.'

The three friends in the book have a fishing house by the water. 'How do you like my river', Piscator asks his friends, 'the vale it winds through like a snake, and the situation of my little fishing-house? ...and here is a bowling-green too, close by it; so, though I am myself no very good bowler, I am not totally devoted to my own pleasure; but that I have also some regard to other men's.' For both Walton and Cotton nothing equalled the pleasure of angling. 'Indeed my good scholar', wrote Walton, 'we may say of angling, as Dr Boteler said of strawberries, "Doubtless God could have made a better berry, but doubtless God never did"; and so (if I might be judge), God never did make a more calm, quiet, innocent recreation than angling.'

It was Cotton who was largely responsible for the advice on fly-fishing in the book after Walton had died in 1683. Among the many hundreds of suggestions for making artificial flies, he recommends the 'hair from the spot on a sow's ear', or otherwise 'the hair of an abortive calf, which the lime will turn to be so bright as to shine like gold'. April was a good month for 'the down of a fox-cub, which is of an ash colour at the roots next the skin, and ribbed about with yellow silk; the wings of the pale grey feather of a mallard'. June was best to gather hairs from a white weasel's tail.

With its combination of dash and of delicacy, *The Compleat Angler* was a success from the start. With five reprints in quick succession, and thereafter over 300 print runs, it is still – three and a half centuries later – in lively and popular print today. Famed throughout the world, it has spawned unpredictable progeny. In 1908 the Izaak Walton Club was founded by streetcar magnate John Roach in his Useppa Island Resort in Florida – enjoyed by the likes of Gloria Swanson and Shirley Temple, it is still flourishing today. Fourteen years later the Izaak Walton League of America was founded in Chicago and today, with almost 300 local chapters from sea to shining sea, it is one of America's oldest and most respected conservation organisations. There are Izaak Walton Fishing Clubs from Mississauga in Ontario to Burslem in Lancashire, various waters are named after him as well as a pub and hotel in his home county of Derbyshire – even a golf club in Staffordshire bears his name. Of all these, the little fishing house is the lone true link with the man; as Charles Cotton wrote in his *Epistle to John Bradshaw Esq*:

> My River still through the same channel glides,
> Clear from the tumult, salt, and dirt of tides,
> And my poor Fishing-house, my seat's best grace,
> Stands firm and faithful in the self-same place.

Lord Byron was not beguiled:

> And angling, too, that solitary vice,
> Whatever Izaak Walton sings or says:
> The quaint, old cruel coxcomb, in his gullet
> Should have a hook, and a small trout to pull it.

## Studley Royal and Fountains Abbey, North Yorkshire

In the adjoining domains of Studley Royal and Fountains Abbey there is surely one of the greatest assemblies of buildings set down in some of the most beautiful gardens and parkscapes in the country. Studley Royal's water gardens were created by John Aislabie who worked

*Below: The Fishing Tabernacles at
Studley Royal in North Yorkshire.*

on them from 1720 until he died in 1742, by which time he had created a masterpiece of formality within the landscape along with a quantity of buildings, including the classical Fishing Tabernacles at the end of a formal canal. Yet, it was when his son William bought the next door estate of Fountains Abbey in 1768, adding the sublime ruins of the 12th-century Cistercian abbey to the fold, that father and son between them could claim to have created a heaven on earth.

John Aislabie was a big noise of his day – a big noise who was silenced by shame. An MP from 1695, he was made a Lord of the Admiralty in 1710 and four years later he was Treasurer of the Navy. In 1718 he was made Chancellor of the Exchequer – a high honour that was to

be his downfall. The South Sea Company had proposed a scheme to take over the national debt; Aislabie was its most ardent supporter and when the bubble burst, so did he. As the *Oxford Dictionary of National Biography* (*DNB*) records, he was accused of ill-gotten gains and his actions were decried by Parliament as most 'notorious, dangerous, and infamous corruption', for which he was expelled from the House and incarcerated in the Tower of London. Every cloud, though, however dark, has a silver lining. It was thanks to this infamous disgrace that the innovative beauties of Studley Royal – the Elysian fields of Yorkshire, largely based on his study of French gardens – were to materialise.

With the River Skell flowing through his parkland, Aislabie was off to a flying start. He created cascades and a lake – in fact a reservoir – as well as the canal, over which he built a rustic bridge. The Temple of Piety, a real beauty of a building, stands over the round Moon Pond which is flanked by two crescent pools – all still cut out of the turf with exquisitely sharp delineation. For the Banqueting House, so rusticated as to look as if it is dripping stone, Aislabie is thought to have been helped by the great architect Colen Campbell. And there is more: a domed Temple of Fame commands fine views from high on a hill, and there is the Gothic Octagon Tower which looms over a grotto of a tunnel.

It was William Aislabie, however, who was to create the grandest shock of all. For after he had embraced Fountains Abbey as part of the estate, he created 'The Surprise View' – a vantage point from which to see a sensational view of the abbey ruins standing like a giant folly in the midst of the planted parkscape and swept around by the River Skell. In William Aislabie's day, visitors were ushered into a little wooden building where when sitting in the dark, the walls would suddenly be slid away revealing – Eureka! – the view.

No helping architectural hand is recorded for the Fishing Tabernacles, although it is known that the stonemasons responsible for their building were called John Simpson and Richard Moor, as well as the suitably Arcadian-sounding Robert Doe and Thomas Buck. Small, square and perfectly proportioned, with pyramid roofs and Palladian windows to the front, they elegantly flank a decoratively built weir, complete with balustrades and stone ball-topped rusticated pillars. Beneath the little buildings are sluice tunnels – as gracefully built as all the rest. To the side of each tabernacle, plainer, multi glazing-barred windows opened up for the angling of trout, grayling and roach (the salmon having been killed

off by the cascade). Most suitably, for our purposes, the gardener of this paradise on earth was called William Fisher.

Studley Royal and Fountains Abbey are now a World Heritage Site.

## Tendring, Suffolk

This temple for fishing from the front and for viewing hare coursing from the back was built in the mid-1700s for Sir John Williams, a merchant known in his day as 'the greatest exporter of cloth in England'. He was also responsible for having earlier created the canal – some 200yds long by 38yds wide – dug out at a somewhat

oblique angle to the house so as to give the illusion of greater length. This is the lone survivor of the Tendring estate, near Stoke by Nayland, named after the medieval owners who bought the great deer park that once covered the land.

Throughout the 15th and 16th centuries Tendring was owned by the Dukes of Norfolk; in the early 1700s it was bought by Williams who built a new house, as well as decoratively laying out his land and building this little gem of a building in the midst of it all. The estate was then bought by Rear Admiral Sir Joshua Rowley, who, between 1784 and 1790 commissioned the young John Soane – it was only his third commission for a house –

to design a new Tendring Hall. Already in command of
the architectural trickeries that were to make his name,
Soane designed a shallow barrel-vaulted ceiling and he
sandwiched in extra levels and built arches galore, as
well as a columned atrium. In 1955 the house was
demolished in its entirety. The Surveyor's Report of 1783
survives at the Sir John Soane's Museum in London,
making haunting reading once you know what is in
store:

> To dig out and clear away the Earth for the whole of
> the Basement Story ... to make the necessary Water
> troughs, and to form a cistern over the Water Closets
> ... the Chimney pieces of the Drawing Room, Library
> & Eating Parlour to be of marble ... The walls of the
> Hall to be of stucco ... etc.

Now everything has gone – everything, that is, save
for the Fishing Temple, for which the architect Sir
Robert Taylor gets the credit.

Originally the canal was filled with trout but it is now
fished for carp. Fishing could be viewed from the
Fishing Temple through a window with glass almost
reaching to the floor in a single and elegantly plastered
room with an overmantel that soars almost to the ceiling.
With a hop, skip and a jump, hare coursing could be
viewed from the other side through an enormous bay
taking up two-thirds of the north-facing wall.

After the death of Sir Joshua Rowley, his son Sir
William Rowley commissioned Humphry Repton to
redesign the park in 1791; Repton produced one of the
first of his famed Red Books (so called as they were
bound in red leather) – watercolours with overlays that
lift to show the effect of his changes – which has now
disappeared. Some remains of Repton's landscaping
have survived at Tendring, along with the earlier canal
which must have caused him acute anguish as by the

end of the 1700s he considered canals to be both old-
fashioned and ugly. It was Repton after all who coined
the term 'landscape gardening'. We must be grateful to
both Rowleys for holding on to this sweep of water and
its Fishing Temple. Today this little building has been
sympathetically converted into a private house. An *oeil-
de-boeuf* window was designed in the mid-1900s by
Raymond Erith to let light into a little kitchen.

## Alresford, Essex

Looking for all the world to be setting sail over the lake
is the 1772 Chinese fishing temple in what were once
the grounds of Alresford Hall. Known as 'The Quarters',
it stands in woods of the same name – said to have
originated from Cromwell's troops having been
quartered there during the Civil War. It was originally
built with its veranda over the water for angling and was
also used as a banqueting and picnic room. The bank
was built up in the 20th century.

An 'Estimate for the Building of Chinese Temple for
Colonel Redbow' survives, drawn up by one Richard
Woods, which tells us that this evocation of the East in
Essex was to cost exactly £343 13s 4d. Such 'Chinese'
buildings had started to appear all over the cultivated
country by the mid-1700s; '[t]he country wears a new
face...', enthused Horace Walpole, in a letter to Sir
Horace Mann, with 'a whimsical air of novelty that is
very pleasing'. There was mockery for such extremes as
'Thatch in the Chinese style' while in Jean Pillement's
*The Ladies Amusement; or Whole Art of Japanning Made
Easy* we read that '[w]ith Indian and Chinese subjects
great liberties are taken, because Luxuriance of Fancy
recommends their Productions more than Propriety,
for in them is often seen a butterfly supporting an
Elephant, or Things equally absurd; yet from their
gay Colouring and disposition seldom fail to please.'

The Alresford fishing temple is sensibly and delicately restrained compared to many such flights of fancy. Here its roof is shaped like a coolie hat – with its swooping shapes taken up in the veranda – sitting atop what was the octagonal 'banqueting room', often an essential feature of fishing temples. Today the room is square to the eye, having had disguised cupboards for fishing tackle built across the corners.

The whole effect is as pretty as a picture – and it was in fact painted by John Constable. In July 1816 he was commissioned to paint it by his first patron and friend of his father, Major-General Francis Slater-Redbow – in part so that the impoverished painter would be able to afford to marry his fiancée Maria Bicknell, or, as Constable wrote to Maria, 'that we may soon want a little ready money'. They were married within six weeks. He was also asked to paint Redbow's other nearby estate, Wivenhoe Hall (today the Wivenhoe House Hotel), along with its deer house, now sadly no more. In his letter to Maria, Constable wrote: 'I am to paint two small landscapes for the General; one in the park of the house and a beautiful piece of water; and another a scene in a wood with a beautiful little fishing house, where the young lady (who is the heroine of all these scenes [Mary Redbow]) goes occasionally to angle.' He wrote too that Mrs Redbow thought him 'very unsociable' but that they in fact made him feel 'quite at home. They often talk of you', he wrote, 'because they know it will please me ... I am going on very well with my pictures for them.' Constable's painting *The Quarters' behind Alresford Hall* is now in the National Gallery of Victoria in Melbourne, Australia, and *Wivenhoe Park, Essex* is in the National Gallery of Art in Washington, USA.

There was a cottage on the site when Richard Woods set to work in 1772 and he incorporated it into the fabric of the temple. In 1951–2 the building was extended and converted into a house, losing not one chip off its charming character. Looking out through its windows, you have unquestionably cast off from the moorings, and with the water all around, have floated to the middle of the lake.

## Kedleston, Derbyshire

When, in 1758, Sir Nathaniel Curzon, Ist Lord Scarsdale – aged only 32 – inherited the vast estate of Kedleston in Derbyshire, he straightway demolished his grandfather's house and had the nearby village moved so as to create the perfect setting for the new house he planned to build for himself. The architect Robert Adam, he decided, was to be the man to create it. At 30, Adam was even younger than his patron, but nevertheless he was entrusted with the whole bang shoot: a Palladian palace planned to rival Chatsworth, set down in Elysian Fields of his creation which would be enhanced with various bridges and buildings, including what must be one of the most beautiful of all Britain's animal buildings – the Fishing Pavilion. Eileen Harris's *Apollo* article tells us that Adam was jubilant, writing to his brother James that Curzon had put

> the intire management of his Grounds ... into my hands with full powers as to Temples Bridges Seats & Cascades. So that as it only is Seven Miles round you may guess the play of Genius & Scope for Invention. A noble piece of water, a man resolved to spare no Expense, with £10,000 a Year, Good temper'd & and having taste himself for the Arts and little for Game.

The 'noble piece of water' was the spectacular canal, 2,000ft long by 6oft wide, that his uncle Sir John Curzon had commissioned from Charles Bridgeman in the 1720s. He had also made various ponds and pools –

all matters of relative ease as Kedleston has two tributaries of the River Derwent coursing through, as well as a good many springs. With the god-like powers afforded to both these young men, the turnpike road was also moved. In 1757, a year before he inherited Kedleston, Curzon arranged that part of the canal be made into a lake with an island, and thereafter Adam was to create two more. It was by Curzon's 'Upper Lake' that the Fishing Pavilion was built between 1770 and 1772. Situated at an angle, it was barely visible from the house, but picturesque perfection when looking towards it. It was the first building that you saw as you arrived, giving depth to the park and the great house beyond.

Fishing was enjoyed from the main window, and if the Curzons so wished, they could bathe in the no doubt icy-cold bath on the floor below, filled with water channelled from the nearby Bentley Well. Cold maybe, but so health-givingly sulphurous that Curzon had set up a small spa here in 1761. The Fishing Pavilion also had flanking boathouses as well as the convenience of an earth closet. While this little building appears chastely classical over the water, the entrance front on the land side is a somewhat different kettle of fish with an altogether fancier façade, including a swag beneath the pediment and George Moneypenny's carved roundels of sea horses ridden by putti on either side of a tall recessed arch around the door. The interior is an Adamesque jewel; a small single room for which the great master saw no reason to reduce his usual degree of decoration. Thanks to Harris's enchanting and scholarly article, I know that, for this relatively modest venture, Adam was aiming high. He based the pavilion's chimney piece, with Venus recumbent on a sea horse, on Piranesi's designs to go above the Earl of Exeter's chimney piece at Burghley House in Northamptonshire! Both fireplaces are also very similar.

And that is not all: a frieze of scallop shells marches round beneath the ceiling and on the walls, above arched niches, there are panels of stucco decoration flanked by paintings of fish. Sadly, Adam's painted ceiling with dancing nymphs, putti and sea horses has gone, although his designs of 1769 survive. Harris tells us of a surprising event that happened here: 'It is worth noting that a large-scale model of the warship *Victory* (later to become Nelson's flagship), made by the sculptor Michael Henry Spring in 1759, was launched in 1765.' For large-scale, I read life-size.

## Virginia Water, Windsor Great Park, Berkshire

George IV's fishing temple at Virginia Water was built as a fashionable fancy between 1825 and 1826 by Sir Jeffry Wyatville (born Wyatt, his grand augmentation was sanctioned by the king when the first stone of his transformation of Windsor Castle was laid), and later lavishly decorated by Frederick Crace. The original estimate of some £3,000 had borne no relation to the sumptuous demands that were eventually made by the pleasure-seeking 'King-Fisher', as the satirists called him, and by 1828 over £15,000 had been spent. Wyatville had created a central columned octagon, flanked by two separate hexagonal pagodas, all three with dragon entwined masts and all three with elaborate Chinese rococo embellishments such as birds and bells, spirals and finials. (By way of an exotic extra, a group of Turkish 'Tents' stood nearby.) It was described by Charles Greville as being 'beautifully ornamented, with one large room and a dressing-room on each side; the kitchen and offices are in a garden full of flowers, shut out from everything. Opposite the windows is moored a large boat, in which the band used to play during dinner, and in the summer the late King dined every day

either in the house or in the tents.' In 1828 he had worried that the king was not well and, when he went fishing and dining at Virginia Water, he would stay out late and catch cold. His beloved buildings, though, were never sound, and in 1860 Samuel Sanders Teulon was commissioned to produce drawings for their repairs, redecoration and redesign. Lamentably they came to naught and by 1900 a mere Swiss Cottage had taken their place.

Other earlier oriental arrangements had stood on the edge of Virginia Water, the great 130-acre artificial lake that had been created for the 'Butcher' Duke of Cumberland – so called after his savage conduct at the Battle of Culloden. His veteran soldiers had been dragooned in for the excavations; we trust not

commanded by the duke with his customary brutality. It was for here, though, that the 'Butcher' commissioned two Chinese fishing pavilions of exquisite finesse – one, in 1753, on water and the other, in 1759, on land. First and most fantastical was 'The Mandarin': a striped-roofed, bell-bearing pagoda, on a 40ft-long converted-to-its-royal-role hulk, with a scaled and fork-tailed dragon painted the full length of its hull. Such was its festive air that from a contemporary engraving by Thomas Sandby, your heart lifts at what appears to be a display of architectural fireworks in the oriental style. Dragons' heads rear into the sky from the crested, lilting roofs; its tall 'mast' is embellished with crescent moons, decorated with 'umbrella'-hatted bells and topped with a bird or some other creature. Vast standards and banners fly forth from the deck, which was surrounded by a wooden 'lozenged' balustrade of the same pattern as the glazing bars on the windows. There was much else besides, including, somewhat oddly, two naked figures reclining against the mast. The duke's second Chinese creation, from which he could fish, was a cluster of three elaborately carved, trellised and tile-covered octagon buildings, again with 'umbrella'-hatted bells on their, this time, star-topped finials. Mrs Lybbe Powys delighted in their curious charm in 1766, writing in her diaries (edited by Emily Climenson) that

> ...we went to the Chinese Island, on which is a small house quite in the taste of that nation, the outside of which is white tiles set in red lead, decorated with bells and Chinese ornaments. You approach the building by a Chinese bridge, and in a very hot day, as that was, the whole look'd cool and pleasing. The inside consists of two state rooms, a drawing-room, and bed-chamber, in miniature each, but corresponds with the outside appearance; the chamber hung with painted satin, the couch-bed in the recess the same; in the drawing-room was a sort of Dresden tea-china, most curious indeed, every piece a different landscape, painted inimitably; in short, the whole of the little spot is well worth seeing.

All three of the royal fishing temples in the Chinese style at Virginia Water must have been very well worth seeing. No trace of them remains today.

## Sherborne, Gloucestershire

The suddenly dead-straight road in the Gloucestershire countryside could be the first clue; the second makes you shout with surprise when you see it standing alone in the fields – a tiny and brilliant little building sparkling with an architectural brio that still sings with

the delight that created it. With a rich assembly of the latest and grandest architectural details of the 1630s jostling harmoniously on its little façade, Lodge Park was built as a beautiful – in spite of its brutal purpose – deer-coursing grandstand on the Sherborne estate. With its mile-and-a-half long coursing enclosure – hence the straight road running alongside – as well as the park in which the creatures were corralled, it is the only such arrangement to have survived in the country.

It was admired from the start – the National Trust guidebook to Lodge Park records that in 1634 a Lieutenant Hammond was full of praise for 'that neat, rare Building, the rich furnish'd Roomes, the handsome contriv'd Pens and Places, where the Deere are kept, and turn'd out for the Course'. Standing there,

*Left and below: Two views of Lodge Park,
the deer-coursing grandstand at Sherborne in
Gloucestershire.*

sparkling and alone in the fields, with crowds of grandly
attired spectators lining the balustrades of both roof
and balcony, it must have been a sensation; a surreal
stage set for a Jacobean masque, set down in the
Gloucestershire countryside.

It was all created by John 'Crump' Dutton – so called,
poor fellow, because of his hunchback – the then owner
of the Sherborne estate. According to Anthony à Wood
in his *Athenae Oxonienses* of 1691–2, Dutton was a man
who was both chaste and wise, 'a learned and prudent
man … one of the meekest in England'. He was also
'one of the richest' and surely in fact one of the most
colourful in having commissioned this dazzling little
building for deer coursing. Originally credited to Inigo
Jones, it is thought to possibly have been built by local

stonemason Valentine Strong, whose master mason son
Thomas was to lay the foundation stone of St Paul's
Cathedral! (His work is recorded there on a tablet as
having 'made shapely the stones' of the building.)

Deer were coursed at Sherborne by releasing a stag
from the (still surviving) beech spinney a full mile away
from Lodge Park. The aptly named 'Teazer' – a mongrel
greyhound – would then get the deer going (known as
'breathing') and the 'slipper' would then release two
staghounds – the French Talbot breed that are now
extinct – to race after their prey. Halfway down the
course was the 'pinching post' – if a dog reached the
deer before it, the race was invalid, or '[i]f the deere
do turne before he cometh to the pinching post, the
match is to be run again.' The rules were laid down in

*The Articles and Orders of the Paddock Course at Shirborn in Gloucestershire*. The ditch in front of the grandstand was of prime interest – the first dog to jump it was the winner. A little further on, a second ditch which was too wide for the dogs but not for the deer was often a means by which the stag could escape, although when over £20 was at stake in wagers, it would become a 'Fleshing Course' when the deer could be killed. Lodge Park could be hired out for the day's sport, with the deer 'put up', according to the *Articles and Orders*, 'at a day's warning for any Gentleman to run his Dogs paying his Fees which is half a Crown a Dog and twelve pence to the slipper for the breathing Course'.

Lodge Park was to go though four centuries of various vicissitudes. Between 1723 and 1733 it was stylishly remodelled by Dutton's great-nephew Sir John Dutton, who employed William Kent for the interior and furniture and Charles Bridgeman for the landscaping of the park. In the early 19th century it was chopped about to make a house and, worse, in the mid-19th century, a row of cottages. In 1899–1902 it was fashioned into a dower house.

Lodge Park has undergone an exemplary restoration by the National Trust and has been given the new and distinguished role of showing off the wealth of 16th-, 17th- and 18th-century paintings and furniture that belonged to the Duttons, who were given the baronacy of Sherborne in 1784. I could go on until the cows come home – or rather the deer, which thankfully they will never again, to be chased by hounds at Lodge Park.

## Dunham Massey, Cheshire

It is extraordinary to say – giving three cheers for the National Trust when saying it – that at Dunham Massey there is an ancient herd of fallow deer still roaming through a 300-acre medieval deer park within the boundary of Greater Manchester. A deer park, furthermore, that was first recorded in 1353. The medieval hall for which it was first established was demolished in 1616 and rebuilt as a vast Jacobean pile, which in 1732 was plunged into another building programme, this time lasting eight years. Dunham Massey was to go on being altered and added to until 1908.

The deer house was built in 1740 – the date is on a beam – by George Booth, 2nd Earl of Warrington, and is oddly plain considering that Booth must have been an architectural buff to his boots at the time it was built, having just finished his grand remodelling of the Jacobean pile. With the deer house, once you know what is what, you see that practicality was paramount. The upper floor is a loft into which hay can be hauled through a first-floor door at the back and then dropped into the mangers below. To air the hay, narrow vents have been cut into the bricks along both sides of the building, with the extra and aesthetic bonus of the *oeil-de-boeuf* opening on the façade. To get their food and shelter, deer come and go as they please through the suitably wide and semi-elliptical arches – three to the front and two either side.

Like a sprinkling of stardust from the gods of architecture, there are 45 listed buildings scattered throughout Dunham Massey – a good few of them for animals. In addition to the deer house, an octagonal brick and stone dovecote of the early 1800s stands in the midst of the home farm, all part of the restored working estate, with the dovecote painted in the crimson livery. Then there are the sparsely handsome brick stables of 1720; their beautiful brick body is cleanly cut with the stone surrounds of circular and segmental windows on the first floor and cross windows on the ground. Their interior survives intact with the finest stalls designed for

*Below: The 18th-century deer house at Dunham Massey in Cheshire.*

riding horses and smaller ones for the cows that supplied the dairy. The small, square brick building nearby was for the stallions to be kept away from the mares. Of the two obelisks, one was built to honour George Booth's mother, while the other – a slender 18th-century sandstone needle terminating the north vista from the house – has always been thought to honour a horse. Most surprising of all is a tiny, brick cottage-like slaughterhouse – a mere wisp of gothicary over its window – that dates from about the 18th century.

Booth had nurtured the medieval origins of his great park, surrounding it with a tall brick wall and planting it with a multitude of trees. When criticised for this extravagance, according to Roger Fisher's *Heart of Oak, the British Bulwark* of 1763, he replied: 'Gentlemen, you may think it strange that I do these things; but I have the inward satisfaction in my own breast; the benefit of posterity; ... and my survivors will receive more than double the profit, than by any other method I would possibly take for their interest.' No 'picturesque' hands were subsequently let loose on his plans and his planting. The hundreds of thousands of visitors who flock to Dunham Massey are a ringing endorsement of those wise words spoken around 270 years ago.

## Bishop Auckland, County Durham

The castellated deer shelter of 1760 in the demesne of the Bishop's Palace at Bishop Auckland was built by Richard Trevor, Bishop of Durham between 1752 and 1771, who also landscaped the park as he altered and added to his palace. His was one of the schemes of innumerable bishops who were to enhance the place from the late 12th to the late 18th century – all of them in their various ways adding layers of would-be 'ancient' contributions to its genuinely medieval core. Bishop Trevor chose the 18th-century 'gothick' revival at its most picturesque, with such additions as the

gatehouse to the park making your spirits dance with its festive air – built incidentally by Sir Thomas Robinson, amateur architect par excellence, who was always likened to a pair of scissors due to the inordinate length of his legs.

Process beneath the gatehouse into the park and after about a quarter of a mile you see a Gothic deer house perched high on a promontory. Decorated with quartrefoils and dummy loops (crosses incised to look like arrow slits) and prickling with pinnacles and castellations, it was designed by Thomas Wright of Durham. No mean claim to fame too is that he

gathered together in the centre so as to be seen from a room high in the tower.

Of Bishop Trevor we learn from George Allan in *A Sketch of the Life & Character of Richard Trevor...Bishop of Durham* of 1776 that '[t]here was a singular dignity in his Lordship's person' and that like his buildings 'he was tall, well proportioned, and of carriage erect and stately. The Episcopal robe was never worn more gracefully.' We are spared no details of the end of the poor man's life after having been attacked by gangrene when 'a mortification of the most fatal kind ensued; his toes sloughed off one after another ... the bark was taken as long and in as large quantities as ever know ... but it was too malignant ... and had already taken a mortal hold'. Bishop Trevor expired on 9 June 1771. Allan recorded the words of 'the animated preacher' John Rotheram, Rector of Houghton-le-Spring, thundering from the pulpit: 'He wore his temporal honours with dignity and ease. Never were the shining qualities of the Palatine more justly tempered by the milder graces of the Diocesan.' Nor were these his only attributes – as well as his 'gothick' embellishments to the Bishop's Palace, he was a scholar and with the genius of an artist's eye: it was Bishop Trevor who in 1756 bought the resoundingly great paintings by the Spanish artist Francisco de Zurbarán, looted from a Spanish ship, that still hang in Auckland Castle today. Incomparably powerful as you stand before them, there are 13 8ft-high portraits of Jacob and his 12 sons, who with their fierce European flash and fire are in thrilling contrast to their northern surroundings. Benjamin is in fact a copy; the original, I discover as I write this, was snapped up by my husband's ancestor Peregrine Bertie, thereby preventing the bishop from owning the complete set. It now hangs at Grimsthorpe in Lincolnshire. The bishop's Zurbaráns had cost him

reinstated the crocketted pinnacles to the western towers and central tower of Durham Cathedral, as well as pinnacles to the towers of the North Transept and the Chapel of Nine Altars.

As was to be expected with the great man, his designing of the deer house was as imaginatively practical as it was imaginatively picturesque: arches march around the walls of a square enclosure creating a passage rather like inside-out cloisters in which the deer could shelter at will. For deer watching – we can only pray that the Lord Bishop refrained from slaughter in so small an enclosure – the creatures would be

£124 and recently sold for £15,000,000.

Mitres off to Bishop Trevor for leaving legacies as diverse as the Zurbaráns and his castle for deer. Worth a mention is that this building is by way of being by divine decree, as until 1836 the Prince Bishops of Durham were all omnipotent in the county, with their own parliament, as well as their own jurisdiction – including the right to inflict capital punishment. They even had their own mint, coined from their mines of gold and silver, as well as immense wealth from the county's iron, lead and 'black diamonds' of coal.

## Willington, Bedfordshire

Willington's stables and dovecote are both stepped gabled beauties of farm buildings on the grand scale. Dating from the 1530s and 1540s, they were built for Sir John Gostwick, the then recently appointed 'Treasurer and Receiver-General of the First Fruits and Tenths for Buckinghamshire, Bedfordshire and Huntingdonshire' – the euphonious name for the collector of certain taxes from the clergy that had been diverted from going to Rome by Henry VIII. Gostwick had been Master of the Horse as well as Comptroller of Cardinal Wolsey's household – most notably accompanying him with Henry VIII to meet the French king, Francis I, at the Field of the Cloth of Gold in 1520. Before Wolsey's downfall, he rewarded his trusty old servant Gostwick by helping him to raise the £1,500 needed to buy the estate of Willington Manor in 1529.

Thereafter he worked for Thomas Cromwell, whose cruel enthusiasm for the dissolution of the monasteries he never shared, thus earning for himself – according to the *DNB* – the sobriquet of the 'stark pharisee'. He may not have liked the job but nevertheless he got on with it and Gostwick was at the forefront of the dissolution – 12 were destroyed in Bedfordshire alone;

he was directly involved in the demolition of nearby Bedford Greyfriars, Warden Abbey, Elstow Abbey and Newnham Priory. There is evidence that he used lead from Greyfriars for Willington's church roof, as well as medieval tiles from Elstow for the floor. Heaven alone knows how many of these ill-gotten gains of holy stones were used to build his stable house and dovecote.

In 1536 Gostwick was one of the chief mourners at the funeral of Katharine of Aragon and that same year was made Paymaster for the king's forces when the royal army was sent north to crush the Pilgrimage of Grace. In 1539, as a Bedfordshire MP, he sailed close to the wind by accusing Archbishop Cranmer of preaching heresy. For this he was denounced by the king as a 'varlett' and threatened with severest punishment. Nothing daunted, within months it was he who was deputed as one of the party to welcome Anne of Cleves to England on the king's behalf. In 1540 Gostwick was knighted by Henry VIII and in 1541 he was made Sheriff of Bedfordshire and Buckinghamshire. All told, a powerful figure, with a position to uphold, as he enthusiastically added ever more buildings to his Willington kingdom.

According to the National Trust, who now owns the stables, the timbers and beams have been dated through dendrochronology to the late 1530s; however, while there is evidence of the building being used as a stable, the brick floor may be no older than 200 years. So was it a stable before 1800? We simply don't know for sure, though I think it must have been – what else would have kept architectural company with a dovecote a short distance from the manor house? Traces of four loose boxes remain on the ground floor, while upstairs there is a large room with a fireplace. This is thought to have been built for extra guests when Henry VIII stayed at Willington in 1541 – with his entourage sadly unable

*Above: The carving cut into a stone above the fireplace in the stables at Willington is believed to be the signature of John Bunyan.*

*Below: The stables and dovecote at Willington, Bedfordshire.*

to avail themselves of the yet-to-be-built and excitingly enormous dovecote nearby. Measuring 20ft by 40ft and 40ft tall, it was able to house 3,000 birds. There is, however, one architectural hiccup in its fine simplicity – when the great march of stepped gables have to give way to the vertical shuttering, this leaves an odd gap.

In 1774 Willington became part of the 5th Duke of Bedford's estates. In 1850 a later duke's steward wanted to tear all the buildings down but, thanks to the urgings of the newly formed Bedford Archaeological Society, it was agreed that these two buildings should remain as curiosities. Due for the chop yet again in 1902, it was

the vicar's daughter, Caroline Orlebar, who ensured that they were taken over by the National Trust (the dovecote in 1914, the stables in 1947).

Carved into the stone above the fireplace in the stable building is the alleged signature of John Bunyan, dated 1650. We can believe that it is authentic if we want to; I do.

## Audley End, Essex

Looking for all the world like a handsome 17th-century manor, the stables of Audley End stand prominent and proud in the parkscape of the great Jacobean house they were built to serve. Built of the finest bricks between 1605 and 1616, they were designed as an architectural force in their own right. However, with their setting making their hierarchical position so clear, they were built with considerably more modesty than the vast palace that was being created at the same time by Thomas Howard, 1st Earl of Suffolk. Not only that, it was also obviously considered more suitable to design them in a Tudor style, which was by then thought to be old fashioned.

In 1603 Thomas Howard had been appointed by James I as Lord Chamberlain of the household; in 1614 he became the Lord Treasurer and royal ambition was to play no small part in the building of what was to be the largest and most magnificent house of the day. Royal 'progresses' had been a great feature of Queen Elizabeth's reign with her court progressing between the grandest of her subjects' houses, and Thomas Howard was to later nurture this tradition with a financially disastrous frenzy – even building separate and splendid suites for both James I and Queen Anne; indeed, the stables are thought to have been originally erected to accommodate the royal servants, though they were soon adapted for stable use. Eventually suspected and found guilty of embezzlement, Howard retired in disgrace to Audley End, surrounded by the grandeur that had ruined him.

In 1666, the great palace – it was nothing less – was bought by Charles II who added a Catholic chapel for his wife Catherine of Braganza. All this was largely because Audley End was so convenient for Newmarket races! The house was returned to the Howard family in 1701 and during their tenure and over the subsequent

years was to be substantially reduced in size, as well as ravishingly enhanced, by such giants as John Vanbrugh and Robert Adam, and with Capability Brown transforming the park.

In 1751 Audley End was bought by the Countess of Portsmouth, who remodelled the building ensuring that only original materials were used. In 1762 it was inherited by her nephew Sir John Griffin Griffin, later 1st Baron Braybrooke, who was responsible for the cobweb-like-in-its-delicacy Gothick chapel, as well as for commissioning Adam to design a ravishing jewel of a drawing room. In 1825 Richard Neville, 3rd Baron Braybrooke, inherited the still great remains of the house – but by now only a third of its original size – and went on to reverse many of Adam's classical interiors in order to restore the Jacobean style. Throughout all these monumentally important changes in the march of its architectural history, the stables of Audley End – with

their steep-roofed gables, their stone window surrounds and their hood moulds – appear little changed. In reality, they have been adapted in various ways over the centuries. The two red-brick bays and central doorway were added soon after construction to convert the building for stable use; in the mid-18th century a castellated parapet was added and later removed; and later still, in the 1880s a lantern was inserted into the roof. The stables have recently been beautifully restored by English Heritage.

## Peover, Cheshire

There are earlier survivals than the 17th-century stables at Peover Hall and there are grander survivals of the same date – there are even those of similar design – but what, most emphatically, there are not, are stables with such an abundance of decorative plasterwork, with strapwork and writhing flowers encrusting the ceiling. Not only that, with ornate wooden arches, supported by wooden Tuscan columns beneath a long strapwork frieze of wood, these are quarters more suitable for humans – decoratively discerning ones at that – than they are for horses. They were built in 1654 as we are clearly told, in letters cut into stone above the main door: 'The Gift of Mrs Ellen Mainwaring to her son Thomas Mainwaring Esq'. The lettering is particularly elegant, as is every aspect of the stables; in fact a little surprisingly so, because during the Civil War, Ellen Mainwaring's husband, Thomas's father, had been a captain of horse in the parliamentary forces, many of whom tended to favour simpler decorative forms.

The family owned Peover from the Norman Conquest to the 20th century. In 1639 Sir Philip Mainwaring was appointed Irish secretary by Thomas Wentworth, Earl of Strafford – doomed to be beheaded before a crowd of 200,000 on Tower Hill. Van Dyck painted a portrait of them together in 1639 – Strafford swarthy and coarse featured, Mainwaring with a face and hands of exquisite refinement. Thomas Mainwaring, for whom the stables were built, was his great-nephew.

It is thought that the craftsmen who worked on the stables were the same as those who carved the screen in the private chapel of nearby Cholmondeley Castle in 1655. Oddly alike – although their setting is so startlingly different – the chapel screen is also marching strapwork arches, but at Cholmondeley they have Corinthian capitals rather than the Tuscan order of the stables' columns. While one frames an altar, the other frames the hindquarters of horses.

The main floor of the stables is made of stone slabs with flint cobbles in the stalls – popular at the time although difficult to keep clean. A rare example of an upright timber hay rack is framed by Gothic arches and the efficient new drainage system of the 16th century can be seen.

The Mainwaring family had already built some comparable stables in 1597 at Whitmore Hall in Staffordshire. With no decorative plasterwork, they are simpler than Peover's although they have the more elaborate details of enormous double wooden balls hanging from the centre of each arch, and of strange applied strapwork rods instead of pillar capitals.

## Penicuik, Midlothian

The stables of Penicuik House were built by Sir James Clerk in the 1760s, slap bang in front of the house. He gave them every bit as much architectural attention as the great Palladian pile that he was building at the same time. And it was fortunate that he did – for when the house was gutted by fire in 1899, the stables were there, more than adequately ready to be adapted as a

house that could reign supreme over the ruin. Here they can be seen through Penicuik's fire-ravaged portico.

Sir James had inherited the estate, with the 17th-century Newbiggin Hall, in 1755. His father, Sir John Clerk, had been too fond of the old hall to make alterations – 'Better in its antique figure than if it was all new built' – and had concentrated on improving the estate. Between 1700 and 1730, he planted over 300,000 trees in the naturally beautiful setting beneath the Pentland Hills. He created lakes and built follies, a bridge, a tunnel with an underground room and a pavilion. When he died the way was clear for his son James to set a palace down in this perfect landscape. Which he did – after having demolished Newbiggin Hall and employing John Baxter as master builder to help him realise his plans. They began work on the house and stables in 1761, and between them created two buildings of both spirit and distinction that hail one another on equal terms. The house, seven bays long and three stories high, has a thumping great Ionic portico. The stables have an arched portico beneath a clock leading you into a courtyard; the stable block formed one side, while the coach house, the brewhouse and the bakehouse formed the other three. Circular stairs were built in all four corners, making the walls bulge out where the angles should be. And once you have walked through into the courtyard, you are faced by a great surprise: a simple pedimented arch supporting a replica of 'Arthur's O'on', a remarkable beehive-shaped structure created by the Romans during their occupation of Scotland (*see* pp 146 and 147).

After the fire in 1899, as full insurance could not be paid on a house that was still standing, the architects Lessels & Taylor were employed to make the stables habitable. Statuary – commissioned in Italy by Sir James Clerk in the 1760s – as well as door-cases (the door surrounds) and fireplaces (one from old Newbiggin Hall) were moved from the ruin. Now, with a fountain echoing in the courtyard, planted as a bright garden and watched over by the tall spire and the hump of 'Arthur's O'on', the atmosphere of the old stables is both rare and strange.

Today a new excitement in the air is the Penicuik House Project, founded in 2008 with the eventual aim of securing the future of Penicuik and its surrounding landscape for locals to enjoy. There are training courses underway on construction, conservation and crafts, and the Scottish Lime Centre Trust is organising workshops for traditional building techniques. There will be apprenticeship training, educational and practical training, and opportunities to work on the house. Incidentally, despite being open to the elements for more than 110 years, much of the masonry of Penicuik House still remains sound.

## Berkeley, Gloucestershire

The 18th-century stables of Berkeley Castle are as festive as the great 14th-century castle they were built to serve is frowning – one contained, light and pretty, the other rambling, bold and immense. Ten Gothic stable doors beneath ten Gothic windows divided by a central Gothic arch march along beneath castellations. At the back of the building, the brick changes to stone, the Gothic windows become latticed and the castellations taller – the whole designed as an eye-catcher to be seen from the castle across the meadows. All in all a charming Gothic exercise, although a surprisingly modest one for the oldest pack of foxhounds in the country. Giles Worsley in his excellent *The British Stable* of 2004 thinks that the architect-astronomer Thomas Wright was probably responsible for their design.

Below: The 18th-century stables at Berkeley Castle in Gloucestershire.

Right: The stables at Seaton Delaval, Northumberland.

The Berkeley Hunt was established in the 12th century and for the next five and a half centuries hunted within a radius that grew to span the lands between the banks of the River Severn and the heights of Islington and Highgate – some 130 miles apart. However, on the death of the 5th Earl of Berkeley in 1810, some of the land was divided and other hunts formed. The area that the Berkeley hunted was reduced but the loyalty of their supporters certainly wasn't – there is a wonderful tale of a 19th-century hunt follower, yeoman farmer Jack Hawkins, who lived over the water from Berkeley Castle on the Welsh side of the River Severn. So eager was he to follow the pack that he would regularly swim from bank to bank, hanging onto his horse's tail. So often did he make this journey that contemporary maps were printed with 'Jack Hawkins Esq' spanning the Severn like a bridge.

It was the 5th Earl of Berkeley who had the stables rebuilt in 1763 – the perfect backdrop for the assembled horses, hounds and huntsmen of the Berkeley Hunt in their unique livery of canary yellow. Frederick Augustus Berkeley was a brilliant horseman, whose marital life was as colourful as his riding to hounds – like his ancestors, hunting as far as London. After having had seven children by Mary Cole, the local butcher's daughter, he married her in 1796 and had six more. Concerned – almost out of their wits it would seem – that their oldest and illegitimate son would not be able to inherit, the earl and his wife forged an entry of an earlier and 'secret' wedding in the church register. It was not believed, and in 1811 the Berkeley Peerage case went to the House of Lords with the by now widowed countess writing her appeal 'with much feeling and elevation of sentiment' according to the Minutes of Evidence. She was turned down. Living in terror of arrest for perjury, Lady Berkeley built an escape route at Cranford – their house in Middlesex – with the arrangement of a trap door in her bedroom, through which she could escape via a rope ladder down to the brick-vaulted cellars, and thence to freedom over the fields. Those cellars still survive today beneath the public playing fields at Cranford. This house has now gone but the accompanying 18th-century Dutch-gabled stables still survive – showing the extent of the hunt's once far-flung territory – within half a mile of Heathrow Airport and within a few feet of the M4 motorway.

Lord and Lady Berkeley had been a formidable pair, particularly in their friendship and support of their local doctor Edward Jenner, pioneer of vaccination against smallpox. They defended him against his critics, introduced him to the royal family and, most importantly, they were among the first in the country to have their children vaccinated.

## Seaton Delaval, Northumberland

The expression 'stone cold' comes to chillingly beautiful life with these stables, which are surrounded by stone on all sides – with walls, floors, stall partitions and, in fact, the whole building made of stone – standing on windswept flatlands hard by the North Sea.

Of a monumental dignity worthy of attribution to Sir John Vanbrugh, who was the architect of the great house that the stables were built to serve, they in fact date from a full 50 years later. The baroque masterpiece of Seaton Delaval Hall was started in 1718; the Palladian masterpiece of its stables was begun in 1768. Admiral George Delaval had commissioned Vanbrugh to build the house (both died before it was finished) whereas the stables, it would seem, were the work of Delaval's dashing great-nephew, Sir Francis Delaval. There is no record of an architect, but a letter he wrote to his brother tells us all. Having seen Lord Hopetoun's 'very magnificent' stables at Hopetoun House in Midlothian, built by John Adam between 1750 and 1756,

Delaval was determined to build some of his own on the same grand plan. Furthermore, he had already built a west wing in front of the house, and a corresponding stable block to the east would complete the desired symmetry.

The result was an equine palace, 68ft long by 35ft wide, that elegantly reflected the new, much to be welcomed, admiration for neoclassical stable design. Three great arches sweep up almost to the full height of the building with the central one spanning the apse, and with a Venetian window looking out into the stable yard. There are 12 stalls, each with a lead-lined feeding trough below the arched niches for the hay racks. The names of the first horses to live here in the late 1760s are still elegantly painted on plaques above the keystone of each niche: Zephyrus, Hercules, Tartar, Regulus, Peacock, Julius, Chance, Prince, Pilot, Captain, Admiral and Steady.

When the beauties were finished, Sir Francis Delaval held a banquet down the main aisle of the stables to celebrate (with, we must hope, at least a few horses nodding over the proceedings). One of 13 children – known as the 'Gay Delavals' for their colourful and outlandish pursuits – Sir Francis was the most colourful of the lot. An MP, Knight of the Bath, soldier and dilettante, he would regularly stage his own theatricals, and they were neither mean nor modest events. When playing the title role in his production of *Othello*, he was given the Drury Lane Theatre for the evening by David Garrick no less. Even more unusual, Parliament was adjourned two hours early for the performance. Sir Francis loved practical jokes and installed devilish devices at Seaton Delaval – one lowered the beds of his unsuspecting guests into tanks of icy cold water in the middle of the night; another slid the walls aside suddenly revealing the occupant of the next-door bedroom. The stables were his last great act of extravagance, matching the splendour of the house itself.

While the stables have remained miraculously untouched, the house has suffered from near fatal disasters – in 1752 there was a fire in the west wing, and in 1822 an inferno ravaged the main central block. Yet every cloud, however dark, has a silver lining. For, with its dividing walls and floors gone, Vanbrugh's skeleton of stone was revealed rising to the full height of the building. So it remained until the 1950s when Lord and Lady Hastings, Delaval descendants, moved into the west wing and set about doing what repairs they could. They died in 2007 and in December 2009 this hulk of a great house was bought by the National Trust. More than £3,000,000 had to be raised and thanks to an unprecedented groundswell of local support – including a 'Hike for the Hall' by the Scouts and 700 local schoolchildren 'Hugging the Hall' – this was achieved. What many consider to be Vanbrugh's greatest work – including Blenheim and Castle Howard – now stands

safe and sound on the outskirts of Newcastle upon Tyne for the use of the local people. With Seaton Delaval, Vanbrugh had produced a triumph of originality – having always loved the north as opposed to what he called the 'tame sneaking south', he has been proved spot on right.

## Brighton, East Sussex

'The dome has not yet fallen' wrote William Porden in triumph to his daughter in 1804, as the supports were removed from the great dome over the stables that he was building in Brighton for the Prince of Wales. He had begun his exotic schemes in 1804 and when they were finished in 1808, the stables were to be the first large building in the 'Indian Style' in the country. Not only that, when these equine splendours ended up towering over the prince's somewhat modest house nearby, they were to inspire and encourage the even more exotic extravagances of the Brighton Pavilion itself. The prince had delighted in 'Brighthelmstone' since 1783 and three years later had commissioned Henry Holland to classicise a modest farmhouse that became known as the Marine Pavilion for him to live in with his mistress, Mrs Fitzherbert. Designed with a dome less than half the size of the one that was to soar up over the stables only feet away, it gave hilarious credence to the rest of Europe's view that the English housed their horses better than they housed themselves – even, to boot, their royal selves!

Influences from the east had started to infiltrate into the prince's plans by 1801, with Porden's unrealised scheme to add a Chinese façade to his house. In the end, first past the oriental post was the equine palace modelled on the general plan of the great Jami' Masjid Mosque in Delhi. The dome, somewhat squat as an evocation of the east, was inspired by, of all things, the

Halle au Blé – a cornmarket in the Paris of 1782 (now
the Bourse du Commerce). The dome is huge – at 80ft
in diameter it is only 20ft short of the dome of St Paul's
Cathedral – hence Porden's terror that it could have
come crashing down when unsupported. Timber
framed, with lotus-leaf shaped panels of glass divided by
stucco panels, it swept over dazzling delights of eastern
promise: a myriad of scallop-arched windows and doors,
great and small, and over the main entrance, a series of
receding arches. There were 44 stables, 5 coach houses
and 2 harness rooms, while upstairs, leading off the
arched balcony were 20 bedrooms for the ostlers, stable
boys and grooms. The cost was enormous, reckoned to
have amounted to £60,000 and the Prince of Wales
never paid the bills. Mr Saunders, in charge of the
timber work, was to die a broken man – heavily in debt
and owed some £10,000. The startlingly beautiful
stable interior can be seen in John Nash's *The Royal
Pavilion at Brighton*, one of an exquisite assembly of
engravings and aquatints done for the Prince Regent.

The Riding House is attached to these stables –
another oriental fancy on the grand scale dreamt up by
Porden and the Prince of Wales between 1804 and
1808. Lit all around by scallop-arched windows and
measuring 178ft by 58ft, it was often described at the
time as one of the largest rooms in the world.

Henry Holland, William Porden, John Nash, James
Wyatt and Humphry Repton, geniuses all, drew up
plans for the Royal Pavilion for the Prince of Wales.
Repton published his *Designs for the Pavillion at Brighton*
in 1808 – as was his enticing way – in a Red Book in
which he painted 12 scenes of the place as he first found
it. All were drawn on flaps, which, when lifted, revealed
his proposed improvements of new buildings set down
in his newly romanticised landscape. One depicts
the exterior of the stables which he described as a

'...stupendous and magnificent building, which, by its
lightness, its elegance, its boldness of construction and
the symmetry of it proportions, does credit to both the
genius of the artist and the good taste of the royal
employer'.

However it was John Nash who got the job. Between
1815 and 1822 he flung fancy dress over the Marine
Pavilion transforming it into the famed Brighton
Pavilion. The new building incorporated the Riding
House in 1823 by joining it to the Pavilion by way of an
underground tunnel – so entirely overcoming the
discomfort of riding in the damp climes of Brighton.
The Riding House later became the Corn Exchange and
is now used for exhibitions and receptions. The stables
were let as cavalry barracks from 1856 to 1864.
Afterwards renamed as 'The Dome', they became a
great concert hall which, with various alterations, it has
remained to this day.

## Megginch, Perthshire

The romantic, rambling pile of Megginch Castle dates
from the 15th to the 20th century. Its Gothic stable yard
and octagonal dovecote – with the sweep of cobbles
beneath your feet – were, on the other hand, built in
one glorious go by Captain Robert Drummond between
1806 and 1809.

He made six journeys to China in the East Indiaman
the *General Elliot*, the first copper-bottomed vessel in the
East India Fleet. In 1783 she had made a record-
breaking voyage to Bombay taking 'two days less than
four months'. And it was also in the *General Elliot* that
Captain Robert's younger brother, Captain Adam
Drummond, had brought the first double red camellia
from China to Britain in 1794, planting it at Megginch.
Two years later Captain Adam, again in the *General
Elliot*, brought the first white Banksian rose to Britain

and also planted it at Megginch. Both continue to flower to this day. The planting of an oak tree on the edge of the stable yard was recorded in 1815 by Captain Robert's sister Jane Athole (and in turn recorded by Cherry Drummond in her mid-20th-century booklet on Megginch): 'On Thursday 30th March 1815 an oak tree was planted in the stable yard in remembrance of our dear brother Robert Drummond by the gardener Duncan Robertson in the presence of my brother Adam and myself.' They put a halfpenny under the root 'for luck'.

Today that enormous oak tree looms large over this most delicate of stable courtyards. With the wealth of Gothic windows and doors – with filigree-fine glazing bars giving such a sense of liveliness and light – it is as if they are prancing the eightsome reel around the lilting roofed pagoda. There is a good deal of enduring beauty at Megginch – most particularly this set piece of the stable yard which is still in happy working use; the only difference today in this pretty-as-a-picture architectural assembly is that the doors are painted palest pink. The dovecote has a contemporary model of the *General Elliot*, obviously proudly cast and put up by Captain Robert Drummond, acting as a weathervane atop its eastern roof.

In 2006 the fortunes of Megginch took a dramatic turn when its then owner – Cherry Drummond, Baroness Strange – changed her will on her deathbed in favour of her youngest daughter Katherine Herdman. It was done at 4 o'clock in the morning and she died the next day. Katherine, her husband Giles Herdman and their children – direct descendants of the Drummonds who came to Megginch in 1664 – now look after and love the estate.

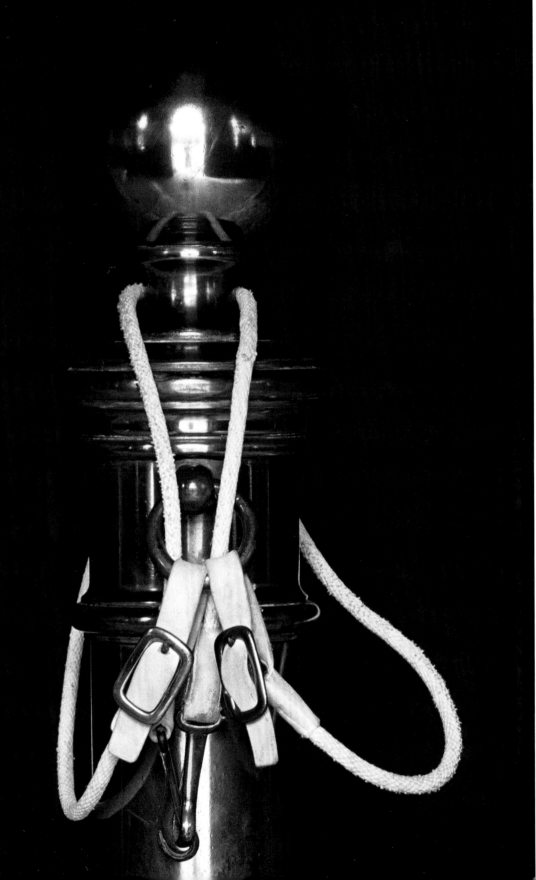

## Manderston, Berwickshire

'There is an air of melancholy interest about the stables at Manderston', reported *Country Life's* 1914 article 'Small country buildings of to-day'. It was lamenting the early death at 43 of Sir James Miller, who had commissioned the buildings for a terrifying sum of £25,000 in 1895. Our anonymous correspondent – going by the name of 'X' – was no doubt also lamenting that within 10 years of these stables being built, the age of the horse was over and the age of the car had begun.

Sir James Miller was a 'King of the Turf'; his horse Sainfoin won the Derby in 1890 and in 1903 Rock Sand won the Triple Crown (the Derby, St Leger and Two Thousand Guineas). He was also inordinately rich – the fortune had been founded by his father trading in herrings and hemp with Russia, and his son determined to spend it on one of the most beautifully built houses of its day in Britain. He succeeded. The architect John Kinross, already renowned for his attention to detail, was mooted as the architect to realise these schemes – but first came the hurdle of building the stables to see if he was up to the job. He was. They are magnificent but entirely restrained. Pedimented ranges of finely cut grey ashlar are built around a quadrangle and you are led through a handsome pilastered archway beneath a coat of arms and great brass bell, past carvings of a hunt in full cry, to find the main stable yard paved with radial patterns of stone set in brick. Directly opposite is another pediment over the arched doorway opening into the stalls. All was, and still is, immaculate with knobs on – literally so, with a shining brass ball atop the shining brass heelpost between every stall. Each one is still hung – if you can believe such a thing – with headcollars of white rope, the softest white kid and brass. Wood blocks are laid in a herringbone pattern on the floor in front of the stalls.

In the tack room, where saddles and bridles hang in abundance, there are lofty glass-fronted mahogany cupboards ranged around the black-and-white chequerboard marble floor.

Both inside and out the workmanship is of outstanding quality using the very finest materials; the woodwork, the barrel-vaulted roof, the carved ventilators as well as the stalls' partitions are all made of finest teak. The names of the horses are in brass filigree frames set into marble above each stall. Like Miller and Manderston, they all begin with M: Melakoff, Mango,

Magic, Monarch, Marsden, Mystery, Matchless, Margot, Milton, Mabel, Mercat, Maiden Erleigh, Monty and Milly. The stables at Manderston have been described by *Horse and Hound* as the finest in the world, while our anonymous 'X' writing in *Country Life* gave them somewhat poetic praise:

> The stables are laid out in the spacious manner of our forefathers ... The stud boxes, the loose boxes for the hunters, and the stalls for the carriage and coach horses are almost perfection in their arrangement and relation to one another ... I can imagine the Master of such a stable might spend many pleasant moments watching his horses enjoy their rest and listening to their slow solemn munching and the rattle of a chain or the stamp of a hoof, which are such pleasant sounds to the ear of a man who loves horses.

His laments though, are not far away: 'Will our grandchildren visit with the same sort of tender regret the deserted garages and try to sniff the odours of petrol?'

At Manderston they might; for almost immediately after this great equine palace was built, it had to be doubled up with an equally grand building for the horseless carriage. Sir James had failed to see the potential of the motor car and found himself having to construct a great 'motor house' for this new mode of transport. Once again no expense was spared – lined throughout with ceramic tiles, even in the working pits, it also has marble inlays around all the taps and radiators.

That the stables were an architectural triumph was not in doubt and Kinross was given free rein with the design of the house, with Sir James's cheering dictum no doubt ringing in his ears that 'money is of no importance whatsoever'.

## Milton, Peterborough

Hounds that were originally thought to have come from Bordeaux under the auspices of Sir Bernard Brocas, a friend of Richard II, have been kennelled at Milton since the Abbot of Peterborough was given the right to hunt the surrounding royal forests in the 14th century. After the dissolution of the monasteries, the hounds were put in the hands of the Fitzwilliams whose family fortune was founded by Sir William Fitzwilliam – treasurer to Cardinal Wolsey – who had bought the land, the estate and the hunt at Milton in 1502. It has all remained with them to this day, with the hounds considered one of the 'governing packs' of England – along with the Brocklesby and the Belvoir – which means that most other packs in the country have been bred from them. Sadly for the hound historian, the Fitzwilliam kennels, with all their pedigree books, were destroyed by fire in 1760. Sadly for the hound historian maybe, but happily for the lover of 18th-century architectural fancy dress as this tiny mock 'medieval' ruined gatehouse was then built as a replacement. With its towers and castellated and bastioned screen, few kennels can be so picturesque – although nothing less should be expected from Sir William Chambers, who many have given credit for their design. After all it was he who designed 25 buildings at Kew Gardens, including a menagerie, a mosque, a Palladian bridge and the 'Great Stove' hothouse – all long since gone; however, his orangery still survives as do his Temples of Bellona and Aeolus, along with a ruined arch. The most ebullient of all, is his great 10-storey Chinese Pagoda of 1761. At Milton, Chambers had made alterations to the house, as well as designing a temple and, possibly, the kennels.

Curiously, there are no records of who did what with the various buildings on the estate. In 1791 Repton made

proposals for re-landscaping the park; indeed it is thought that he collaborated with John Nash on a richly ornate Gothic lodge that stands nearby. So at least, declared the eminent architectural historian Christopher Hussey. Today, in a clash of the Titans, John Martin Robinson attributes this to William Wilkins Snr.

At the end of the 20th century there were new Gothic – and glorious – improvements to the lodges, designed by Philip Naylor-Leyland, descendant of the Fitzwilliams whose family have lived here since 1502. He is joint master of the Fitzwilliam (Milton) Hunt. His wife Isabella is my sister.

Since the hunting ban was imposed, the Fitzwilliam have been dedicated to carry on with the chase. As Philip says: 'Hunting has the overwhelming support of the countryside, so it seemed inconceivable that it could be successfully outlawed. Fortunately, its continuation has been assured by poorly drafted legislation, which has served mainly to increase its popularity.' With joint master George Bowyer announcing that he was prepared to go to jail rather than hang up his saddle and with more than 100 members of the hunt protesting in London, a way was found to keep the hunt going. Under the Hunting Act of 2005 dogs can be worked, as long as the killing of the fox is done by either a gun or a bird of prey.

The kennels now house 38½ 'entered' couples (hounds that have been hunted) and 14½ couples of puppies. There are three yards behind the castellations – the main one and two 'draw yards' where the hounds are sorted out. The 'feed house' is from where the 'fallen stock', collected by the hunt as a service to local farmers, is daily distributed to the pack. There are three 'lodges' where the hounds sleep. The valeting room in the tower – where boots, coats and whips are cleaned – is painted from floor to ceiling with a local artist's murals of the old favourites of the Milton Hunt – human, equine and canine.

## Nunwick, Northumberland

The hound kennels at Nunwick are as pretty as a picture; indeed a picture is what you get in this book – a delicate ink and wash by William Beilby of Newcastle upon Tyne – as atrocious weather made it impossible to photograph the building. It was built by Sir Lancelot Allgood, a magistrate and MP who was knighted by George III. (His half-sister was Hannah Glasse, whose *The Art of Cookery, Made Plain and Easy* of 1746 made her the first cookery writer in the country to achieve nationwide fame.) Between 1748 and 1752 Daniel Garrett built Sir Lancelot's house, described in

Eneas Mackenzie's *An Historical, Topographical and Descriptive View of the County of Northumberland* of 1825 as 'a remarkably genteel structure of white freestone'; in 1768 Sir Lancelot arranged that this little castle be built to house his hounds. Gothic and with lancet windows, it was designed to be seen as a pleasingly romantic ruin from the house.

In 1782 Sir Lancelot was succeeded by young James Allgood who put the kennels to active use with the beguiling addition of a 'guinea hen' who exercised daily with the hounds – racing along to the front of the pack for as far as 70 miles. She even went out hunting and when exhausted would perch on the back of the huntsman's saddle as the chase jolted on. Delighted in to this day, the bird is stuffed in a glass case at Nunwick – with one claw missing, trodden off by a horse. A far worse fate eventually befell the bird, as I was told in a letter from a more recent Lancelot Allgood in 1991. Apparently its head was bitten off by a young hound who did not know it.

James Allgood had been famed in his undergraduate youth as 'The Celebrated Gentleman Jock' who raced under the name of 'Captain Barlow'. As a grandee aspiring to the cloth, it was thought to be a questionable activity; furthermore, according to John Fowler in his *Recollections of Old Country Life* of 1894: 'It was considered inadvisable that the university authorities or their parents should know that they were riding races.' There were many such 'Varsity men ... accustomed to ride their aristocratic mares ... in the Aylesbury Aristocratic Steeplechases' who revelled in their anonymous notoriety. In his earlier *Echoes of Old Country Life* of 1892, Fowler describes how James Allgood had won a wager to jump his horse over a table laden with food and drink at the White Hart in Aylesbury:

The horse answered to his cry of 'Come up,' and just cleared the table, but caught one of its heels on its edge, and pulling the cloth over smashed a few plates and glasses, which fell with a loud clatter, whereupon the ride struck the gallant steed with his open hand, and again he cleared the whole in much better style than before.

Fowler's account in *Recollections of Old Country Life* of a perforce anonymous 'sporting rector in the extreme north' must also surely be James Allgood:

who was *facile princeps* as a rider over our Aylesbury course, and who won more races as an undergraduate than any other at the 'Varsity'. Amongst his sporting parishioners his horsemanship was greatly admired ... The rector often rode to church, sometimes across country ... and the parishioners assembled in the churchyard, waiting for his advent, would watch his progress ... with keen relish, expressing themselves enthusiastically as one fence after the other was safely negotiated. One of them would say 'He's safely over the single;' another, 'Now he's at the double;' 'Yes, he's all right;' 'What will he do at the rails?' 'He's well over;' and the last thing he jumped was the churchyard wall. I am writing these anecdotes with no irreverent spirit, as I am told there are no more devoted men to the wants of their poorer parishioners than these very men, and they are no mean preachers from their pulpits. I never could see why exercise on horseback and the reasonable sports of the field should be loudly condemned, any more than exercise on the river or the cricket-field. Muscular Christianity is human and full of good omen, and oftentimes unites the parson and his flock.

Below: The 'Elevation and Plan of a Dog House designed for a nobleman' by Sir John Soane.

Having fallen into a state of disrepair, the kennels have recently been restored, as well as festively planted with flowers, so as to be even more eye-catching from the house.

## Sir John Soane's dog houses

The 'Elevation and Plan of a Dog House designed for a nobleman' of 1778 hangs in the almost-too-narrow-to-walk-through study of Sir John Soane's extraordinary house in Lincoln's Inn Fields. It is a building where real magic seems to have been wrought; where every conceivable – and inconceivable – architectural trick has been employed. With its endlessly curious series of spaces – enhanced by mirrors – it seems like some beautiful yet crazed jigsaw, made complete by having missing pieces. Soane had lived here between 1792 and 1837, honing his home into 'A Temple of Art' by obsessively furnishing and filling, rebuilding and extending – in his own words 'distending its little body to the upmost endurance of its skin'.

In 1833 he had the house protected by the Soane Museum Act of Parliament, ensuring that all his idiosyncratic arrangements were protected in perpetuity. The house is therefore exactly how he left it – and the kennel was the first thing he saw when he looked up from his desk.

The 'Residence for the Canine Family of Ancient times', as Soane liked to call it, was designed in 1778 for the disreputable Lord Bishop of Derry, Frederick Augustus Hervey, who was then soon to be elevated to be the 4th Earl of Bristol. They had met in Italy, when the 25-year-old Soane was on a three-year long grand tour scholarship from the Royal Academy, and the Lord Bishop had bewitched the young architect with grand proposals for his Irish estate. First amongst them was to be a dog kennel for the hounds of his eldest son.

Inspired by a visit that they made together to the site of Lucullus's Villa near Terracina on Christmas day in 1778, the idea of classical kennels had appealed to the bishop – and Soane was his man, on hand, determined to show the convenient charms of the style. Without unsightly concessions to its working role, a circular exercise yard embraces three wings that splay forth from the central rotunda. One is a residence for the kennel man, another the veterinary sick bay and the third is for the bitches – while the dogs were kept beneath the dome. With the Doric order – so simple, clean and clear – the bishop and Soane had made a handsome case for the general use of the neoclassical style. As a proud cheer, or rather bark, four dogs sit tall

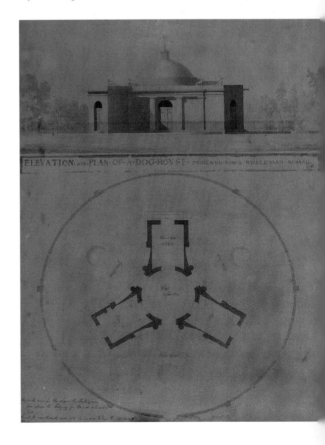

on the parapet, while another leaps high in the sky on the weathervane. Although the original architectural drawings were lost – no doubt purloined by the Lord Bishop – Soane made a copy of them from memory in 1781, to be exhibited in the Royal Academy. This is what hangs in his house in Lincoln's Inn today.

Nothing was to come of any of it: cock-a-hoop with such important commissions on the horizon, Soane cut short his precious studies in Italy and sped to work on the bishop's estates at Ickworth, Suffolk, and Downhill, Ireland. It was all to be in vain. His proposals were rejected and he returned to England without payment – not even for every penny spent on travel! He never got over it; in his memoirs nearly 50 years later he wrote: 'Experience ... taught me how much I had overrated the magnificent promises and splendid delusions of The Lord Bishop of Derry.'

Despite rejecting the great Soane, the bishop was a builder on the grand scale – creating not only palaces and houses, but also an abundance of roads, bridges and monuments. His road works alone were likened to those of a Roman emperor rather than an Irish bishop; and William Childe-Pemberton's biography records a description of him when in Italy that suggests that it was not only his building that would liken him to a Roman emperor:

> He was a reprobate with profane conversation ... always giving himself the airs of Adonis. He is the strangest being ever made with all the vices and foibles of youth, a drunkard and an atheist, although a Bishop, constantly talking blasphemy or indecency at least, and at the same time very clever and with infinite wit. He courts every young and every old woman he knows.

Heaven alone knows why young Soane was not warned.

## Belvoir, Leicestershire

'I have seen many kennels in my day, but none so picturesque as the home of the Belvoir pack', wrote Thomas Francis Dale, the decidedly unpoetic chronicler of *The History of the Belvoir Hunt* (1899) who, at the sight of this building, abandoned his stolid prose for poetry:

> ...coming to it as I did the first time, along the road through the park ... the eye is first attracted to the Castle, with its absolutely unrivalled position and its splendid grouping of massive towers, amid the rich foliage of the Belvoir woods; while on the right, near the River Devon, which flows through the park, lie the ... large and handsome ... kennels... .

Claimed to date between 1802 and 1809 they were built for the 5th Duke of Rutland who had inherited Belvoir in 1787 when he was only nine years old. With no ducal figure at the helm, the hunt was to grind to a halt and during what was called 'The Long Minority' it was left to his mother, the Dowager Duchess Isabella (known as 'Was a bella' after she lost her looks), to press for its revival. After cross-breeding with hounds from such established packs as the Fitzwilliam, the Beaufort and the Brocklesby, by the time the duke attained his majority in 1799 his hunt was up and running once again. Becoming master in 1805, he took on the celebrated 'Gentleman Shaw' as huntsman; a man 'of superior attainments and possibly superior birth' who, above all others, was to nurture the Belvoir Hunt to nationwide fame. Dale tells us that 'Gentleman Shaw' was especially noted for his relationship with his hounds and that to give them confidence when they were clustering around him, 'Shaw would take his cap off and cheer them with enthusiasm ... And when the chiming pack, heads up, sterns down, started to race over the grass, Shaw, riding beside them, his face alight

with pleasure was in his glory.' The stuff of hunting
legend, his runs were written of in both prose and
poetry; one anonymous admirer penned a saga of
21 verses which was faithfully reproduced in Dale's
book, and included these lines:

> Written in commemoration of a most famous fox-
> chase run by the Duke of Rutland's hounds,
> December 10th 1805:
>
> Ye sportsmen, attend to my song,
> Which to please you I hope will no fail:
> It's a fox-chase full three hours long,
> And was run over Belvoir's sweet Vale.
> 'Twas Tuesday, the 10th of December,
> The Duke fixed at Waltham to meet,

> But the frost was so hard, I remember,
> The horses could scarce keep their feet.
>
> The huntsman came on his grey,
> And rolled his eye round like a hawk;
> Not a second in that place would he stay,
> As your sport he never will baulk,
> He then made a cast with his hounds,
> When the fox jumped quickly in view,
> And like pigeons they skirted the grounds,
> And left Craven,* Vanneck, and a few.
>
> In three miles this noble chase ended,
> We whipped off at Barton Slade Wood;
> To the Castle we then our pace mended,
> And trotted as fast as we could.

The ladies (God bless their sweet faces!)
With smiles came to welcome us home;
Their looks were like those of the Graces
And old Belvoir Olympus's dome.

Now a bumper we'll drink to his Grace,
A full bumper to him and his hounds,
And long may he live at the place
Where health and good humour abounds.
May his family flourish for ages,
Such a noble sport to pursue,
And the poet to be hanged now engages,
If this song in all points be not true.

*Berkeley Craven, one of the dandies in Beau Brummel's set.

As hunting became an ever more prosperous activity, money was to be made and spent: in 1822 the Duke of Rutland gave 800 guineas for a hunter that, according to *The Sporting Magazine,* had cleared the River Swift – 9yds wide. More than 20 years earlier, £60,000 had gone towards celebrating his marriage and thereafter countless thousands of pounds were to be poured into schemes for rebuilding the castle and estate. With his wife Elizabeth as the driving force, the architect James Wyatt had been employed to recreate a 'medieval' castle at Belvoir, and they no doubt collaborated on the many and various buildings of the demesne – the dairy (*see* pp 112–14) and the kennels, both with central-roofed octagons, are unquestionably architectural kin.

Stone balls seem to leap around the kennels – on stone piers standing regularly between the wooden railings around the yard, above the entrance arch as well as supporting the fox weathervane on the peak of the roof. The great sweeping double-roofed octagon with an arch on each wall at ground level was built as a place for boiling the hounds' food and for giving it out.

The hounds' 'lodging-houses' were also built here, as well as the living quarters for the feeders. Square flagstones covered all the floors. Two little stone buildings, like lodges on guard at either side of this 20,000sq ft enclosure, were built as the straw house and granary. There are also two houses built for the huntsman and the whipper-in. Nor is that all; beyond these main quarters there are many more modest buildings, such as the kennels for the young hounds. 'No hounds have a sounder constitution than the Belvoir', wrote our friend Dale, 'though something is due to a long continuance of first-rate kennel management, so that it is an old Belvoir joke that a hound seen to scratch himself is drafted.'

Duchess Elizabeth, who had been largely responsible for the kennels, died in 1825 aged only 45 and with her died a particular brilliance at Belvoir. As a landscape gardener she had enhanced its already tremendous terrain; as an agriculturalist she had masterminded the estate farms and livestock; and most extraordinary of all, as an architect she had twice instigated the 'medievalisation' of the great castle – in 1816 it had burnt down and had to be rebuilt. The life she created at Belvior was later to be the inspiration for *Coningsby* by Benjamin Disraeli, who often stayed there. How delightfully odd to imagine him hunting from these kennels, dressed in a topper, velvet coat and grey trousers; and odder still to think of Beau Brummel – who came so often that there was a room reserved for him. Beau Brummel never hunted though – instead he strolled about the estate in deep winter, dressed in such extravagant furs that he was mistaken for the Prince of Wales and cheered by gathering crowds. To be considered and cheered most admiringly of all though is Elizabeth, Duchess of Rutland, for having created such a kingdom of fine buildings.

## Brocklesby, Lincolnshire

In 1782 the architect James Wyatt designed one of his greatest masterpieces with the neoclassical mausoleum at Brocklesby, and in 1810, having done various other work on the estate, he turned his attention to the kennels for the Brocklesby Hunt. The huntsman's house was designed to take centre stage, while, on the other side of the yard, there are the various working offices. Towers stand proud at all four corners. Built of rusticated brick – echoing the gate piers between the coach house and the stables, as well as being the same form as the church porch – two of them are hospital lodges for the hounds, another is for the puppies and the fourth for the kennel staff. A small fireplace and bath is on hand for the 'knacker's car'. The stone flags on almost all the floors are enormous and kept spanking clean. In one room two giant boilers make oatcakes for the hounds which are laid out on the stone flags to cool; next door there is a slate floor on which the cakes are laid to set firm. These are fed to the hounds mixed with their staple diet of flesh, either to hasten its progress through the hounds' digestive systems or otherwise to bulk out their feed if the meat is scarce. Downstairs in the feed house, Grimm's fairytale-like in its grimness, there is a set of boards to which have been fixed some hundreds of snouts and whiskers of dead foxes. There they all are: row upon row of the noses of every fox caught since 1882.

The Brocklesby Hunt, covering the area between the Humber Estuary to Market Rasen in Lincolnshire, was founded in 1714 by Charles Anderson Pelham, who became its joint first master. He was succeeded by his great-nephew Charles Anderson Pelham, 1st Baron Yarborough – who built these kennels – and to this day the pack has been continuously hunted by the earls.

Today, Charles 'Abd al-Mateen John Pelham, the 8th Earl of Yarborough, who has converted to Islam, is joint master of the Brocklesby Hunt.

The great George Stubbs did three paintings of the hunt in the late 1700s: one of the handsome *Ringwood, a Brocklesby Foxhound*; another of the heart-melting nose-to-nose *Old Pony and Hound at Brocklesby Park*; and a third of the famed *Thomas Smith the elder and Thomas Smith the younger of the Brocklesby Hunt, with the hound Wonder*. This last one captures a moment in the hunt's history, when the retired old huntsman handed the reins of rule over to his son. The old man, with his long white curls, was said to be an exact likeness – down to the detail of him always having one hand in his pocket. Mounted on a sturdy brown horse called Gigg, he sits by his son on his sleek cream hunter Brilliant. The younger Tom Smith, looked up at adoringly by a hound, had succeeded his father in 1761 and was to remain huntsman for 59 years, enjoying the benefits of these new kennels for the last six years before he retired, on full pay for life.

His son Will Smith moved into the kennels as huntsman in 1816. According to George Collins in his *History of the Brocklesby Hounds, 1700–1901* – dedicated to the farmers in the Brocklesby Hunt – there was no better-known name in the history of fox hunting 'until a simple toss at an insignificant fence spelt ... dire misfortune'. An obelisk was erected in Smith's memory where he had fallen at Barnoldby-le-Beck:

> This stone the name of 'WILLIAM SMITH' records,
> The huntman skilled of two of Yarborough's Lords; –
> Honest and true, of temper well approved,
> By 'Master' honoured, and by 'Field' beloved!
> No need to paint that well-known form and face,

Which, stampt on memory, find a welcome place
In the warm hearts that knew him, – *they* recall,
By covert-side – in cottage, farm and hall,
(When friend meets friend beside the yule-log's glow,
And kindly feelings swell and overflow,)
Those happy days, when on the breeze were borne
'WILL'S' tuneful holla and his echoing horn,
Cheering his gallant pack, so stout and bold,
A perfect horseman as e'er crossed the Wold!
And as the vision fades, too bright to last,
They sigh to think those days are now 'the past.'
No need of aught for such as knew him best
To keep in mind their valued friend 'at rest;'
But, for posterity, this stone shall tell
The fatal spot where, midst his friends, he fell,
And bid them ponder, both in Faith and Fear,
How frail the tenure of Man sojourn here!

His son, the second Will Smith, took over the kennels until 1845 when he was succeeded by his brother Tom who was huntsman until 1862. The Smiths had reigned supreme in the Brocklesby Hunt for almost 150 years. There were many more such legendary figures – Nimrod Long who, when only five years old, hunted on a donkey; Alfred Thatcher; Will Dale etc – their names are all remembered. Today it is John Goode who is in charge.

The names of the many hundred of hounds also still resound throughout these walls: Tippler and Trickster; Royal and Drunkard; Frater, Phaeton, Furrier and Jerker; Jumper and Bumper; Merryman and Twinkler – all rolling like poetry off the tongue. Today's hounds are often named after their ancestors in this 300-year-old hunt, one of the two surviving private packs that are left in England.

# PLATE & PALATE

Previous page: The dovecote that once served
Wilcot Manor in Wiltshire.

Below: A castle for bees at Berthddu, Powys.

THIS CHAPTER reveals some remarkable
buildings designed for animals destined, I fear,
to satisfy the stomach. Others were built for the
creatures such as bees who provided sustenance for our
very survival. Hilda Ransome in *The Sacred Bee in
Ancient Times and Folklore* of 1937 writes that in the
classical world of northern Europe, honey was thought
to come from heaven, with the bee as a medium for
bringing it to man. They certainly have had some god-
like structures built for them. In her encyclopaedic *The
World History of Beekeeping and Honey Hunting*, Dr Eva
Crane tells us of a giant 50ft high by 10ft square stone
tower that was built for bees in the 1200s by a Nicholas
de Verdon in Clonmore, County Louth, Ireland. She
wrote too of another early Irish 'bee tower' at Moira
Castle in County Down. Known as 'honey pots', these
vast buildings were not only confined to the grandees;
for example the Cistercians also built a 50ft-high tower
for their bees at Mellifont in County Louth. And an
unidentified castle for bees used to stand at Berthddu,
Powys, Wales (*below*). The date is not known, but
judging from the clothes of the top-hatted old
gentleman and the lady hiding from the camera in the
photograph, it is the mid-1800s.

The most usual way of housing bees, however, was
in a simple straw hive known as a 'skep', which was

then placed in a niche or 'bole' in a wall – 'bole' is the Scottish word for alcove and it became synonymous with sheltering bee skeps. Earlier alternatives to bee boles as protection for the hives had been old crocks, or otherwise little stooks of thatch with sloping roofs, like Chinese temples of straw. Cow dung, too, was used 'tempered with gravely dust or sand or ashes' according to Charles Butler, 'The Father of English Bee-keeping' and author of *The Feminine Monarchie* of 1609. To thwart thieves, there was sometimes an iron bar locked across the wall. Bee boles were in fact considered a convenience rather than a luxury and were used by one and all – hundreds survive all over the country. There are a good many regional names that are still used instead of bee bole, including 'bee niches' in Derbyshire, 'bee keps or shells' in Cumbria and 'bee walls' in Gloucestershire.

In *Rural Rides*, the great William Cobbett wrote that you needed two bushels of 'clean unblighted straw' to make a skep: 'The cost is nothing to the labourer. He must be a stupid countryman indeed who cannot make a bee-hive; and a lazy one indeed if he will not.' Not all skeps were made of straw – our old friend Butler recommended 'wicker made of privet, withy or hazel'. His rewards were great since he claimed to be able to hear bees singing; even transliterating every tone of their buzzing, which he wrote into the musical score *Melissomelos* or *Bee's Madrigall*. Convinced that musicians would hear it as music – that 'Musicians may see the grounds of their Art' – he made his observations:

> When the prime swarm is gone ... the next Prince, when she perceiveth a competent number to be fledge and readie, beginnith to tune, to sing in hir treble voice, a mournfull and begging note, as if shee

did pray hir Queene-mother to let them goe. Unto which voice, if the Queene vouchsafe to reply, tuning hir Base to the young Prince's Treble ... then does she consent ... This song being conteined wihin the compass of an Eight (from C-sol-fa-ut to C-sol-fa).

And on it goes, with page after page of musical annotation, ending up with the four-page 'madrigall'. It was the first book in the English language on beekeeping, although with his English almost as odd as his methods, I doubt that it was hugely popular.

Beekeeping was revolutionised by the invention of the movable-comb beehive in 1851 by the poetically named Reverend Lorenzo Lorraine Langstroth, who was known throughout America as 'The Father of Modern Bee-keeping'. In his *A Practical Treatise on the Hive and the Honey-Bee*, published in 1853, he claimed that the bee was capable of being tamed and that 'anyone favourably situated may enjoy the pleasure and profit of a pursuit which has been appropriately styled, "the poetry of rural economy," without being made too familiar with a sharp little weapon which can speedily convert all the poetry into very sorry prose'. With the easy charm of such observations as '[b]ees cannot under any circumstances resist the temptation to fill themselves with liquid sweets', he also knowledgeably addressed every aspect of tending the apiary. In 1862 the movable-comb beehive arrived in England and the old bee boles became redundant.

Some of the richest sources of inspiration for Britain's buildings for animals were the dozens of pattern books on rural architecture that began to appear in the mid-1740s and continued until the 1830s. The books were filled with piggeries, sheepcotes, cattle byres and dairies, suggesting that they all could and should be given architectural fancy dress. The names of

Below: One of the painted glass windows from the Chinese Dairy at Woburn Abbey, Bedfordshire.

Right: The 18th-century dairy at Milton Park near Peterborough.

their authors should be made into a song, praising their enchanting, and enchanted, creations: Timothy Lightoler, William Halfpenny, Robert Lugar, Isaac Ware and many more – not forgetting John Plaw who suggested that a dung pit would be greatly improved by an obelisk rearing out of its midst! These books were hugely influential in setting the scene for architectural extravaganzas and it often seemed that the more extraordinary they were the better. A popular proposal was to disguise the whole farm – haystack and all – as a lofty Gothic ruin. In his *Georgian Model Farms*, John Martin Robinson tell us of a spoof advertisement for such architectural forays that was published in 1755 by Robert Morris:

> There is now in the Press, and speedily will be published, A Treatise on Five Barr'd Gates, Styles and Wickets, Elegant Pig-Styes, beautiful Henhouses and delightful Cow-cribs, superb cart-houses, magnificent Barn Doors, variegated Barn Racks and admirable Sheep-Folds: according to the Turkish and Persian manner ... to which is added some Designs of Fly Traps, Bee Palaces, and Emmet Houses, in the Muscovite and Arabian Architecture; all adapted in the Latitude and genius of England.

A spoof maybe, but not far from the truth, when you consider that a Grecian temple with tapering Egyptian windows was built for pigs at Robin Hood's Bay in Yorkshire and that a 'Chinese' dovecote was built in a Gothic stable yard at Megginch in Scotland.

The most elaborately decorated of all buildings associated with animals were the dairies. Often thatched for insulation and with decorative glass windows (as at the Chinese Dairy at Woburn Abbey, *right*) and verandas to keep out the sun, they were off to a good picturesque start. Once inside – this being the domain of the 'Lady

of the House' – their refinement knew no bounds. Some, such as at Manderston in Berwickshire, had marble walls, floors, ceilings and fountains, while at Shugborough in Staffordshire Samuel Wyatt turned the Tower of the Winds into a dairy in 1803 and covered it from floor to ceiling in brown-veined Derbyshire alabaster. Josiah Wedgwood was to make a fortune with his cream-coloured Queen's Ware pottery, much of which was created especially for dairies.

The 18th-century dairy at Milton Park near Peterborough (*opposite*), thought to be by William Chambers who had worked here in the 1770s, has

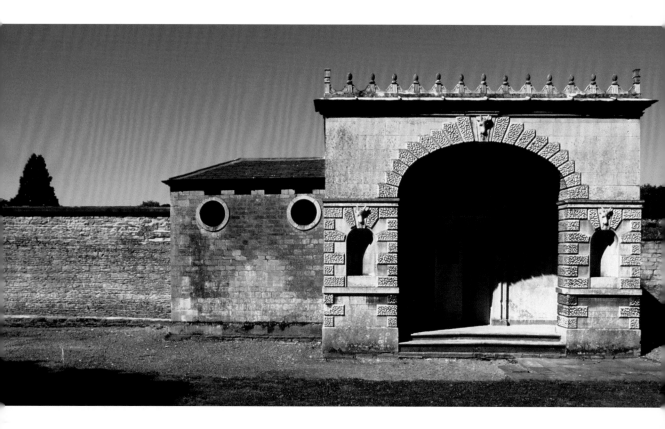

recently been restored both inside and out by my brother-in-law Philip Naylor-Leyland (who gave my sister Isabella a complete new set of 'lipped' dairy 'pans' for her birthday). Inside the walls are covered with white Wedgwood tiles with ivy borders and, as if all of this was not enough – which it is – the floor is a real Roman mosaic. Removed from the Roman 'palace' at nearby Castor, it was laid here in 1821. In 1999 the mosaic was brilliantly restored in what were the original materials of stone and terracotta.

It is satisfying to write that the English dairy was on the go long before Marie Antoinette's Petit Trianon. Eventually, though, it was Queen Victoria and Prince Albert's dairy at Windsor that would beat all England's 18th- and 19th-century dairies into a cocked hat. There cannot be another room with such extensive decoration in the country.

It never fails to cheer that however humble the creature, it was not beneath the attention of their owners, whether architects or enthusiasts, to design them beautiful buildings. Both brick and stone

pyramids were created for pigs in the 18th and 19th century, as were castles for cattle and even for salmon. The Triangular Lodge at Rushton in Northamptonshire – one of England's great architectural masterpieces – was built in the late 1500s to house a keeper of rabbits. Nor was this merely a historic exercise – a small kingdom of Gwelfic battlemented houses for goats, as well as castles for pigs, have been built at Larchill in Ireland today.

A building which, extraordinary to say, has barely changed in its design or use in Britain from the 14th to the 19th century is the columbarium or dovecote (known as the 'doocote' in Scotland). Although the ancient Egyptians had left decorative images of doves as long ago as 2,700 BC and although these 'fowls of Heaven' were considered sacred throughout most of the ancient world, it seems that there was never a mention of the columbarium until the Romans weighed in with knowledgeable and picturesquely alarming accounts of pigeon husbandry. They had been passionate about their pigeons; 'many were mad with

love of these birds', wrote Pliny the Elder in his *Natural History*, noting that 'they build towers for them on the tops of their roofs and will relate the high breeding and ancestry of each after the ancient fashion'. Varro in his *Rerum Rusticarum* wrote of the need for windows in dovecotes so as to admit light and air, lest 'saddened by the slavery of continued confinement' the pigeon might become ill.

Great was the interest taken in the pigeons of Rome – not only for their delectable fare of meat and eggs, forever fresh in these 'living larders', but also for providing various and valuable medicaments as well as their droppings (guano), which was an excellent fertiliser. The bird's ability to carry messages was of course of paramount importance, most particularly in the field of battle; it was Pliny who, in his *Natural History*, admiringly wrote of 'the winged messengers traversing the air' between Decius Brutus and Mark Antony in the Siege of Mutina in 43 BC. A dead interesting outcome of the invention of the Roman columbarium was its adaptation to contain human remains, with cinerary urns housed in the same layout as the doves' compartments.

Today, whether containing live doves or the ashes of humans, the design and the name of the building has remained the same. So too have almost all of the architectural features of those first ancient columbaria. The buildings were usually round with small entrances to minimise the size and shadow of a human appearing at the door. Their walls were made smoothly resistant to the climbing paws and claws of vermin and they were built with nests from floor to roof. Alighting ledges were often part of the design, either continuously sweeping around the dovecote for the promenading pigeon, or individually in front of each nest opening which would be round, square or oblong.

In southern climes the buildings were open to the skies with a round opening called the 'oculus', but when the dovecote travelled north – first to France with Caesar's invasion of Gaul, then to England with the Norman invasion – these later pigeon houses were designed with little roofed cupolas to allow the birds to fly in but to keep the rain out.

The earliest dovecotes built in Britain were round as with their Roman predecessors, but thereafter the sky was the limit: oblong, square, hexagonal, castellated, crenellated, gabled, crow-stepped, spired, pyramided, pinnacled, domed, towered and even built as cones. From our earliest precisely dated dovecote of 1326, built of sandstone and rubble at Garway in Herefordshire – and there are many thought to be earlier – these pigeon houses are like a living architectural pattern book with a huge array of materials and architecural styles – black-and-white timber framing, brick and flint, cob construction, sandstone and limestone and so on; the whole bang lot is there. Little beacons of the local vernacular, they were often built in styles and materials honouring the land on which they stood. For example, a little brick and stone dovecote, dating from 1737 and now beautifully restored and re-thatched, once served the ancient Wilcot Manor in Wiltshire (*see* pp 74–5). Nor was it only the local builder who exercised his wits on the dovecote – John Nash designed quarters for doves as part of his overall picturesque schemes for Blaise Hamlet, near Bristol, in 1812, while Scotland was well served by Robert Lorimer in 1911 at Balcaskie in Fife.

The trouble was that dovecotes not only bred doves but also resentment. When the dovecote crossed the Channel with the Normans they brought the same French rules of feudal privileges, which meant that the building of dovecotes was for many centuries the sole prerogative of the owners of castles, manor houses and monasteries. However it was the birds' appetites for crops that caused the most problems. With one pair of pigeons consuming four bushels of corn a year and with between 500–2,000 nest boxes per dovecote (Lewes Priory's church-like pigeon house had 3,328) such crop destruction was untenable for the common man. In the 1600s the polymath Samuel Hartlip reckoned that there were some 26,000 pigeon houses disgorging birds to daily pillage the land.

Something had to be done and it was the turnip and

the swede, of all unlikely saviours, which first came to the aid. When these two humble root crops were introduced into British agriculture in the early 18th century, livestock was suddenly able to survive throughout the winter months. No longer was November to see wholesale slaughter, with its horrifying Saxon name 'Blodmonath' (the month is grimly represented with a stone carving on Carlisle Cathedral, showing a farmer pole-axing an ox). A later and death knell deterrent for the dovecote was the founding of the Board of Agriculture in 1796 encouraging the very latest methods of 'progressive agriculture'. Nevertheless dovecotes went on being built for a good further hundred years; indeed they are still being built today, although now for more decorative purposes. No better example can be found than the tower at Westcote Manor, Warwickshire (*opposite*). Used partly as a glass-walled study and partly as a traditional roost for doves, it soars high over the surrounding countryside.

As for the Scottish doocotes, theirs is an 18th-century legacy of unusual refinement. As England's leading agricultural reformers were agitating that the pillaging occupants of the cotes made them no longer viable, the Scots went on building them regardless, determined to continue in their traditional ways. Many and graceful were the results, none more so than the Gothic Chinese doocote at Megginch in Perthshire or otherwise the domed grandeur of the pigeons' quarters atop the entrance arch to Conon Mains Farm in Ross and Cromarty. Surrounded by working agricultural buildings, it bears a startling resemblance to Tom Tower at Christ Church, Oxford!

Collectively the dovecote or doocote – also known as a pigeon cote, culvery or culverhouse – is a pantheon in miniature of British architecture.

Below: The bee shelter at Hartpury in Gloucestershire.

Right: Bee boles set in 17th-century walls at Packwood, Warwickshire.

## Hartpury, Gloucestershire

The uniquely strange and seemingly ancient bee shelter in St Mary's churchyard at Hartpury has been given two wildly different histories – one dating it from 'pre-1500' and the other, very precisely, from between 1824 and 1852. Every instinct tells me that the earlier version is the right one, even though Paul Tuffley, a 19th-century stonemason, claimed he carved it. Perhaps he rebuilt it and felt justified in claiming the strange structure as his own.

It is enormous – 30ft long and 8ft feet high with 28 hives fitted into the carved and scalloped niches and space for five more hives to stand under the arches on the ground. The bee shelter is made entirely of stone – Cotswold stone, if you favour the 19th-century version of it being locally built, or otherwise Caen stone from Normandy, if you are rooting for its pre-1500 origins. What is not disputed is that a shelter originally stood in the grounds of the Manor of Minchinhampton in Gloucestershire. This had been granted by William the Conqueror to his daughter when she had become the first abbess of the newly established Abbaye aux Dames at Caen in Normandy. With regular toing and froing to France for the abbey's dues and rents, it is thought that stone quarried in Caen could well have been brought back to England; especially after it had been seen that bee shelters like this had been in successful use in Normandy for hundreds of years. Not only that, honey and beeswax were of course valuable commodities and such a vast hive would have been lucrative. The stone caps are of Cleevehill Peagrit and the 'plates' of Purbeck stone – later and English decorations. The crosses, as well as showing the attachment to the abbey, might also have been made to proclaim the God-given nature of the bee.

The Victorian version of the story is that the bee

shelter was carved out of stone from the nearby Ball's Green quarry by Paul Tuffley – a Nailsworth stonemason whose family worked on the rebuilding of the Palace of Westminster. A simpler story, but one that in no way belittles the unique beauty of the bee shelter. Later the two histories have a complicated convergence: in 1968, after the bee shelter had spent many unappreciated years in what had become the grounds of Nailsworth Police Station – once the stonemason Tuffley's garden – the shelter was dismantled for safety by the Gloucestershire Beekeepers' Association. It was found that the panels were held together with thick oak pegs and that the stones weighed a total of over 5 tons. The shelter was rebuilt in the grounds of Hartpury Agricultural College and a sealed plastic container for posterity was put into a cavity carved out of a pier. It held an account of the rebuilding, with the names of all those who worked on it, a bottle of mead, some coins –

both decimal and pre-decimal – and a copy of the Gloucestershire Beekeepers' Association *Year Book*. But once again it started to deteriorate and the college also wanted to build over the ground on which it stood. After a red alert by English Heritage, the shelter was taken over and restored – this time definitely with Cotswold stone from the Minchinhampton as well as the Ball's Green quarries – by the Hartpury Historic Land & Buildings Trust who have given it a safe home in St Mary's churchyard. It makes a curious contribution to the graveyard, but no more curious than it would look wherever it was put.

## Packwood, Warwickshire

There are 30 bee boles built into the sloping beauty of the 17th-century walls that divide the terrace from the famed yew garden at Packwood. Two by two, they march along on either side of a handsome 18th-century wrought-iron gate, with both walls ending up at a gazebo. In one of these little buildings there is a fireplace that fed heat through horizontal pipes along the peach wall, encouraging a succulent harvest for the inhabitants of the skeps. Packwood is remarkable for the number of bee boles that were built and also for their prominent position in such distinguished surroundings.

The yews make Packwood one of Britain's greatest topiary gardens. Created in the mid-19th century by Graham Baron Ash, there are over 100 trees planted so as to represent the Sermon on the Mount. 'The Master' stands on the summit of a mound with the 12 Apostles and the four Evangelists in two rows on either side of him, leading down to the 'multitude' on the lawn.

## Peckforton, Cheshire

A big surprise. A beehive in the shape of a castle atop an elephant's back standing in a garden on the edge of a farmyard in Cheshire. Dating from about 1859, it was carved out of only two blocks of richly red sandstone – one for the elephant and the other for the hefty howdah in the shape of a three-tier castle on its back. Why was it built? I will hazard a guess. John Watson was the local stonemason responsible and he had been working between 1844 and 1850 on the gigantic and fake medieval Peckforton Castle nearby. Faced with flaming red sandstone, this was a building so elaborate that, as Pevsner and Hubbard's *The Buildings of England: Cheshire* reports, Sir George Gilbert Scott described it in 1858 as '[t]he largest and most carefully and learnedly executed Gothic mansion of the present' and 'the very height of masquerading'. So John Watson had spent six years honing his craft on a red sandstone castle and perhaps – during what must have been a painfully empty aftermath – he decided to build one of his own.

Supported by a stone saddle with stone straps and tassels, the castle on the elephant has a turreted gatehouse with arrow slits; its keep has three turrets and the walls have courses, as well as arches over the windows. These were glazed – all taking a cue from the great Peckforton Castle, which, according to the *Illustrated London News* of 1851, exhibited all the beauties of an ancient stronghold without its inconveniences. Once John Watson had decided on his castle, what inspired him to carve his elephant? The history of the 'elephant and castle' is long and varied, from Roman war elephants to 19th-century pubs. Most pertinent, for this purpose, is that the elephant and castle was depicted on the coat of arms of the Corbett family who owned Peckforton Castle up until 1626. I leave you to guess what caught his fancy.

*Left: An elephant-and-castle-shaped beehive near Peckforton in Cheshire.*

*Below: The bee pavilion at Hall Place near Hurley in Berkshire.*

## Hurley, Berkshire

The central support of the 10-sided pavilion for bees at Hall Place near Hurley in Berkshire is a tree trunk – a rustic feature so often suggested by architects in 18th- and 19th-century pattern books, but so seldom seen. Turned upside down so that the buried branch stubs act as anchors, it is surrounded by a bench on which the beekeeper can sit to tend the hives. These stood one at each window, which can be opened or closed. Beneath the windows and in the eaves are bands of trelliswork decoratively concealing panels of perforated zinc which allow the air to be constant and the hives draught-free. Good ventilation and an even temperature are essential for bees.

The exact date this little building was constructed is at first unclear. The cheerfully graceful Chinese lilt might suggest an 18th-century date but this is misleading. There are two clues: the roof timbers have been cut with a band saw, which was not used in England before 1859, and the pavilion appears to have been built for movable-comb beehives which were developed in America in 1851 and not brought to England until 1862. And so a late 19th-century date has now been put forward for the bee pavilion. The delicacy of the building could be explained by the fact that there were traces of another bee house on the site and so this pavilion – no doubt created to celebrate the arrival of the new types of hives – was rebuilt in the same style as an earlier and much-loved predecessor.

The history of Hall Place, originally known as La Halle, goes back to 1234 when it was the manor of Hurley (*see also* p 138). John Lovelace acquired the manor in 1544, but not the actual house; he (or possibly his son Richard) therefore built a new manor house, called Ladye Place, and the manor and Hall Place went their separate ways. (It is now called the manor of Hurley once again.) The estate was purchased in 1728, the old house demolished and a new Hall Place – plain, pretty and of pink brick – was built between 1728 and 1735 by William East, whose descendants were to own the estate for another 221 years. In the early 1800s Sir East George Clayton East created a deer park in which he built brick pyramids and planted oaks in the formation of the French and English fleets in the Battle of Trafalgar. Sir Robert and Lady Dorothy Alan Clayton East Clayton were the last of the line; adventurers both, their search for the lost oasis of Zerzura in the Libyan desert gave Michael Ondaajte the inspiration for the key characters in his novel *The English Patient*, also made into a film. On Sir Robert's return to Hall Place he caught polio and died within a week.

## Rushton, Northamptonshire

There can be no more exquisitely crafted building in the British Isles than the Triangular Lodge at Rushton built between 1594 and 1596 by the devout Catholic convert Sir Thomas Tresham as a testament to his faith. Designed at a time when to be a Catholic was punishable by imprisonment, even death, it was coursed through with symbols of the Holy Trinity including his all-important family emblem of a trefoil – a pun on Tresham's name (Tresham, 'I am three'). The triangle itself is, of course, also a symbol of the Holy Trinity and, as well as being the shape of the little building itself, it is decorated with an abundance of triangles. This is, though, not merely a

Catholic conceit – it is the all-Christian belief in the glory of God that trumpets forth from its walls.

For our purposes, it must immediately be said that it was, in fact, built as 'Warrener's Lodge' to be lived in by the man who looked after the rabbits! In a contemporary engraving of Tresham's nearby Rushton Hall – now a hotel and spa – the Triangular Lodge can be seen on the eminence of the 'Connegerie', brimful of 'coneys' as warrens and rabbits were also called at this time. As well as satisfying the Treshams' stomachs, the rabbits made for a profitable business with their meat and fur. Furthermore, it was an excellent way of making use of poor land, and there were many estates that took to rabbit farming on a large scale. Mark Girouard gives alarming examples in the English Heritage guidebook for Rushton Triangular Lodge: 'The great warren at Thetford in Norfolk, once covered 3,000 acres and was 8 miles long'; another at Methwold, also in Norfolk, was four miles long. He also tells us that Sir Francis Bacon's warren at Gorhambury, near St Albans in Hertfordshire, was of 72 acres and that it yielded £60 a year. Sir Thomas Tresham was in the business too, dispatching rabbits to London to be sold – the grey 'coneys' for £3 per hundred, the black for £5 per hundred and the black-and-white and plumper 'rich' rabbits for £10 per hundred. The Triangular Lodge's warren was so successful that he created another at Pipewell, a few miles away.

The little three-sided building, despite its myriad of refined complexities, is in fact built along the lines of a working warrener's lodge with a top floor from which the warrener could watch over his charges, and rooms below for the equipment required to dispatch them and for hanging their skins. All the corpses would have been kept in the cool basement. The bare bones of a 'Connegerie Lodge' it may be, but most decidedly not in design or decoration.

Tresham designed every aspect of the little building to revolve around the number three. The plan is an equilateral triangle with each side being 33ft 4ins long (one-third of 100ft) tapering up to 33ft at the upper storey. There are two storeys, plus a basement, with three windows on each side. The three main rooms are hexagonal, each with a triangular corner chamber. Nine gables soar up to the sky, 'ablaze' with stone 'flames', creatures and three-sided pinnacles topped with trefoils.

Each side of the building represents one member of the Holy Trinity, with unifying inscriptions carried round all three facades. Eighteen letters, 'MENTES TUORUM VISITA' ('Visit the minds of thy people'), are incised above the first-floor windows and 'RESPICITE

NON MIHI SOLI LABORAVI' ('Look, I have not worked only for myself') is written above the sundials in the central gables. There are carvings on the gables to either side of the central gable on each front: on the south-east face are the emblems of a seven-branched candlestick and seven eyes, perhaps symbols of the Apocalypse in the Book of Revelation; on the north face are representations of a dove with her chicks and a pelican feeding her young with her blood, representing God's care and Christ giving his blood on the cross to save humankind; and on the south-west face can be seen a dove on a serpent with its coils winding round a globe and a hand coming forth from the sun to touch the earth, the latter representing the hand of God. The entablature, 33ft long on each side, has three passages from the Bible, each with 33 letters: 'APERIATUR TERRA & GERMINET SALVATOREM' ('Let the earth open and bring forth a saviour') on the south-east face; 'QUIS SEPARABIT NOS A CHARITATE CHRISTI' ('Who shall separate us from the love of Christ?') on the north, and 'CONSIDERAVI OPERA TUA DOMINE ET EXPAVI' ('I have considered thy works, Lord, and been afraid') on the south-west.

Whereas the Holy Trinity was acceptable to the Protestants, the worship of the Virgin Mary was not; as for participation in the Catholic Mass – this could be punishable by death. These therefore, were the two elements of Tresham's faith most important to conceal on the building. Mary was symbolised by a dove. Dicing with danger were the nine stone angels with lead spouts sticking from their stomachs, draining water from the roof. With the letters and triangles incised on their chests, they read 'ss sd ds' and 'qee qee qve', the initials of 'Sanctus Sanctus Sanctus Dominus Deus Sabaoth' ('Holy, holy, holy Lord God of Hosts') and 'Qui Erat et Qui Est et Qui Venturus Est' ('Who was, and who is, and who will be'). In other words the opening of the hymn of praise as the congregation is bidden to join the choir of angels during the most solemn part of the Catholic Mass, just before the Host is transformed into the body of Christ.

The chimney, topped with trefoils of Tresham and the Trinity, soars defiantly into the sky, carved with emblems on each of its three sides – the sacred monogram IHS with the cross and three nails; the Lamb of God bearing a cross that symbolises Christ; and enclosed in a pentagon a Tau cross rises out of a chalice to symbolise salvation. Tresham family shields surround the windows with a variation of trefoils on the top floor and crosses with trefoils at the end of each

arm on the ground. Little trefoils with a triangular opening light the basement. The words 'TRES TESTIMONIUM DANT' ('The number three bears witness' or 'Tresham bears witness') are incised over the front door.

Sir Thomas Tresham was to spend nearly 12 years, plus a few extra months here and there, either in prison – or in confinement or under surveillance – due to his religious beliefs. The Triangular Lodge was his sermon in stone that still speaks to us with brilliant eloquence after more than 400 years. It is an astonishingly beautiful building, so sharply defined that it quite slices into your senses.

## Netherby, Cumbria

The Netherby estate is the site of the Roman fort Castra Exploratorum (The Fort of the Scouts), which served as an outpost to Hadrian's Wall. Netherby Hall itself is an architectural amalgam par excellence – an ancient pele tower that has been overlaid with 17th-, 18th- and 19th-century additions. A long stone's throw away is the pink sandstone salmon castle, only one of the grand improvements to the area that were instigated in the 18th century by Netherby's then owner, the Reverend Robert Graham. A leading agriculturalist of his day, he built a harbour at Sarkfoot near Gretna from which to send his fish and the rest of his produce to Liverpool; he was also responsible for the pleasingly wide-streeted and tree-lined model town of Longtown nearby. Keeping elegant company with the salmon castle, on the other side of the river, is his Kirk Andrews of 1776 with its rotunda of columns atop the bell tower.

The salmon castle was built in the mid- to late 1700s. With the back of the building rearing high over the River Esk, it was designed so the salmon coops that formed part of a dam over the river below could be watched from a projecting bay. One of its four stone waterways was blocked off to trap salmon – which are unable to turn round – then a door was dropped behind them to secure their capture.

Not only is the castle as picturesque as it is practical but, with its apparent fortifications, it appears to have been built into the historic fabric of a landscape that had witnessed both the Scots and English 'reivers' – the border raiders – vigorously plundering one another's lands for many centuries. In 1783, a good century after such troubles had died down, this little castle, as if built as bait to do battle, was subjected to a sudden and seemingly full-scale border raid. In *Redgauntlet*, Sir Walter Scott marvelled that such a story was by no means improbable fiction: Shortly after the close of the American war, Sir James Graham of Netherby [Robert Graham's grandson] constructed a dam-dyke, or cauld, across the Esk, at a place where it flowed through his estate, though it has its origin, and the principal part of its course, in Scotland. The new barrier at Netherby was considered as an encroachment calculated to prevent the salmon from ascending into Scotland, and the right of erecting it being an international question of law betwixt the sister kingdoms, there was no court in either competent to its decision. In this dilemma, the Scots people assembled in numbers by signal of rocket lights, and, rudely armed with fowling-pieces, fish-spears, and such rustic weapons, marched to the banks of the river for the purpose of pulling down the dam-dyke objected to. Sir James Graham armed many of his own people to protect his property, and had some military from Carlisle for the same purpose. A renewal of the Border wars had nearly taken place in the eighteenth century, when prudence and moderation on both sides saved much tumult, and perhaps some bloodshed. The English proprietor consented that a breach should be made in his dam-dyke sufficient for the passage of the fish, and thus removed the Scottish grievance.

Leading the way had been 200 'armed and disorderly' men, according to William Hutchinson's *The History of the County of Cumberland* (1794), disbanded from the Duke of Buccleuch's regiment of the 'South Fencibles', but they 'had been repelled by the Netherby tenants with all the spirit of ancient times'. At the time the then beleagured salmon keeper was living upstairs in modest quarters – the same quarters which in the early 1900s were occupied by a family of ten, whose eight owls – each child had a pet apiece – would all sleep in a row on the end of their beds at night.

By the 1980s the castle had fallen into a sad state of decay, but in 1992 it was saved by John Smith for the Landmark Trust – saved and sympathetically restored. The only architectural addition was a gabled porch around the front door. Now known as Coop House, it can be rented and stayed in any time. I tried in vain to photograph the building in its new garb – driving three times from Buckinghamshire to Cumbria to so do, but every one of those three days it poured with rain. What you see in the photograph is the building as it was when John Smith was inspired to save it.

## Badminton, Gloucestershire

Thomas Wright of Durham – astronomer, antiquary, mathematician, instrument maker, landscape and garden designer, and architect – designed a delicate castle for pigs as well as the thundering citadel known as Castle Barn, for cattle and doves, in the park of Badminton House. His was a genius that encompassed the first analysis of the Milky Way, as well as innovative garden design and strikingly individual buildings, both often coursed through with celestial themes. Is it any wonder – according to Eileen Harris in her brilliantly produced facsimile of Wright's *Arbours and Grottos* – that the poet Elizabeth Carter addressed him as 'Your Worshipful Conjurship'!?

He worked at Badminton for 36 years, producing a quantity of garden plans and architectural oddities for 'The Great Proprietors', as the 4th and 5th Dukes of Beaufort were known. The 4th Duke, as well as commissioning William Kent to enhance Badminton, was also one of the grandees who first gave work to

Left: The castellated pigsty
in the park of Badminton
House in Gloucestershire.

Right: Castle Barn –
built for doves and cattle –
at Badminton,
Gloucestershire.

Canaletto in England. The 5th Duke rebuilt the parish church in the style of London's St Martin-in-the-Fields. It was, though, the 4th Duchess Elizabeth, who between 1750 and 1786 was the greatest supporter of Wright's schemes as their complex planting and rustic architectural fancies writhed into interweaving life. A few of the buildings were thatched – a hermit's cell, as well as a 'Root House' made entirely of logs with an arcade of contorted tree trunks. He designed one rustic domed temple with pediments, as well as another with a rotunda, standing high on an artificial mound, with a large pedimented grotto at its base. The 'Ragged Castle' of 1750 was made of rubble and is still deserving of its name. For Swangrove, a *maison de plaisance* of 1703 that had been built on the edge of the park, Wright designed a Chinese façade and two pavilions – which were never built – as well as a pigsty – which was, but which, although elegant, was discreetly out of sight. Incidentally, his 'Chaple garb' (sic) for the stables, sadly never saw the light of day.

However sensational his architectural and garden designs, both modesty and mismanagement were Wright's middle names. Forever in the firmament of astrological discoveries that were eclipsing all else, he was barely known outside the small commissioning circle of grandees.

In the 1750s, after most of his scientific patrons had either died or disappeared, he had wholeheartededly taken up design – much to the mockery of the poet William Cowper, who railed that the fashionable world had at first lauded and then abandoned his friend. Harris tells us of Cowper writing to Wright that his celestial erudition had been

but laying a lane before them which concentrated all their greatness into an atom ... Now you lay before them their own greatness, and what is really the fruit of your genius shall hereafter be shown as the contrivance and art of the great proprietor ... I am sorry the stars have treated you ill.

They were to deal him more blows, in that after his death in 1786, Thomas Wright was forgotten. It has been largely thanks to the sleuthery of my friend Eileen Harris that Wright's dazzling aesthetic oeuvre can once again be enjoyed.

## Sway, Hampshire

These concrete pigsties – with an eastern air of roofs that lilt gently skywards – were built in the late 1860s by Andrew Thomas Turton Peterson, a singular man who built singular buildings years ahead of his time. Born in Yorkshire in 1813, he ran away to sea when he was only 13 years old and after many adventures – at one point finding himself in charge of a ship during an attempted mutiny – he ended up in India. There he rose to the top of the legal tree, eventually becoming acting judge in the High Court of Calcutta. Not only that, greatly to Hampshire's – and our – benefit, he applied himself to a thorough understanding of Indian building construction, most particularly of the mud and cement funeral towers that were created by the Parsi Zoroastrians. So it was that when in 1868 he retired to England as a rich man, he determined to prove the viability of unreinforced concrete by building an immense funeral tower in the material for himself. It was to be the tallest unreinforced concrete building in Europe, rising out of the Hampshire countryside along with a smaller tower, various farm buildings and a model piggery.

Every aspect of his concrete kingdom was designed by Peterson and he headed a workforce of 40 of the local unemployed to build it. With no scaffolding, wooden frames, horse-drawn pulleys and no work during winter, all his schemes took 17 years to be realised. His two handwritten diaries, including his building instructions and descriptions of the still-primitive building methods, survive in the Hampshire Record Office and are full of such laments as: 'I am afraid that this book, if read at all, is chucked aside and nothing is thought of it ... I find that either my orders

Left: The 19th-century concrete pigsties at Sway, Hampshire.

Right: The Grecian temple for pigs at Fyling Hall near Robin Hood's Bay in North Yorkshire.

An unlikely footnote of the whole affair is that Peterson was in fact convinced that his building of the tower had been directed by the spirit of Sir Christopher Wren. The great man, impatiently determining that concrete should take up its rightful role as the prime building material, had supposedly supplied Peterson with architect's plans and details of the content of the concrete. Peterson had been bewitched by a Mrs Girling – a self-proclaimed prophet and a fervent spiritualist with a religious sect, known as the 'Children of God' (or the 'New Forest Shakers' for their gyrating dance), in the New Forest. Mesmerised by her powers, Peterson had held séances to which he claimed Wren appeared with his architectural instructions for the tower. Peterson's plans for it to become a spiritualist laboratory came to naught, but it can nevertheless be claimed as a socking great shrine to spiritualism.

The latest and happy news is that the buildings that are clustered around the base of the tower can now be stayed in as a bed and breakfast.

## Robin Hood's Bay, North Yorkshire

In 1883 Squire John Warren Barry of Fyling Hall built a Grecian temple for pigs on a hill high over Robin Hood's Bay from where the sea sweeps off to the horizon. It was described in endearing local lore – in a sadly anonymous scrap of a newspaper cutting – as '[t]he most elegant home for porkers in Britain ... A pig-sty that looks like the Temple of Diana standing sentinel on the Yorkshire coast.'

Squire Barry was an inveterate traveller, often returning to Yorkshire with some new plant, tree or architectural plan. With the Fyling Hall temple it is supposed that his inspiration came from the Mediterranean. It is a tiny temple with an Ionic-columned portico supporting an anthemion-topped

are not read, or if read, are never attended to.' He had spent years experimenting with concrete and he triumphed, although it was to be some 50 years before the benefits of the material were fully recognised. At 218ft 'Peterson's Folly', as the funeral tower is also known, is enormous. With its 13 concrete floors, can it be that this flight of fancy is one of the world's first skyscrapers? The good judge's ashes were put in it when he died aged 93 in 1906; an arrangement that was obviously disapproved of by his family as in 1957 they removed them.

Peterson's buildings at Sway were suffering somewhat by the 1980s. Seeing them then, I wrote in *Beastly Buildings* that as 'an advertisement for its [concrete's] excellence they fail, since the towers have had to be reinforced and the farm buildings are of interest rather than beauty. A grim warning of concrete, and high-rise concrete at that, they appear exotic and strange in the Hampshire countryside.' The buildings have now been restored – the tower thanks to English Heritage and the local council – and are proud proof of Peterson's belief in concrete.

pediment, as well as a fluted frieze and acanthus-leaf drainpipe heads – all concocted for two Large White Yorkshire pigs. To the rear of the building they could poke their snouts through small tapered Egyptian windows. The pillars and their capitals were of wood; the base on which it was built was of stone, cut from the estate quarry and hauled forth by horse and sledge. In 1948 Matthew Hart, a stonemason from Scunthorpe then aged 90, recalled the frustrations as Squire Barry was forever changing his mind as to the classical variations. So relieved was Hart when it was finished that he danced a jig for joy on the roof but fell off and broke his nose. It had taken three men two years to build the sty.

In 1932 the squire was described – by our same poetic old pal – as 'a very courteous old man who used to wear what we called a Daily Mail Hat – a top hat cut short – that was very popular at the time'. As well as courteous, he was a character. What a difference it would make if only a mere fraction of the effort that he had put into the design of his little sty was applied to our agricultural buildings today which so often are brutalising rather than beautifying. Historically, farm buildings have been fine buildings that fit into, even enhance their surroundings – why can't they be so again? At a time too when the pig's lot has become so particularly grim, how hugely pleasing it is to think of Squire Barry's Large White Yorkshire porkers wallowing in the luxury of their classical temple for some 50 years. Today, thanks to the Landmark Trust having saved this unique little building in 1998 and revived it to its full-whack glory, we humans too can stay in the sty. Three grateful cheers for Squire Barry.

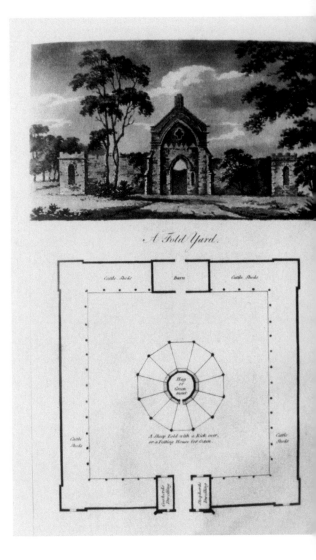

A Fold Yard.

## John Plaw's sheepfold

In 1795 John Plaw produced the pattern book *Ferme Ornée; or Rural Improvements. A Series of Domestic and Ornamental Designs*. It was jam-packed with his schemes for improving the countryside with his buildings, and a very idiosyncratic collection it was too. The faux ruin of the 'Fold Yard', it was ensured, 'will be very useful to fold sheep in, in severe weather, or for cattle and horses needing extra feed'. Built as an enclosure it would have a wall 'built of rough old materials to give a monastic character'.

He proposed three designs for a cattle shed: one classical, another Gothic and he also suggested that 'the grotesque or fancy character may be adopted ... whichever character may accord with the adjoining buildings, or whichever shall best please the fancy of the builder'. The 'Grotesque', wrote Plaw, could commemorate 'some favourite animal for past services ... The skull of a horse may be placed over a mural tablet, where may be recorded the feats of that noble animal, and the water trough may represent the sarcophagus.' Plaw avoided eastern influences, but otherwise all architectural avenues were explored. His 'Gothic' design has a rustic cattle shed with gnarled Doric pillars and Gothic doors, built around a tree that sprouts out of its thatched roof. His 'Monastic Farm' was built with a stone-ached entrance way and an enormous tower of a dovecote 'calculated to ornament an extensive domain, and to unite the useful with the agreeable ... The entrance gates, with the turrets and towers, have a monastery-like appearance: these embosomed with stately trees give an air of antiquity, consequence and grandeur.'

Plaw and his pattern book were in tune with the times. He was one of the many architects in the late 18th and early 19th century who were to produce these delectable volumes – Robert Adam and John Soane, as well as Joseph Gandy, Thomas Wright, Robert Lugar and many others, all of them sallied forth into this venturesome and tolerant field of rural architecture. Timothy Lightoler in his *Gentleman and Farmer's Architect* of 1762 had 25 copperplate engravings for 'Cowhouses, Stables, Sheepcots etc' including a classical cow shed with wings. He designed a Gothic barn – to be built with or without arrow slits – as well as, if you can believe such a thing, an elaborate Gothic screen to hide a haystack. Three illustrations are shown, one with an unadorned stack, the other two disguised by different Gothic ruins. You could be as fanciful as you liked without fear of defying tradition.

Right: The oyster pool on the shore at
Culzean in Ayrshire.

## Culzean, Ayrshire

For our own particular purposes Culzean has few
rivals for wealth of animal architecture – from a
modest oyster pool on the seashore to the lofty
eminence of the Home Farm. The oyster pool was
created by the 9th Earl of Cassillis, a renowned British
'connoisseur' who lived for years at a time in Italy
from where he sent home crates of statuary as well as
works by such artists as Piranesi. In 1773 it is recorded
that he replanted his oyster bed on the Maiden's shore
below Culzean, having hired Norfolk oystermen at
great expense rather than employing men from the
local oyster industry, which had been flourishing since
the 13th century. To create this private oyster pool,
great stone flags were embedded into the rocks. They
still survive, along with traces of the iron posts that
had a metal mesh attached to them to prevent the
matured oysters from being swept away by the tide.

The 9th Earl made great improvements to the
estate but he was never able to get his hands on
developing the Home Farm, as it remained in the
hands of his mother with whom he was on virulently
bad terms. However, when he died in 1775, the estate
was inherited by his brother David, an equally
cultivated figure who was to spend even more
prodigiously on the place. In *The 'Magnificent Castle' of
Culzean and the Kennedy Family*, Michael Moss tells us
all: It was to be first things first, with David's land
steward John Bulley writing that his 'chief concern at
present is only to put the land in the proper condition
for a more perfect system of husbandry' and
lamenting that 'several things are wanting. I have not a
proper farm-yard, nor a house or shed for feeding
cattle ... but these things will come in course ... Lord
Cassillis has extensive and very commodious plans ...
which he intends to build soon.' And so he did,
immediately and well – for this was the 'Age of
Improvement' when a distinguished architect in
charge of the house might well then be asked to design
all the farm buildings, although at Culzean it was to be
the other way around.

The distinguished architect was none other than
Robert Adam and his design of the Home Farm was
of striking originality. Built in local sandstone of
various hues, four crow-stepped buildings surmounted
by stone crosses stand at right angles to four arched

and turreted ranges, which together form a hexagon enclosing a large central yard. His plans survive – with buildings symmetrically shooting forth like a cartwheel – showing a long '*Ox house*' and '*Stables*', as well as a '*Stable for cattle*' flanked by the '*Tool house*' and quarters for '*Swine*'. A '*Byre*' was between a '*Calf house*' and the '*Pigs*'. Even four '*Privys*' were marked and carefully drawn by Adam to be built behind the '*Cart Shed*'; as well as seven more – all of them appearing to be holes in a plank of wood – on either side of the '*Pigs*'.

There were two 80ft-long barns, as well as houses for the land steward and dairyman and also a '*Boiling room*' and a '*Poultry maid's room*'. A local minister of Kirkoswald wrote charmingly of the cows' contentment in these buildings, telling us that they were '...in the house by night or by day ... fed with fine cut red clover and put in parks sown down with white and yellow clover'. A year later Cassillis gave Adam the job of both classicising and castellating his medieval stronghold a few hundred yards north along the cliff top. There they both stand, along with the great stable tower – all given equal pride of place, all stupendously beautiful, all in stupendously beautiful positions.

Another colossus of Culzean built the monkey pagoda (*see* pp 179–81) and a Gothic duck house – no mean pairing of buildings that hail one another across the park. Archibald Kennedy, 12th Earl of Cassillis, later 1st Marquess of Ailsa – a handsome-as-hell American – took over the estate in 1794, aged 24, only two years after his father, New Yorker Captain Archibald Kennedy, had inherited the earldom. Both of them had had to grapple with their forbears' alarming debts, as well as doing battle with a rival Kennedy cousin claimant. As a result the affairs of the estate had become frozen and it was to be years before the 12th Earl was able to realise his schemes for the place. When he did, he did so with a vengeance – landscaping, building and beautifying on the grand scale and, as with the earls of the century before, once again diverting public roads and levelling lands.

With the damming of the Hogston Burn, Culzean's only natural stream, a 13-acre pond was formed. An island was created, planted with trees and given the added charm of an octagonal Gothic duck house as a nesting place convenient for collecting eggs – the pond could, and still can, be waded through with ease. Robert Lugar was in rhapsodies: 'The buildings themselves stand at the head of a large sheet of water or lake which is entirely surrounded by plantations and wood, the surface of the water enlivened by swans and various kinds of fowl, together with wild fowl which frequent it in considerable numbers.' Lugar's description still holds good to this day, with over 600 ducks and a good many swans enjoying the company of the world and his wife out for day trips from Glasgow.

In 1945 the Kennedy family gave Culzean to the National Trust of Scotland and in 1969 the grounds were declared Scotland's first country park. The new buildings needed for visitors would have wrecked Adam's great 18th-century cliff-top architectural assembly, and so it was decided to restore the Home Farm, re-christening it the Park Centre. Salt-stirred wind had eroded the stones and the slates were in ruins but with a 75 per cent grant from the Countryside Commission of Scotland and with a good deal of skill, the building was saved and beautifully restored between 1971 and 1973. In 1975 it won the European Architectural Heritage Award.

## Larchill, County Kildare

Although in Ireland rather than in the United Kingdom, Larchill is irresistible for its display of architecture for animals and most particularly for its palaces for pigs. Known today as the Larchill Arcadian Garden and open for all to see, it is a rare, if not unique, survival of a complete 18th-century ornamental farm or 'Ferme Ornée', as it was called since first written of by Stephen Switzer in the 18th century. In his seminal work *The Nobleman, Gentleman, and Gardener's Recreation* of 1715, he pioneered the delights of 'mixing the useful and profitable Parts of Gardening with the pleasurable', shown off by elaborate illustrations of fine and judiciously placed buildings in the farm, garden and park. Agricultural estates, in particular, could and should be aesthetically pleasing.

It was the Prentice family, Quaker farmers from the north, who with a flax pit and mill made the fortune that created the pastoral paradise of Larchill. It was the dawn of the 'Age of Improvement', when enthusiasm was high for architectural adventure. Pattern books were appearing with such outlandish plans that they seemed the stuff of dreams. At Larchill such dreams were given reality – better still they have gone on being built well into the 20th century.

In 1994 the by-then ruinous Larchill was bought by Michael de Las Casas and his wife Louise, who set out to revive the place – a worthy aim in which they have triumphed, both with the restoration of the 18th-century architectural oddities, as well as with their building from scratch. The new castles for goats and the Saddleback and Berkshire pigs – when photographed it was the magnificent Beatrice who reigned supreme – stand in happiest harmony with an old Gothic model farm, an 18th-century Gothic

Left: A 'fortress' for ducks in a lake at Larchill in County
Kildare.

Below: At Larchill, castles for pigs and goats were built
in the 1990s.

boathouse and, most remarkable of all, a five-towered
castellated fortress for ducks in the middle of a lake.
This is known as 'Gibraltar', as from the air it is
the same shape as the rock. Odd as can be is the
18th-century stone eel house in the eel pond, where the
creatures – then considered a great delicacy – would be
harvested in the darkness of a little stone tower. Even
odder though is the temple for a reincarnated fox,
which is gleefully described on pp 210–11.

With the Wicklow Mountains as a backdrop and
with winding scenic walks, here is a vision of the
picturesque at every turn. Larchill is a key link in the
history of Irish landscape gardening created at the
onset of the Romantic movement when agriculture and
architecture were to develop in aesthetic unison. So
they most marvellously did in Larchill's 26 acres of
parkland – furthermore, the gardens are still giving as
much pleasure today as when Larchill was described in

1830 by an Ordnance Survey publication as 'The most fashionable garden in all Ireland' – a proud claim on Larchill's website today. As if that were not enough, both farm and parkland are filled with rare and exotic breeds of domestic farm animals. When photographed in the Gothic farmyard, the black Vietnamese pot-bellied pigs were suffering the public humiliation of one of the sow's infidelity revealed by the arrival of 16 pink piglets!

A surprising footnote to all these Irish architectural fancies is that they were not the only ones, nor were they the first. Another and very similar assembly had already been built at nearby Dangan Castle, home of Lord Mornington, grandfather of the Duke of Wellington. It was undoubtedly the inspiration for Larchill, yet it is no more, whilst Larchill continues to go from strength to strength.

## Rousham, Oxfordshire

In 1737 James Dormer inherited Rousham (*see also* pp 234–6); a year later he called in the architect and landscape supremo William Kent to apply his softening genius both to the house and grounds – which he did to glorious and enduring effect. *The Buildings of England: Oxfordshire* trumpets Kent's work on the house and garden 'as a landmark in the history of the Romantic movement' and describes his drawing room as 'one of the most exquisite small rooms of the c18 in England'. No small claims. By opening up the grounds to the countryside at one point, and by placing a temple or a statue within an enclosed fold or unexpectedly around a corner, a painterly scene could be admired at every turn. The poet Alexander Pope had perfectly penned the 'picturesque' ideals – with its extra edge of giving shock and surprise – to Lord Burlington in 1731:

To build, to plant, whatever you intend,
To rear the column, or the arch to bend,
To swell the terrace, or to sink the grot;
In all, let Nature never be forgot.
But treat the goddess like a modest fair,
Nor overdress, nor leave her wholly bare;
Let not each beauty ev'rywhere be spied,
Where half the skill is decently to hide.
He gains all points, who pleasingly confounds,
Surprises, varies, and conceals the bounds.
Consult the genius of the place in all;
That tells the waters or to rise, or fall;
Or helps th' ambitious hill the heav'ns to scale,
Or scoops in circling theatres the vale;
Calls in the country, catches opening glades,
Joins willing woods, and varies shades from shades,
Now breaks, or now directs, th' intending lines;
Paints as you plant, and, as you work, designs.

At Rousham it materialised with obelisks and sham ruins, and with eye-catchers on distant hills that planting was flung open to reveal. One nurtured view was of the medieval bridge over the River Cherwell. There are statues of fauns by John van Nost, who also sculpted Mercury, Bacchus and Ceres. A large Apollo stands at the end of the Long Walk, which culminates with a view of the Praeneste – a remarkable building, often and enticingly visible through clearings. With seven pedimented arches that are alternately filled with seats or busts, and flanked by urns, this is a rare sight standing high over the river. William Townsend created a neoclassical Temple of Echo, in which you find a Roman tombstone – you come upon it out of the blue after following the Watery Walk beside a winding stream. Kent's Pyramid House was also placed so as to suddenly loom into view at close quarters. Standing big

and bold in the grounds are two statues by Peter Scheemakers – the *Dying Gaul* and the terrifying *Lion Attacking a Horse*.

On the very edge of Rousham's Elysian Fields is a stone Gothic seat; walk around it and lo and behold, on the other side it becomes a castle for cows. Its inmates are the ancient and magnificent Longhorn cattle – among England's oldest breeds. Despite their fearsome appearance they are exceptionally docile and easy to handle and, according to the Longhorn Cattle Society, are beyond equal as suckler cows due to their abundance of milk and ease of calving. The high butterfat of the milk is also said to give a 'bloom' to their calves. Longhorns were bred at Rousham between 1910 and 1927 and the herd was refounded in the early 1970s by Charles Cottrell Dormer, who lives at Rousham today. With this castle for cows designed by William Kent, again let it be said that architecture for animals was never beneath the art of the great architect.

## Woburn, Bedfordshire

The Chinese Dairy at Woburn in Bedfordshire was designed by Henry Holland for the 5th Duke of Bedford, whilst working on Woburn Abbey between 1787 and 1802. The long, covered walk was originally even longer, sweeping a full quarter of a mile to Woburn Abbey, whilst revealing surprises at every turn: a 'lofty palm house', a statue gallery 'with very beautiful pillars from Italy' and thence through 'an interminable plantation'. This was all seen and recorded by Prince Pückler-Muskau, a German grandee exponent of landscape gardening. His letters to his ex-wife (both in penury, they had separated so that he might come to England to find a rich wife) while on a tour of England – published in his *Tour in England, Ireland and France* – have left us with delightful details of his often odd but always charmingly chosen discoveries. On his stroll down the dairy's covered walkway in 1826, he found

an unbroken arcade clothed with roses and climbing plants ... over the arcade are partly chambers, partly the prettiest little greenhouses. One of them contains nothing but heaths, hundreds of which, in full blow, present the loveliest picture, endless multiplied by walls of mirror.

As well as being so suitable for English climes, the long corridor was in fact a traditional Chinese architectural form, whether vertical as with pagodas or horizontally winding away from buildings.

The dairy's interior, as delicate as Wedgwood's bamboo-decorated ducal porcelain that once filled it, is painted in the Chinese manner with faux bamboo trellis work and filigree of gentlest hues – all dimly glowing from the light of the oriental glass windows (*see* p 78) dating from 1789 to 1791 and painted by Theodore Perrache for Crace, the famed firm of interior

decorators. Once again the prince gives it life when he describes 'a profusion of white marble and coloured glasses ... hundreds of large dishes and bowls of Chinese and Japanese porcelain of every form and colour filled with new milk and cream'. The floor – as well as panels around the walls – is of marble.

With its fretted balustrade and octagonal lantern, Holland had drawn heavily on William Chambers' scheme in his *Designs for Chinese Buildings, Furniture,*

*Dresses, Machines, and Utensils* of 1757. Chambers had already created a Chinese 'Banqueting House' at Woburn for the 4th Duke of Bedford. Big enough for 30, it sat proud on an island in the midst of the nearby 10-acre Lower Drakeloe 'Pond'. Then Humphry Repton, with stupendous ambition, proposed that this be moved to stand on a great mound of rocks built over the boathouse by the dairy. In 1804 Repton also painted a watercolour of another oriental companion

*Previous page: The Chinese Dairy at Woburn Abbey, Bedfordshire.*

*Left: The interior of the Chinese Dairy at Woburn.*

*Right: Humphry Repton's design for the aviary and ornamental poultry yard at Woburn.*

for these two buildings – a lilting roofed 'Chinese Porch' appearing to be forever waving at the dairy across the water.

Good fortune is ours that the English chose to embrace the Chinese style to the colourful extent that they did – such fancies seldom took flight in Scotland and as far as I know, never in Northern Ireland or Wales. The European version of Chinese style, mocked by so many for its unruly flights of fancy, was by its very nature invigoratingly original.

Before Woburn's dairy was finished Repton was called to concoct exotic plans to surround the building with, as he put it 'the first specimen of a Chinese Garden in England'. He thought that the dairy had a 'gay singularity and that its appearance justified the novelty of an attempt to extend the character of the building to the scenery in which it is placed', the view towards the dairy being '*riante*' (gay) and the view away '*trieste*' (sad). He had painted one of his famed Red Books for Woburn, filled with watercolours of Woburn's gardens and parkscapes. His tempting trick was that they were painted on a flap – which when lifted revealed how it would look once Repton had added his schemes.

Repton also designed the aviary, which incorporated an ornamental poultry yard as well as a menagerie. The aviary and menagerie were picturesquely linked with a double-fronted entrance between them. Each side was architecturally different: rusticated Gothic in the form of a semicircular bower from the aviary into the menagerie; grandly pedimented in the Doric style (and decorated with a palm-like ornament) from the menagerie into the aviary. Our friend Prince Pückler-Muskau was again entranced:

The fourth or fifth attendant awaited us ... and showed us first several gay-plumed parrots and other rare birds ... As we walked out upon the open space our Papageno whistled, and in an instant the air was literally darkened around us by flights of pigeons, chickens and heaven knows what birds. Out of every bush started gold and silver, pied and common, pheasants; and from the little lake a black swan galloped heavily forward, expressing his strong desire for food in tones of a fretful child.

Often built with a fragility that added to the prettiness of it all, the tree-trunk columns of Woburn's aviary are typical of the air of rustic romance that it wished to convey. Ordinary poultry were very much part of the picture, with broody hens performing the useful service of hatching the pheasants' eggs. Poultry yards were often integral with ornamental aviaries – both of them areas in which the 'ladies' could feel at home. At Kimnel Park in Wales, the prince was quite overcome with 'a sort of pastoral sensibility' when seeing Fanny, a daughter of the house, feed the poultry with 'dainties from her apron'.

## Fort Putnam, Cumbria

The cow house is part and parcel of Fort Putnam Farm
at Greystoke Castle, which was built in the late 1700s
by the 11th Duke of Norfolk – an ardent Whig, a
supporter of the rebel forces in the American War of
Independence (he turned down the American
ambassadorship) and a notoriously colourful figure. In
large part to taunt his neighbour, the Tory Earl of
Lonsdale, with whom he was on fiery terms, he named
his farms to celebrate the American cause. 'Jefferson'
honoured the 3rd President and principal author of the
Declaration of Independence; 'Bunker's Hill' marked
the devastation of the British Army in the battle of 1775;
and then there was 'Fort Putnam' honouring the
bravado of Colonel Israel Putnam throughout the
American war, a man who was admired for his bravery
by fellow rebels, American loyalists, the French and the
English alike.

Architecturally as fanciful as their names, the farms
were built in Britain's heyday of agricultural adventure.
During the 18th century England's population had
doubled, her equine population had trebled and the
affluent landlords, both educated and enterprising,
were ready to rise to the challenge. Furthermore, as
aesthetic improvement was for them as important as
agricultural improvement, new farm buildings would
have to be beautiful and old ones would have to be
disguised.

Fort Putnam was entirely screened by battlements,
with a turret and a large Gothic window, as well as
three castellated walls with curiously bland and blank
Gothic windows that join onto this arched screen of
*oeil-de-boeuf* openings and stiff stone petal coronets.
Bunker's Hill was more simply built, with a three-sided
castellated stone screen. Then there was Spire House,
another folly of a farm, built with a church steeple for a
non-churchgoing tenant farmer. If he would not go to
church, then the duke decreed that the church should
go to him.

Norfolk and Lonsdale were in constant rivalry,
standing as Whig and Tory candidates for Carlisle
whilst trying to undo one another with building after
building on the neighbouring estates. A picture of the
duke was penned by Sir Nathaniel Wraxall in his
memoirs: 'Nature, which cast him in her coarsest
mould, had not bestowed on him any of the external
insignia of high descent. His person large, muscular,
and clumsy, was destitute of grace or dignity ... He
might indeed have been mistaken for a grazier or a
butcher by his dress and appearance.' His richly
swaggering portrait by Gainsborough, painted in 1784,
of course, shows us otherwise, although his jet-black
short hair reveals a startling difference in the man. 'At a
time when men of every description wore hair-powder
and a queue, he had the courage to cut his hair short
and renounce powder.' The duke proposed to Prime
Minister William Pitt that a tax should be put on hair-
powder but was told that there were too many
individuals who were compelled to use it – 'Indeed, few
gentlemen permitted their servants to appear before
them unpowdered.'

Norfolk was clever, hard working, energetic and well
liked. He represented Carlisle – as well as Arundel in
Sussex and Hereford – in Parliament and he reached
high office with such appointments as Lord of the
Treasury as well as being given a host of country posts
of distinction. However, despite these overt obligations,
according to Wraxall, the duke 'led a most licentious
life, having frequently passed the whole night in
excesses of every kind, and even lain down when
intoxicated ... to sleep in the streets...'. What trumpets
the tabloids would blow today!

It was recorded too that '[i]n cleanliness he was negligent to so great a degree, that he rarely made use of water ... He even carried the neglect of his person so far, that his servants were accustomed to avail themselves of his fits of intoxication for the purpose of washing him ... being wholly insensible to all that passed about him, they stripped him as they would have done a corpse, and performed on his body the necessary ablutions.' Wraxall does not stop there, writing that in public affairs the duke showed 'a certain amount of political talent, but we look in vain for any redeeming qualities in his private character. He was heartless in his dealing with men, and worse than heartless in his relations with women. Gross in his tastes, he affected low company and low pleasures... .'

His drunkenness, decreed Wraxall, 'was in him an hereditary vice, transmitted down, probably, by his ancestors from Plantagenet times, and inherent in his formation'. As he advanced in age, the duke increased in bulk – 'such was his size and breadth, that he seemed incapable of passing through a door of ordinary dimensions'. Wraxall concluded that: 'His talents were neither impaired by years nor obscured by the bacchanalian festivities ... His death has left a blank in the Upper House of Parliament.'

The footnote should be told that Lonsdale, whose enmity inspired the naming of Fort Putnam, was a man whose temper was so bad that he was judged as mad. When his mistress died he kept the corpse by his side, dressing her and dining with her daily.

## Ham, Surrey

There are few rooms in England that seem as enchanted as the late 18th-century dairy at Ham House – as if only a wizard's wand could have created cows' legs of cast iron supporting a marble slab for milk and cream, all surrounded by tiles of entwined ivy. (These same tiles can be seen in the dairies at Endsleigh in Devon and Milton near Peterborough.) It was built attached to one of the lodge gatehouses that lead into the cobbled backyard of the house and probably replaced an earlier building. According to the National Trust's guidebook, the 17th-century inventories of the house showed that the 'Wash House', 'Bakhouse', 'Still House' and 'Dayry' were downstairs, 'although one would expect them to have all been in the yard outside'. There was also a 'Brewhouse' and a 'Confection Roome', all part of the village-like assembly of services on which a great house of the day would have depended. Nor must we forget all the buildings for the agricultural estate, such as the cow yards, pigsties etc.

Ham, dating from 1610 – seemingly still in the midst of countryside yet surrounded by solid suburbia – has had a life of frenziedly fluctuating fortunes from stupendously unrestrained riches to abject poverty. Yet for more than 400 years it has had the good fortune to have always been held by conserving and preserving hands, by maintaining and retaining hands – at worst by hands that, through lack of interest or poverty, have left it alone.

How loudly we should huzzah the hubbub of history that seems to roar throughout Ham. There were heroes aplenty who created the house and its still bucolic surroundings, both dark and delightful characters, to whom we must be grateful for its extraordinary survival. It was built by the poetically named Sir Thomas Vavasour – the skeleton of his building can still be seen beneath later additions – and was taken over in 1626 by William Murray, later Earl of Dysart. Favourite and friend of Charles I since childhood, he had had the unenviable role of being the young prince's 'whipping boy'. This meant Murray being soundly beaten whenever the young prince erred. It was Dysart who created Ham's great interior, coursed through with an exotic splendour. Thanks to a madcap and abortive mission made to Madrid in 1623 to enable the future king to woo the Spanish Infanta, he spent six months immersed in the great art collection and treasures of King Philip IV. These were six profitable months for the future of Ham.

His daughter Elizabeth was Countess of Dysart in her own right, later to become the legendary Duchess of Lauderdale. She was first married at Ham to Sir Lionel Tollemache, but it was from 1672, with her new husband John Maitland, 1st Duke of Lauderdale, that the house was enriched with splendours that, according to John Evelyn in his diary entry of 27 August 1678, were 'inferior to few of the best villas in Italy itself; the house furnished like a great Prince's; the parterres, flower-gardens, orangeries, groves, avenues, courts, statues, perspectives, fountains, aviaries, and all this at the banks of the sweetest river in the world, must needs be admirable'.

In starkest contrast to the exquisite creation of their house, the Duke and Duchess of Lauderdale were cast in the coarsest of moulds – although both were exceedingly learned. The duke was a master of Latin, Greek and Hebrew, while the duchess was mistress of divinity, history, mathematics and philosophy. M J Routh's edition of *Bishop Burnet's History of His Own Time* records Burnet's observation that Lauderdale 'made a very ill appearance: he was very big: his hair red, hanging oddly about him: his tongue too big for

his mouth, which made him bedew all that he talked to: and his whole manner was rough and boisterous, and very unfit for a court'. The bishop wrote too that the duchess had 'a restless ambition, lived at a vast expense, and was ravenously covetous; and would have stuck at nothing by which she might compass her ends'. He also described her as 'violent in every thing she set about, a violent friend, but a much more violent enemy'. Described as a great beauty by some and by others as 'a vulgar full blown virago', her lovers were legion – it was said she even captured Cromwell's heart whilst at the helm of this ardently Royalist household!

With her descendants, the fortunes of the estate alternately sank and soared. Her great-great-grandson, the 5th Earl of Dysart, married Charlotte Walpole, niece of Horace Walpole. Walpole wrote about Ham when he came to see the house in 1770, telling George Montagu that '[t]he old furniture is so magnificently ancient, dreary and decayed, that at every step one's spirits sink, and all my passion for antiquity could not keep them up ... In this state of pomp and tatters my nephew intends it shall remain....' And so it did.

In 1799, when his brother Wilbraham became the 6th Earl, he was to haul Ham back into the limelight, respecting and restoring it with antiquarian verve. Ten years on though, Queen Charlotte was to give rather a sad assessment of his progress, writing that Ham was magnificent and beautiful but very melancholy. His sister lived here into old age making few changes and then Ham was inherited by her grandson who lived as a miser and recluse in London. His son in turn 'debauched' his way through life, according to a leader in *The Times* in 1881: 'having done all in his poweres before he was thirty to wreck the noble inheritance of his ancestors'.

Once again the fortunes of the house were floundering – Augustus Hare in *The Story of My Life* wrote that when he went there in 1879 '[n]o half inhabited château of a ruined family in Normandy was ever half so dilapidated as this home of the enormously rich Tollemaches. Like a French Château too is the entrance through a gateway [he was passing the dairy] to a desolate yard with old trees and a sundial and a donkey feeding.' Later revived and then once more doomed to a dismal downturn, Ham was saved by the National Trust in the mid-1940s, its final and successful saviour.

When Walpole had seen Ham in 1770 – the house having twice swooped and soared from riches to rags in between times – he had also lamented that '[e]very minute I expected to see ghosts sweeping by; ghosts I would not give sixpence to see, Lauderdales, Talmachs, and Maitlands...'. So strong were the imprints made by these individuals on the estate during their lives, they could not possibly have been erased by their deaths. They have undoubtedly all enjoyed the delicacy of the dairy.

## Belvoir, Leicestershire

Belvoir, with its outline of battlemented towers, turrets and crenellations rearing high on a hill over the Vale of Belvoir, is a flamboyant, yet refined fake of a castle – a Regency creation by Elizabeth, 5th Duchess of Rutland, who employed James Wyatt between 1801 and 1813 to restore medieval magnificence to the place. The pink dairy was to be part of this great demesne.

The first castle at Belvoir (*bel voir* meaning beautiful view) was built around the 11th century, the land having been granted to William the Conqueror's standard bearer at the Battle of Hastings. It was fortified in the 13th century, rebuilt in the 1500s, then as a Royalist stronghold was destroyed – 'slighted' – by the Cromwellians during the Civil War. After the Restoration it was rebuilt yet again as four plain blocks making up a square house, which by the late 1700s had deteriorated into rack and ruin. Such were the architectural stepping stones that in 1800 the 5th Duke and Duchess of Rutland were inspired to restore 'medieval' magnificence to the place. It was done with aplomb, but in 1816 a fire almost destroyed the lot. Once again it was rebuilt, again with Duchess Elizabeth in charge. A raven-haired beauty with a passion for agriculture as much as for architecture, she would have applied herself assiduously to the design and workings of her dairy. Not only that, whilst beautifying Belvoir, she was at the same time drawing up many and various architectural schemes in London, as well as plans for improving the capital's parks. At Belvoir she landscaped extensively in the already dramatic terrain.

In his elegiac *The History of Belvoir Castle* of 1841, the Reverend Irvin Eller writes:

I have in vain endeavoured to find a more appropriate word to describe the marvellously beautiful territory which surrounds the Castle ... Besides the affectation of the expression, 'Ferme Ornée', it is far too limited to comprehend the character of the Belvoir domain; which does indeed include an ornamental farm, but a great deal besides, of a much more imposing nature.

Eller later noted:

...as it is known, that the Duchess herself, imagined, planned, and superintended the execution of the designs, which have now ripened into such luxuriant beauty ... I would even go so far as to assert, that it would require a combination of the diversified talents of the three greatest landscape painters the world ever saw, to do justice to the subject. The grace of Claude, the depth and simplicity of Poussin, and the wildness of Salvator Rosa, combined in one individual, could alone portray on canvas, a faithful character of the Belvoir scenery.

Bang in the middle of all this beauty is her dairy, illustrated here in this 1836 engraving by James Sands after Thomas Allom. 'There is a combination of Norman massiveness in the details ... which is particularly pleasing', wrote our romantic friend Eller. 'This building is indeed a beautiful object at various distances, and in various directions. Viewed from the garden gate ... it appears the terminal point of a superb avenue ... From more open points it might be

mistaken for the mansion of a small ornamental farm... .' All, he thought, 'in perfect keeping with the elevated conceptions impressed upon the mind, by the contemplation of the universally magnificent features of the Belvoir demesne.'

Duchess Elizabeth died on 29 November 1825. Three days before her death, she rode on horseback over her extensive farm and plantations, and viewed fat stock intended for exhibition at Smithfield in London. On her return, Eller tells us that she walked for the last time to her beloved dairy.

In 1833 John Claudius Loudon, one of the greatest exponents of agricultural efficiency, gave the dairy an honourable mention in his definitive *Encyclopaedia of Cottage, Farm and Villa Architecture and Furniture*. It would seem therefore that the duchess' dairy was a source of inspiration to Loudon, as similar versions of this building appear in his encyclopaedia as the most desirable up-to-date designs, although the Belvoir dairy was built some 30 years before.

## Port Eliot, Cornwall

The building at Port Eliot was part of Sir John Soane's grand sweep of alterations and additions between 1802 and 1806 to what had originally been the 13th-century Priory of St Germans. He had been commissioned by the second Lord Eliot, a man of taste and action, who had done much of Port Eliot's landscaping himself. Soane's work was to embrace the whole estate, making considerable alterations and additions to the house, as well as designing heavily machicolated Gothic stables, along with a dairy and this ingenious cow house. Beneath the eaves, what seems like a fluted frieze is in fact a pleasing-to-the-eye ventilating system, operated by pulling a knob to slide panels aside and thus opening the 'flutes'.

Elihu Burritt, the American Consul in Birmingham, came to England in 1863, writing in *A Walk from London to John O'Groats* that he was 'determined ... that a walk through the best agricultural counties of England and Scotland would afford opportunity for observation which might be made of some interest to my friends and neighbor farmers in America as well as to myself'. The self-educated son of a Connecticut cobbler and a philanthropist, pacifist, emancipationist and writer, he was otherwise known as 'The Learned Blacksmith', having apprenticed as a blacksmith. He had mastered some 50 languages including Hebrew, Syriac and Chaldaic. His English was peerless – in *A Walk from London to Land's End and Back*, he described his first taste of clotted cream from the cows of Port Eliot as 'that most delectable of luxuries ... I remember meeting with an old musty volume many years ago, containing a learned disquisition in Latin on the question whether the butter of Abraham placed before the angels was really butter or this very cream.'

One of Soane's first buildings ever to get a public airing was also for cows – the 'Elevation of a Dairy House in the Moresque Stile' that appeared in his *Designs in Architecture* of 1778. It was produced when its author John Soan was only 25 years old – he had yet to add the extra 'e' of distinction to his name. The book was his debut publication, allowing him to commit fantastical and high-flying ideas to paper before having set up an architectural practice, let alone having built any building. Hurrah, though, for such gall. Only two years earlier, as a student at the Royal Academy, his quite stupendous design for a Triumphal Bridge – a veritable city of colonnades – had won him the Royal Academy's Gold Medal. Not only that, it had so impressed George III that the young student was sent on a three-year-long Grand Tour, paid for by the Royal

Top: Sir John Soane's cow house at Port Eliot in Cornwall.

Bottom: Sir John Soane's 'Elevation of a Dairy House in the Moresque Stile'.

Academy's travelling scholarship. In Rome he met Piranesi himself and the mould was cast for Soane to become the greatest Romantic classicist of all time.

He was a colossus in all matters architectural, not least for our purposes with his designs for animal buildings. At Wimpole in Cambridgeshire, he drew up plans for the Earl of Hardwick to have 11-bay classical façades on his chickens' nesting-boxes, while the 1794 thatched farm on the estate managed to be both rustic and grand at the same time. Wimpole was also blessed with 'capital piggeries', as well as deer-pens, all designed by the great man himself.

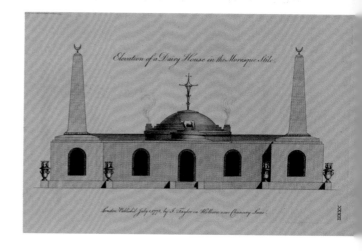

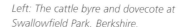
*Left: The cattle byre and dovecote at Swallowfield Park, Berkshire.*

## Swallowfield, Berkshire

Standing in the home farm of Swallowfield Park, near to the house but discreetly out of sight from both the front and back doors, is this wildly roofed cattle byre and dovecote – looking for all the world as if it is about to lift off into the sky. At its core an octagonal dovecote dates from the 18th century; its oddly charming 'skirt' dates from the 19th century. There are other and tempting possibilities as to both their origins – that there was something afoot between 1689 and 1691 when the architect William Talman rebuilt the house for the 2nd Earl of Clarendon; otherwise, could it be that a contribution was made in the late 1700s when Sylvanus Bevan, one of the founders of Barclays Bank, made picturesque alterations to the place? The octagon core is barely visible, with the cote rising up the full height of the building to the ball finial on its peak, and embraced all around by the cattle shelter with its wooden posts and curved brackets. The outlandish octagonal hipped roofs of tiles and slates sweep overall. Inside the dovecote, brick pillars stand at each angle with 535 brick nests in rows five abreast between them. The main beam supports the 'potence' – a French invention which consisted of a central pole with an arm attached on which was fixed a ladder to climb up to collect the eggs. They could be gathered at ease, when, at a mere flick of the wrist, you rotated yourself round the full circle and at speed. Outside, the walls have had to be restored as their angles had been worn away by the cattle rubbing themselves, softening all the bricks to the height of their backs.

All manner of other buildings were also part of Swallowfield Park, including a brewery, a slaughter house and a building in which water – from a deep well – was pumped up by a horse attached to a beam to service both the kitchen and the laundry. This was then stored in a thrice-arched building with a cupola adorned by a rare one-handed clock of 1757.

The benefits of the buildings on this estate have been enjoyed by an interesting lot. In the 17th century Swallowfield was lived in by the Rosicrucian philosopher William Backhouse, who 'adopted' Elias Ashmole – the scholar, collector and founder of Oxford's Ashmolean Museum – as his son. 'Mr Backhouse told me I must now needs be his son', wrote Ashmole in *The Diary and Will of Elias Ashmole*, 'because he had communicated so many secrets to me.' One of those secrets was 'the true matter of the Philosopher's stone, which he has bequeathed to me as a legacy'. Then there was Thomas 'Diamond' Pitt – grandfather and great-grandfather of Williams Pitt the Elder and the Younger – who, in 1702, as Governor of Fort St George in India where he was making a trading fortune, bought a diamond that had been smuggled out of a mine in a wound in a worker's leg. He sold it to the French Regent in 1717 and it was later set into the French crown. Today it is in the Louvre. No doubt largely from the proceeds of this great gem, Pitt bought Swallowfield from the Earl of Clarendon in about 1717. Sir Henry Russell, who bought the house in 1820, had been the Chief Justice of Bengal.

In 1965 Swallowfield was bought by Mutual Householders Association when the house was sensitively converted into self-contained private apartments. Today it is run by the Sunley Group, offering 'Luxury Apartments' for 'Country Estate Living'. They have beautifully restored the place and were responsible for the excellent *Swallowfield Park, Berkshire: Landscape and Building Study* by Wessex Archaeology.

## Welbeck, Nottinghamshire

The cow houses and poultry house at Welbeck Abbey are part of what can be cheeringly hailed as a village of buildings for animals, and a stately one at that; all created between 1857 and 1878 for the 5th Duke of Portland – as strange a man as ever lived. He was an obsessively secretive recluse who employed many thousands of men on gargantuan building programmes, a good many of which were underground. For example, the chickens that were reared in this handsome poultry house were dispatched daily from the kitchen, where they had been cooked, on an underground railway to the few rooms that he occupied in the abbey. Known as the 'perpetual chicken', there was one that was forever ready on the spit to be trundled off whenever the duke felt peckish. It would be delivered to a hatch of double doors so that the duke would never have to see a soul.

He eventually built 15 miles of tunnels beneath the Welbeck estate, including one of a mile and a quarter long, to Worksop Station. This was wide enough for two carriages to pass and provided a swift and secret route for him to leave the place unnoticed. There were underground stables and there were underground pigsties, often attached to one of the 41 'Jacobethan' lodges – the architectural term used for the 19th- and early 20th-century revivalist mix of the Elizabethan and Jacobean styles. As had been decreed by the duke, these were designed to be identical back and front, with one side having a dummy chimney and porch. White-tile-hung tunnels led from the lodges to quarters for cows, calves, chickens and pigs and sometimes even a donkey. A pierced quatrefoil cast-iron grille allowed the animals air. The duke even created underground greenhouses, as well as a curving sweep of a magnolia house. These were in fact semi-subterranean and with

snug shelter around them and light pouring in from above, how could they fail? Certainly from photographs, they were bulging with blooms. Most sensational of all, though, was his series of underground reception rooms – but to receive whom? These were connected by statue-filled and glass-topped galleries to a vast quarter-of-an-acre room that had originally been planned as a chapel. It became a picture gallery and hung heavy with oil paintings and

later ended up as a ballroom, although the reclusive duke, of course, was never to dance a single step on its quarter acre of floor. Strangest of all there were hydraulic lifts installed for the would-be guests to descend from their carriages above. As no one was asked, no one came. When the huge room was finished, its 65ft-span of iron-girdered flat roof, complete with plate-glass skylights, was reckoned to be the largest unsupported roof in the world.

Victorian technology had been one of the driving forces behind all these fantastical schemes. What were the others? One of them was giving work to the local unemployed, including hordes of Irish navvies to each of whom he gave a donkey and an umbrella. No one, though, was allowed to acknowledge him if they passed – even the vicar. The most likely explanation that I have found for all his underground work is that he obsessively liked to hide his buildings as much as he obsessively liked to hide himself. 'His love of building tunnels came perhaps from an exaggerated desire for privacy' was the view of Lady Ottoline Morrell, the stepsister of William Cavendish-Bentinck, the next duke. She went to Welbeck after the 5th Duke had died and wrote an account of all that she saw, recorded in Cavendish-Bentinck's *Men, Women and Things*. Her most haunting evocation of the duke was after she had discovered the old riding school hung with many hundreds of mirrors and crystal chandeliers. 'The sudden mood of gaiety that had made him decorate it as a ballroom must have soon faded', she wrote, 'leaving the mock sunset to shine on the lonely figure reflected a hundred times in the mirrors around him.' She found that most of the rooms at Welbeck '...were absolutely bare and empty. They were all painted pink, with parquet floors, and all bare and without any furniture except that almost every room had a "convenience" in the corner, quite exposed and not sheltered in any way.'

So much for his own modest-to-a-fault arrangements. For his animals he built a prodigious number of buildings, and all of them lavish. The somewhat rare 'tan gallop' (tan, the outer shell of a coconut split and shredded into strands) was laid on the ground of a utilitarian shed-like structure of an alarming 422yds length. The hunting stables covered a whole acre of ground and there were coach house stables, racehorse stables and fire stables. At the ring

*Left: Welbeck Abbey's riding school.*

*Right: Houses for cows at Welbeck Abbey.*

of the alarm bell, the firemen would slide down a brass pole and with a flick of a switch would release complete harnesses suspended from the ceiling. Down they dropped onto the horses' backs and, with just one buckle to do up, they were off, with six horses pulling a brass boiler. As for the riding school, which could be reached by two underground tunnels, one for the duke, the other for those who worked for him – it too was enormous. With a glass and iron barrel-vaulted roof and with cast-iron columns, it had all the appearance of a delicate railway station. In the 1860s it was reckoned to be second in size only to one in Moscow; measuring 385ft by 112ft and 51ft high, it was proudly claimed by Cavendish-Bentinck as being 'capable of holding two cavalry regiments, both manoeuvring at the same time'. It is built – as is the rest of this harmonious village for the duke, his tenants and his animals – with limestone quarried on the estate. Mostly in the Jacobethan style, there are buildings great and small, in groups and at various angles, that are shown off to perfection on immaculate greenswards.

The ogee-domed poultry house has more of the by-now-to-be-expected grandeur with two of its original four stone birds – a grebe and a stork – still atop stone pillars standing sentinel over the enclosed grass yard with an ornamental fountain. A stone turkey also survives in the yard. Two cottages flank the main building, one for the poulterer, one for the dairyman. (The dairy, one of the few buildings to have been demolished, stood nearby.) The chickens roosted in the middle of the poultry house, with rows of nesting and feeding boxes on either side of the dovecote tower. Marching along the façade is a wooden arcade, allowing the birds to take the air. The original plans show a squat tower instead of the dome – the change of heart

was for the better – and are signed C C and A Dunnet. There have been no birds here since 1982.

Three cow houses were also built; two of them for cows in their individual stalls and the third for the milking parlour. While the stone that built them is the same, these elevations, with their pierced stone balls and daintily proportioned pediments, have a delicacy that all the other, more lumpen, buildings lack.

A little lumpen maybe, but what a magnificent assembly nevertheless and all thanks to a visionary recluse. Today the buildings have been given various and successful roles, such as an art gallery, museum, restaurants, craft shops and more, all abuzz with life and of the highest quality.

*Left: The beautifully decorated Royal Dairy at Windsor, Berkshire.*

## Windsor, Berkshire

'THE QUEEN AS A FARMER'. The most Perfect Dairy in the World' ran the headline in New Zealand's *Otago Witness* on 11 February 1897. It went on to say that 'the Queen is one of the most enthusiastic amateur farmers in the British Islands, and it is not too much to say that there is not a dairy in the three kingdoms that can hold a candle to the dairy at the Shaw farm, Windsor'. The inhabitants of southern New Zealand were then spared no details of this distant – albeit royal – dairy, designed under the auspices of Prince Albert between 1858 and 1861. 'Walls of Minton tiles of delicate hue ... fountains tinkling ... great racks of old Worcester and Crown Derby china, fitter you would think, for a drawing room than a dairy – nothing more beautiful could be imagined.' It was all true – the cooling room at Windsor's Royal Dairy was a trumpeting testament to the wonders of 19th-century faience decoration. No detail should be left out. Set in a sky-blue frieze on high are ceramic roundels of Queen Victoria, Prince Albert, their children and the husbands of their two eldest daughters – all supported by sea horses while dolphins flank medallions of the crossed V R. There are majolica tableaux – orange and white, brilliant and bright – of babies prancing through the seasonal pastimes: skating and sheep shearing, dancing around the maypole, ploughing and gathering in the harvest with goats. Friezes abound, one with tiny china oranges, their leaves entwined with blue-and-white ribbons, weaving round the walls. These are repeated, double size, in plaster on the ceiling.

Such wealth of decoration is made all the more extraordinary when so much of it is sculpted in relief – giving a general sense of materialising magic to the place. Two Minton fountains even appear to have heaved forth from the walls; one is a merman, the other a mermaid, both holding shells on high whilst sitting in shells held aloft by herons amid arum lilies, water lilies and bullrushes. These are thought to be by the prince's favourite sculptor John Thomas. Adding yet more lustre to the room, all the windows are of stained glass, decorated with arches of harebells and hawthorn and each with a Tudor rose bearing the thistle and shamrock leaves on its stem. A pin cannot be pricked between the decoration.

All the faience work was made at the Minton china factory in Stoke-on-Trent, which had been founded in 1793 by Thomas Minton. It was son Herbert who was our man; he invented artistic techniques that were to capture the admiration of such giants as A W N Pugin and Henry Cole, as well as Prince Albert when he created this dairy.

Moreover, behind all this beauty was sound practicality; the model dairy had been designed as part of the working Home Farm and was soon to make a profit – one would expect nothing less from the great royal champion of the arts and sciences. (Such was the Prince Consort's agricultural acumen that he also multiplied the revenues from the Duchy of Cornwall estates held in trust for the Prince of Wales.) For his dairy 'he introduced all modern improvements and tried all modern experiments', according to the *Chicago Tribune* on 13 June 1869 (the dairy was written of worldwide!). It was built with double walls and the windows were double-glazed throughout to maintain an even temperature. It was air-conditioned by a paddle that drew fumes from the oil-fired lighting up through the pierced ceiling tiles and out through the Italianate 'air tower' on high. All the shelves were made of solid marble while beneath the floor a warren of pipes flowed with cold water to keep everything cool. The width of the doors allowed for the yoke and buckets.

*Left and right: Two views of the Royal Dairy at Windsor.*

Fifty cows were milked here daily with the milk from the Alderneys kept aside for Queen Victoria. As for the butter – according to the *Chicago Tribune* 'tempting to the eye and sweet to the tooth' – 20lb was produced daily and wherever the queen went so too went the Home Farm butter. (Balmoral was the exception, where they made their own pats of butter stamped with a royal crown and the word 'Balmoral' beneath crossed sprays of flowers.)

As befits such opulence it has been described with reams of extravagant prose, none purpler than what was written by Elihu Burritt, the American Consul in Birmingham, appointed by Abraham Lincoln. His description of the dairy – written soon after it was built and published as a 'selection' in *Elihu Burritt; A Memorial Volume* – is a period piece and a half!

'*The Queen's Dairy!*' How Saxon and homelike sounds that term! ... The Queen herself, in straw bonnet and thick-soled shoes, walking up and down the dairy-room, dropping happy and smiling looks into pails and pans of milk and cream; perhaps anon stamping a roll of new-made butter with her wife's seal manual for the royal table ... *The Queen's Dairy!* The very name seems to link her queenhood to the happiest and homeliest experiences of rural life; to attach her, by a sensible lien of industrial sympathy, to all the farmers' wives in the British Empire ... The milk-room ... is perfection in itself. Its internal structure and arrangements are exquisite in every feature and fitting. To say that it is a little marble temple, 'polished after the similitude of a palace,' would convey a sense of its cool whiteness and purity, but not its aspect of softness. The walls, the long marble tables, the fountains, the statuary of rustic life, and all the finely-sculptured allegories look as if wrought from new milk petrified just as the cream began to rise to the surface. Or as if, looking into the basined pools of the soft white fluid circling around the interior, like great fluent pearls strung for a bracelet, they had gradually assimilated themselves to the medium that reflected their faces, and had taken up both its softness of look and sweetness of savor. It was truly a beautiful sight ... The pans or dishes are of oblong shape, with a lip to them, which saves many an unlucky splash in pouring their contents into other vessels. Then they are all made of the finest stone china, with gilt edges, each holding two gallons ... There were ninety-two of them, placed in double rows on the long marble tables, which run around the room over a flowing sheet of clear spring water rippling in its wide marble channel ... No description I could give would convey any adequate idea of the refined taste, fertile genius, and exquisite art brought to bear on this little palace.

No detail escaped his praise, even the names of the cows: 'The floral and fairy kingdoms of nature, heroes and heroines of ancient mythology, history and poetry, supplied most of this interesting nomenclature; and this made it all the more interesting to me to see that *Uncle Tom's Cabin* had furnished two or three names, and that "Eva" and "Topsy" had their place in the rank of chosen celebrities.'

It is pleasing to be able to write that this is still the queen's Royal Dairy and that milk, cream and cheese are still dispatched daily from the Home Farm; the milk in large wide-necked glass bottles emblazoned with E II R in brilliant royal blue.

By the by, on the sloping greensward that surrounds the dairy, are bronze effigies of two of Queen Victoria's favourite dogs – Boy, a dachshund, and Boz, a Skye terrier – a modest pair among the many canine bronzes that were put up by her throughout the Home Park at Windsor.

## Manderston, Berwickshire

Sir William Miller of Manderston House made a prodigious fortune when, as honorary British Consul in St Petersburg in the 1860s and 1870s, he traded in herrings and hemp with the Russians. It was left to his second son Sir James Miller – fate decreed that the elder son choked to death on a cherry stone – to spend that fortune between 1903 and 1905 recreating a house that for quality of workmanship and materials would have no equal in the British Isles.

His case was made with the dairy alone. A Gothic room, built entirely from marble and alabaster from seven different countries, it is no ordinary sight. So sleekly solid that you want to stroke its every contour, it soars forth from an elaborately inlaid floor up to vaulting of finest cut marble stripes. At its apex is a great stone boss, weighing half a ton, of a milkmaid milking a cow. With her hair in a bun, her beribboned straw hat on the ground at her side and her long skirt

*Left: The Gothic dairy at Manderston House, Berwickshire.*

*Right: Coo Palace – a model dairy farm, near Kirkandrews, Dumfries – was built for only 12 cows.*

flung back over the three-legged stool, no detail has been left out. Leaves are thick on the trees and the grass is clearly delineated. The cow's backbone is clear to see, as is its swishing tail. Everything was perfect, but it was all wrong. When she was first hauled into place it was realised that the milkmaid was not sitting on the right side of the cow. Down she came, to be carved all over again.

Nor is this the only spot that knocks you for six in the assembly of buildings that make up the dairy: to get to this 'poem in seven marbles' – as the room is proudly called by Manderston's present owner Adrian Palmer – you progress through cloisters around a central fountain. The cowshed was to be seen next to the dairy, then afterwards tea could be taken in a panelled room in a mock border keep, known as the Tower. All the decorative work was by Italian and French craftsmen, and it was all designed by the attention-to-detail supremo John Kinross. The architect had already built the estate buildings – including the stables (*see* pp 62–4) – before he thundered on with the house.

It has been suggested that Sir James Miller's passion for building such splendours was in part to keep up with his wife's family. He had married Lord Curzon's sister Eveline; she had grown up at Kedleston – by Robert Adam and no grander stately home in the land – and so Sir James created a gargantuan Adamesque front hall at Manderston. 'Keeping up with the Curzons' must have been an arduous business.

## Kirkandrews, Dumfries

Although the Coo Palace in Dumfries is now sadly decaying, it is still a palace nevertheless – Gormenghastian in scale and with a wealth of complex architectural detailing. It was created between 1911 and 1914 as model dairy farm for a herd of only 12 cows. James Brown was the Mr Big who built it. He was a successful Manchester shopkeeper who moved to Dumfries in 1900 to build a plain neo-Georgian house for himself and 11 years later he saw to it that his cows were rather more sumptuously housed than he was. As excellent an example as ever there was of allowing yourself full whack architectural indulgence when building for animals.

Rearing out of the desolate coastline of the Irish Sea with scarcely another building in view, the Coo Palace is an uncommon sight. With the surrounding walls inlaid

with panels of pebbles and slate, and capped with pebbled roofs, all, at first, seems sound. Thereafter the devil is in the detail, all of which, for a dairy in Dumfries, should be described. The main block, with an enormous segmental arched roof, was the milking parlour; stone buttresses march around the walls and its entrance is heavily hooded; Maltese cross 'arrow slits' are everywhere; and rearing overall is the water tower, with battlemented corner turrets and a smaller round tower on top. Arts and Crafts features abound, such as lead lanterns and a curiously Egyptian-like stone trough. There are stone balls galore, atop gabled arches and on corners of the various buildings. All the roofs are covered with ornamental terracotta tiles, some of them edged with what looks like terracotta piping intercut into patterns, and many of the walls are inset with triangles of crazy paving-like mosaics of stone. It is altogether a startling concoction! The drainpipe heads which are flanked by fleur-de-lys give us its date of 1911.

So much for the exterior; walk somewhat nervously inside and you are surrounded by white-tiled walls with turquoise-tiled dados beneath stripes of brown. Each room is connected by an arched entrance with a fanlight. The stalls for the cows – queens of this castle – still have their handsome iron-ball posts with walls that are covered with brilliant green hexagonal tiles.

In 1996 this extraordinary assembly of buildings was boldly bought by local hero Rex Pyke, who so far has been unable to find a use for them.

## Tong, Shropshire

Here is a story and a half – of fortunes made from slavery, sugar and captured booty in the Caribbean, and spent on a multi-domed palace in the eastern style, set down in grounds designed by Capability Brown; of subsequent years of grotesquely debauched scandal;

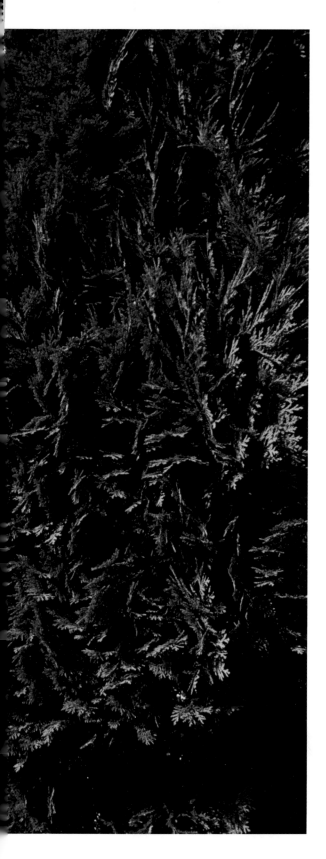

of the creation of buildings, most particularly for beasts, that for eccentricity would be hard to beat – and all this in a few square miles of Shropshire.

It was George Durant I who made the money and it was he who built Tong Castle in 1765. With its forest of domes great and small, its fancy 'gothick' and ogee windows as well as castellated roofs and gables, it must have been an exotic sight on the Shropshire skyline. In Frederick Calvert and William West's *Picturesque Views ... in Staffordshire* of 1830 we read that it was 'fancifully composed, partly of Moorish, and partly of Gothic architecture, and produces a grand effect from the numerous and widely extended minarets and pinnacles, and the stately crown given to the whole by the lofty and magnificent Turkish domes'.

Such was the architectural influence exercised on George Durant's son, also called George, who grew up in the castle – an influence which he put to exciting and often childlike-in-its-jokiness effect. For instance, there was a dovecote, now demolished, inscribed with the words 'PIGEONS ONLY DO KNOW WOE WHEN A-BEATING THEY DO GO' as well as a water well emblazoned with 'ADAM'S ALE LICENSED TO BE DRUNK ON THE PREMISES 1838.' There was a coffin decorating the carpenter's shop with the words 'IN MORTE LUCRUM' (Profit in death) and 'GARDE A VOUS' (Attention!); a stone ball atop a stone pedestal was emblazoned with 'AB HOC MOMENTO PENDET AETERNITAS. GEO. DURANTAN. 1821' (On this moment hangs eternity) and a Gothic arch made from the jaw of a whale decorated with 'MORS JANUA VITAE' (death, the door [or gateway] of (eternal) life) and 'POST TOT NAUFRAGIA PORTUM' (after so many wrecks a haven). And there was more, much much more. Surely one of the most surreal creations was a weeping willow made of iron with concealed water pipes throughout its branches. If you sat on the iron seat

beneath it, you were immediately drenched by the
'weeping' willow tree.

Most elaborate of his schemes was Convent Lodge of
1821, flanked on either side by dark pink sandstone
walls that had been carved by the village workman John
Vaughn. A sculpted stone rope rose and fell over the
castellations until it reached the 12ft-high pyramidal
gate piers, which it then twisted around into tassel-
ended knots. Flowers, leaves and fruit such as figs and
pineapples writhed throughout the multitude of
carvings – a serpent biting a foot, ships, a skep of bees,
kneeling legs, a Roman lamp and book and so on and
so on. It was all pious and personal symbolism for the
strange George Durant II who built a pulpit onto the
lodge's wall containing a stone lion on which he would
sit and talk to passers-by. The lodge keeper's wife was
ordered to dress as a nun.

Nor were these his only eccentricities – as far as it is
possible to tell, it seems that he had upwards of 40
children. He had 14 by his wife while concurrently
having three more by the nursemaid, and at the same
time a baby by another maid – 'making a brothel out of
his own house', thundered his wife's lawyer in the
divorce courts, whilst 'connecting with the dairy maid in
the fowl yard or shrubbery; or with the labourer's wives
on the floors of their own cottages'. He was reputed to
have fathered a child in every cottage on his estate,
calling himself their 'Godfather' and giving them such
discreet names as Napoleon Wedge, Columbine
Cherrington, Luther Martin and Cinderella Greatback.
A child by his first wife was christened Anguish, as a
reminder of his mother's sufferings during his birth.
George Durant II married again in 1830 and had six
more children by his second wife. When he died in
1844, the *Shrewsbury Chronicle* did not beat about the
bush about his private life: 'Although blessed with an

amiable wife and family of children any gentleman
might be proud of, he like that fallen Majesty of
Denmark left the feast to prey on garbage... .'

He did, though, create the pyramid for poultry, the
star for our purposes in his architectural show. At 20ft
high, it is built in yellowish brick and, to allow breezes
through the pyramid, some of these have been taken
out to create variously shaped openings. It has dark-
blue vitrified quoins tapering up to a stone cap with

egg-shaped aerating holes. To one side the top is inscribed with the name and date of the building, 'EGYPTIAN AVIARY 1842', while to the other are the letters 'AB OVO'('From the beginning, the origin, the egg') – a Latin reference to Helen of Troy being born in an egg from the union between Leda and Zeus disguised as a swan. After this sole stab at scholarship, the inscriptions are more countrified and cosy: 'SCRATCH BEFORE YOU PECK', 'LIVE AND LET LIVE', 'BETTER COME OUT OF THE WAY LOVE', and best of all 'TEACH YOUR GRANNY.' They have now all gone, as too have the swarm of sandstone carvings including a cat carrying a kitten called 'TRANSPORTATION', a swan amongst bullrushes and a bas relief of a cockerel.

At Acorn Cottage in nearby Bishop's Wood – what once must have been part of the Tong Castle estate – there is another pyramid, this time for pigs and of rough-hewn brown stone with the welcoming inscription 'TO PLEASE THE PIGS' over the door. Only a foot away stands a Gothic and crow-stepped little castle for cows with the words 'RANZ DE VACHE' on it – the name for the simple melodies played by Swiss mountaineers on the Alp horn *pour ranger des vaches*, to drive their herds to pasture or bring the cows home.

Other than these three, George Durant II's buildings have long since gone. In the early 1980s, I ran to ground the fast deteriorating sandstone carvings of the Convent Lodge walls and gate piers and even sat on the lion in the pulpit. Today the fates of those piers are in a curious limbo – in a failed bid to save them, Villiers Engineering Co Ltd demolished and rebuilt them in Wolverhampton as the grand entrance to their works in Marston Road. Too narrow for lorries, they were set wider apart, but even then one was bashed asunder by a great juggernaut – at the time of writing they were still lying in pieces by the roadside.

Tong Castle itself deteriorated into decay and, in 1954, when a child was killed in the ruins, it was blown up. Photographs were taken just before and after the explosion; one with the towers, pinnacles and gothicary still upright but sinking, the next with a great long heap of rubble and dust. The castle for cows and the pyramids for pigs and poultry are therefore the lone survivals of George Durant II's little kingdom.

## Flintham, Nottinghamshire

Flintham Hall near Newark has been through many architectural phases – all of them perfect for their period. Originally a plain-as-a-pikestaff medieval cum Jacobean multi-gabled stone manor, it was trimmed and mainly rebuilt into a chastely classical box in 1798. In 1829 it was enlarged with stern brick additions by Lewis Wyatt and, only 24 years later, it was transmogrified into a Victorian potentate's palace of golden stone, designed by the architect T C Hine. The pheasantry, like a slice out of that architectural progress, is also by Wyatt – a miniature version of his red-brick north front of the house that still survives today.

Beneath the eaves of an octagonal bay is a dovecote, while on either side there were aviaries once filled with pheasants and other birds. So as to enable you to stroll unhindered from end to end, each was subdivided with doorways of hanging chains. Both aviaries were heated from pipes that were built within the walls – by then a long-established practice for heating walls so that the most exotic fruit could be grown in the English garden. Outside, two of the original oval ponds survive, although only stumps remain of the posts to which mesh was attached, creating a vast tennis-court-size enclosure for the birds in front of the building – taking up all the ground that is in the photograph and more.

While everything but the building and ponds have disappeared, the gardens all around it have been beautifully restored by Myles Hildyard, who lived in and loved the place for most of his life, until he died, aged 90. In the late 20th century he made the electrifying decision to commission the Argentinian artist Riccardo Cinalli to paint reproductions of his favourite paintings as murals on the pheasantry's walls. Thus it is that on the walls of a small 19th-century building for birds in Nottinghamshire, we find life-size naked figures taken from *The Raft of the Medusa*, originally painted by Theodore Gericault between 1818 and 1819. Cinalli

worked at speed. 'It was quite extraordinary how quickly he worked', said David Rowbottam, who lived at Flintham with Myles. 'He sloshed it on, and as for the marbling, that only took a morning!'

Flintham's greatest enrichment of all was the conservatory, designed by Hine when the house was rebuilt in 1853. It was a remarkable embellishment that has now become, by virtue of its survival, unique – a gargantuan barrel-vaulted conservatory, the lunette of which is a reincarnation of the Crystal Palace. (The Great Exhibition had taken place a couple of years before Flintham was rebuilt, and the house is filled

## Leighton, Powys

The estate of Leighton Hall was a triumph of scientific experiment and advanced technology, built on a stupendous scale. Sir John Naylor, a Liverpool banker, was responsible for it all – for creating what in its day must have seemed like a small city of agricultural industry. Having made enormous sums of money, he determined to spend it wisely, and did so wildly well. Streams were channelled to drive turbines and part of the River Severn was diverted to drive a water ram pumping water up to a great tank on Moel-y-Mab, a spur of the nearby Long Mountain. A funicular railway would haul the raw materials up to the tank to make liquid manure, which would then flow forth in copper pipes throughout all of Naylor's farms. He also built a private gas works that sent gas through pitch-fibre pipes to his house, the home farm and the church. Not satisfied with just the funicular, he built a broad-gauge railway linking the threshing barn with the hay and fodder stores.

The poultry yard of 1861, with its fowl house, storm shed, pond and scratching yard, was designed with fitting splendour to be part of the home farm. Today, the home farm, with its huge brick circular cow sheds, appears in a sorry state; however, the fowl house in the poultry yard, along with the nearby poultryman's cottage (which you can now rent to stay in), have all been restored by the Landmark Trust. According to the alluring account of the place in their handbook, '[e]very species, whether large or small, ornamental, water or humble hen, had its own meticulously designed quarters in the Fowl House: a thorough attention to detail, which is typical of the whole estate'.

The architect for this festive building might well have been the Liverpudlian W H Gee who designed Naylor's lofty towered house – with interiors by J D Crace and A W N Pugin – as well as the lofty spired

with such Crystal Palace exhibits as a town-hall-sized fireplace.) It is a conservatory with a sturdy rather than a flimsy presence, for, in keeping with the rest of the whacking great house, the same stone was used between the conservatory's glass. Thus the two are united.

Myles died in 2005, after both he and David had restored the house to its original and alarming splendour. It is seldom that you love a house as much as its owner, or an owner as much as his house. Flintham was the exception. Here they were both fused with dash and distinction in equal measure.

church. A claim should be made, though, for the possibility of this fowl house having been designed by the architect of the Windsor aviary and poultry farm. They are so startlingly similar – C R Stanley's royal buildings were built a good deal earlier in 1845, so we should at least give him the credit of having influenced the jolly style of this Welsh fowl house.

A dastardly footnote: Sir John Naylor was also a passionate forester and it was under his guidance at Leighton in 1881 that the Leyland cypress – a hybrid between the Montery cypress and the Nootka cypress –

was first propagated. Having been brought up in Northumberland, there has always been the shadow of Captain Leyland, a fellow Northumbrian, as the first person to produce the sanitising-of-the-suburbs tree. Once, I'm ashamed to say, my sister and I danced on his grave. What a relief to discover that the real villain was Sir John Naylor – not a Northumberland man after all. It was his son Christopher John Naylor, a naval man who, having changed his surname to Leyland for an inheritance, moved to Northumberland where he further developed the *Leylandii*.

Left: The fowl house at Leighton Hall, Powys.

Below: The restored Ovaltine egg farm at Kings Langley in Hertfordshire.

## Kings Langley, Hertfordshire

Speeding along the M25 and just east of the Kings Langley exit, you spot it: a huge white horseshoe of a building, which was the first battery chicken farm in the country. This, though, is a misnomer if ever there was one. For the building, designed in 1929 to the highest agricultural and architectural standards, can best be described as a late Arts and Crafts palace for poultry. Ovaltine was behind it, or rather Dr George Wander from Berne in Switzerland was. He was a pharmaceutical dietician who, in 1904, believing in the health-giving properties of malt extract, had invented what was originally called 'Ovomaltine'. His son Albert brought the business to Britain in 1909 where an office clerk mistakenly called it 'Ovaltine'. So the never-to-be-forgotten name was born.

In 1913 the first Ovaltine factory was built in Kings Langley, which was so successful that between 1924 and 1929 it was replaced by a giant Art Deco masterpiece – with, to boot, a ballroom where regular tea dances were held for the workers. This building ran for a full quarter of a mile along the Grand Union Canal, used by an Ovaltine fleet of narrowboats in pairs to bring coal from Birmingham, each of them named after the factory workers – *Albert* and *Georgette* were the first pair, *Mimas* and *Enid* the last. Today its façade – on a par with the Hoover Factory at Perivale – has been retained, in front of 215 newly built apartments.

In 1932, by now no doubt on its architectural high horse as well as at its peak of popularity, Ovaltine laid down grand new schemes – buying two local farms to create new kingdoms, one for cows, the other for chickens so as to provide the firm with enough barley, eggs and milk. The first, Parsonage Farm, was to be a model dairy farm designed as an exact replica of one built by Louis XVI for Marie Antoinette – including a

thatched silo! The second, Numbers Farm, was to be the Ovaltine egg farm. There had been nothing like it before; the architectural detailing was superb, as were the working arrangements. The cockerel battery house and the pullet battery house stood tall – each with a towered end, a two-storied arch and sweeping roofs – at either side of the entrance to the farm. Joining them from behind was the unique pullet-rearing house, shaped like a horseshoe to ensure that the birds caught

*Left and below: Kings Langley: the Ovaltine egg farm today (left) and as it was in the 1930s (below).*

as much sunlight as possible. Better still, they had the bonus of 'sun parlours' – large cages protruding from the building – in which the White Leghorns, with plenty of space to strut, could enjoy 'clement weather'. All around the horseshoe-shaped building, little wooden poultry houses stood between avenues of apple trees, mature oaks and woodland. There the chickens were tended by white-capped and coated 'maids' wearing jodphurs; one of them later wrote an account for the BBC website *WW2 People's War*, noting that

'[t]here was a complete absence of smell in the Model Poultry Farm'. Ovaltine's archive of photographs could not lie – chickens cannot pretend to be perky – this was a paradise for poultry! How sad to think that this was the beginning of the end, that this would develop into the monstrous battery farms of today.

As was inevitable, by 1980 the relatively small scale of the farm was overtaken by mass-market production and it was forced to close – making a tantalisingly odd ruin as it stood empty for 20 long years. But in 2000 its

Left: The sun parlours at the Ovaltine egg farm.

Right: The interior of the dovecote at Hurley in Berkshire.

fortunes changed – ironically and dramatically. Having been the first battery chicken farm in the country, the building was taken over by Renewable Energy Systems (RES) – who have renamed it Beaufort Court – as their up-to-the-minute zero-emissions flagship head office! It has since undergone an exemplary – and exhilarating – restoration and rebuilding by Studio E Architects, with RES practicing what they preach. Not only that, they have published many papers online detailing their success: 'By means of sustainable building techniques, high standards of energy efficiency and several types of clean renewable energy to provide all of the heating, cooling and power requirements, a world first has been achieved.' In other words, they have created a 21st-century version – on a vast scale – of the passive solar design of the chickens' 1930s 'sun parlours'. RES is one of the most successful wind-energy companies in the world; proud proof of which is a giant wind turbine standing overall.

What a first to have chalked up – to be able to claim that what were once cockerel and pullet battery houses have now become the first commercial zero-emissions offices in the country; that a huge and beautiful battery chicken farm has somehow bypassed all its attendant horrors to become, in the words of RES, '[a] model of low carbon building design and energy generation, capable of replication across Europe'. It is a modern miracle.

## Hurley, Berkshire

The dovecote at Hurley, allegedly dating from 1307, is claimed by some to be the oldest in England though others are thought to be even earlier, with Garway in Herefordshire the oldest that is authentically dated (1326). Hurley's dovecote was originally part of the priory of St Mary – a small cell to the Benedictine house at Westminster – founded in the mid-11th century by Geoffrey de Mandeville, who had been given the manor by William the Conqueror.

The Tudor manor of Ladye Place, built over the prior's infirmary, was lived in by Richard Lovelace who greatly enriched the place with Spanish bounty gathered on forays with Sir Francis Drake. A later seafaring shaft of history associated with the place came in the 1700s when the dovecote was owned by the brother of Admiral Kempenfeldt of the *Royal George*, one of George III's fleet that met with disaster off Spithead in 1782. She was being loaded with stores and listed over with a loss of 900 lives, including the admiral himself.

The dovecote is 88ft in circumference with 3ft-thick walls and 600 L-shaped nests of chalk, round which its potence can still whirl. Outside four buttresses climb up to its cone-shaped roof with a square cupola on the top. Later and interesting additions are the jambs and lintels dating from 1642 with the inscription 'CR' ('Carolus Rex') still visible above the door. Standing today in the garden of newly built and named Tithecote Manor, the dovecote is a Grade I listed building.

## Sibthorpe, Nottinghamshire

The simplicity of the Sibthorpe dovecote standing in flat countryside gives it a haunting isolation. It dates from the 14th century and is enormous, standing 60ft high, with 1,260 nesting boxes in 28 tiers. It was built to serve a college of chantry priests, which, with the creation of St Mary's Chapel, was founded here by Sir Thomas de Sibthorpe in 1324 – thriving for years under the protection of Edward III. The advowson of Sibthorpe had belonged to the Knights Templar from 1185 and Sir Thomas managed to obtain it in 1341. Save for the splendid chancel of St Peter's Church nearby, nothing but the lone dovecote survives. Originally it had two dormers and a wooden louvre on the top, but these were not replaced when it was part of the admirable dovecote restoration programme by the Nottinghamshire County Council in the 1970s.

Left: The 14th-century dovecote at Sibthorpe, Nottinghamshire.

Below: The dovecote that served Minster Lovell Hall in Oxfordshire.

enjoy it was his son Francis Lovell, about whom there is a terrible tale. He was an ardent Yorkist who supported Lambert Simnel, the imposter claimant to the English crown, but faced with their final defeat at the Battle of Stoke in 1487, Lovell was seen fleeing across the River Trent on his horse and presumed drowned.

In the early 1700s, when building work was being done on Minster Lovell Hall,

> ...there was discovered a large vault or room underground, in which was the entire skeleton of a man, as having been sitting at a table, which was before him with a book, paper, pen &c, and in another part of the room lay a cap much moldered and decayed, which the family and others judged to be this Lord Lovell, whose exit had hitherto been so uncertain.

So relates Francis Peck in his *Memoirs of the Life and Actions of Oliver Cromwell* of 1740.

## Minster Lovell, Oxfordshire

The manorial dovecote stands in the grounds of the 15th-century Minster Lovell Hall, the house that it was built to serve, now romantically ruinous amidst trees on the banks of the River Windrush. An even more ancient manor belonging to the Lovells since the 1100s had been incorporated into a new house by William, 7th Lord Lovell, between 1431 and 1442, when it is thought that he built the dovecote as well. The last to

*Below: The flint and stone dovecote at Monks Risborough, Buckinghamshire.*

Today, thanks to English Heritage, the dovecote – with its lantern atop a conical roof of Cotswold slates, supported from the inside by wooden rafters, above tiers of stone nesting boxes – is in tip-top order.

## Monks Risborough, Buckinghamshire

Monks Risborough's dovecote, thought to date from the 16th century, stands hard by St Dunstan's Church. It is built of flint and coursed rubble clunch – as satisfying to say as to see. Handsomely large stone quoins march up each corner and make up a chamfered arch around the little door. Their quality suggests that this cote must have been attached to the monastery of Christchurch Priory that was here from the 10th century to the dissolution of the monasteries. Place Farm was subsequently built here but was demolished in the mid-1970s, leaving behind the dovecote to be used as a cattle shelter. It was restored in 1980 and is now a listed building standing on protected open land in the middle of the village.

## King's Pyon, Herefordshire

If dovecotes are miniature examples of the vernacular, then the dovecote built to serve the Butt House, Butthouse or 'Buttas' – as the 17th-century house is variously called – at King's Pyon, is a miniature of all these miniatures, measuring only 11ft by 12ft. As befits its gem-like qualities, it is rich with ornate carvings; inscribed on its north face is the date 1632, while to the south are the initials KGE standing for its builders George and Elizabeth Karver. Here the dovecote's great chronicler A O Cooke should be quoted:

> There are three stories, only the upper one being fitted with nest-holes. It has been called the Falconry, and the suggestion made that the middle chamber of the three was intended to be occupied by hawks. It seems a somewhat sinister arrangement, that of placing hawks and pigeons side by side – like caging lambs and lions cheek by jowl. But, always provided that the intervening floor was strong, the gentler occupants might in time grow fearless of their foes.

Cooke reckons that it was designed by John Abel, whose tomb is in Sarnesfield churchyard, with its inscription possibly written by the architect himself:

THIS CRAGGY STONE A COVERING IS FOR AN ARCHITECTER'S BED,

THAT LOFTY BUILDINGS RAISED HIGH, YET NOW LYES LOW HIS HEAD;

HIS LINE AND RULE, SO DEATH CONCLUDES, ARE LOCKED UP IN STORE;

BUILD THEY WHO LIST, OR THEY WHO WIST, FOR HE CAN BUILD NO MORE.

HIS HOUSE OF CLAY COULD HOLD NO LONGER,

MAY HEAVEN'S JOY FRAME HIM A STRONGER

JOHN ABEL ... WHO DIED IN THE YEAR OF 1694 IN THE 97TH YEAR OF HIS AGE.

## Hanbury, Worcestershire

Pumphouse Farm and its dovecote, near Hanbury, were both built in the early 17th century. Whereas the house has been largely camouflaged by changes made during the 18th and 19th centuries, its dovecote remains pure and true to its architectural origins. With its brick and timber framing intact, along with its gable and lofty flight lantern, the little building stands alone and apart, lording it over the Worcestershire countryside.

## Queniborough, Leicestershire

Looking small enough to be held in the palm of your hand, Queniborough dovecote was in fact recently 'picked up' and moved to stand within the grounds of Queniborough Hall. In 2004, after Charnwood Borough Council reported that this locally listed building was in danger of collapse, it was dismantled and rebuilt nearby, taking up a prime position in a new prize-winning local Heritage Award Scheme. The house too had been in need of restoration and the whole estate was revamped, including reinstating a lake and giving this rebuilt dovecote pride of place. The roof is of local Swithland slate, the first recorded use of which is in the 13th century and no doubt the bricks

Top left: The dovecote near Hanbury, Worcestershire.

Bottom left: This dovecote was rebuilt in the grounds of Queniborough Hall, Leicestershire.

Right: A dovecote at Castletown in County Kildare.

are local. Many of them are in delicate relief, giving the dovecote's date as 1705, along with ww – the initials of its builder. The tiny door has an arched hood mould and there is little string course above the dormer window. Embracing all the building is a string course designed as an obstacle for creeping vermin.

## Castletown, County Kildare

Not strictly within the geographical remit, but too extraordinary to leave out, the 18th-century conical dovecote at Castletown is one of two that were built to keep company with a larger and castellated seven-storied stone cone known as the 'Wonderful Barn', with a helter-skelter-like stairway of 94 steps. They were all built as part of the Castletown estate, begun in 1722 by William 'Speaker' Conolly, Speaker of the Irish Parliament. He commissioned Alessandro Galilei to design Castletown House, the first and the finest Palladian house in all Ireland. Edward Lovett Pierce, armed with Palladio's *Quattro Libri dell Architettura* of 1570, was left to supervise its construction. Conolly died before it was finished but his widow lived on, remembered to this day for still being able to read a newspaper without spectacles and by the light of a single candle at the age of 90. The description of her also lives on to this day – as being a plain and vulgar woman, but with very valuable qualities. Her legacy was immense, in that in order to provide employment during the severe winter and subsequent famine of 1739–40, she commissioned various and extraordinary buildings. She arranged that a 140ft-high obelisk, perched atop two tiers of arches should close a vista to the north of the house, while to the east there was to be the 'Wonderful Barn' and its flanking dovecotes. A stone plaque above the barn entrance reads '1743 EXECUT'D BY JOHN GLINN' (with the second N as small

Left: The domed doocote at Penicuik, Midlothian.

Below: A brick dovecote standing in the grounds of
Antony House in Cornwall.

as a full stop), so presumably the cotes were also built by him. In 1960 the obelisk, known as the Conolly Folly, was taken over by the Irish Georgian Society and is now in the care of the Office of Public Works. The house, saved by the Irish Georgian Society in 1967, is now owned and immaculately run by the Castletown Foundation. However, the 'Wonderful Barn' and its attendant dovecotes are in dire distress. These curious buildings have now all been separated from the house by the M4 motorway.

## Penicuik, Midlothian

This great dome, lording it over what was once a chastely neoclassical stable yard, is a replica of 'Arthur's O'on' – a Roman temple built on rising ground above the River Carron in Stirlingshire, 'up a height' presumably so as to be admired from the nearby Antonine Wall of AD 140s. This beehive of a building was 22ft feet high, with a circumference of 88ft and with walls 10$^1$/$_2$ft deep at their base. It survived until the 18th century, when it was considered to be the most remarkable and best-preserved Roman monument in all Britain, only to be wantonly destroyed in 1743 by Sir Michael Bruce of Stenhouse – a philistine who should be named and shamed to this day. He had wanted the stones to line a mill dam, but within hours the whole lot had been swept off down the river. Scotland was scandalised by the destruction of what, according to Robert Gillespie in his *Round About Falkirk* of 1879, Walter Scott had called '[t]he great glory of the Roman remains in Scotland'; no one more so than Sir John Clerk of Penicuik who vowed to reconstruct the building. Eventually his son Sir James Clerk was to do so in 1763, when he ordered that an exact replica be built of the exterior, whilst converting the interior into a doocote. It has served this function for many years,

complete with a smoothly working potence, which can be swung around the full circle of the building, allowing eggs to be gathered at every level.

## Antony, Cornwall

The circular brick dovecote stands in oddly happy harmony with the Pentewan stone of Antony House on which building began in 1770 for Sir William Carew; the dovecote is of the same date. Humphry Repton produced one of his famed Red Books in 1793 and was responsible for landscaping the grounds although many of his suggestions were not carried out. The Carew Pole family have lived on this land since 1432 and still live in the house, although it was given to the National Trust in 1961. Over the last 25 years, the National Trust and the trustees of the Carew Pole Garden Trust, together with the family, have commissioned sculpture by contemporary artists which can be seen in the formal and wider gardens.

Too sinister to leave out is that John Carew, born at Antony in 1622, was one of the leading regicides of Charles I. Boldly determined not to flee after the Restoration, he was also one of the 10 who were hung, drawn and quartered for treason at Charing Cross in 1660. Edward Bower's painting of the king's trial hangs in the house.

The dovecote was restored, with a new potence installed, between 1982 and 1983 by the Manpower Services Commission under the supervision of the National Trust.

## Blaise Hamlet, Bristol

In 1810 a Quaker banker, John Scandrett Hartford, commissioned John Nash to build a village of nine dwellings, one of them a double cottage, for the old retainers on his Blaise Castle estate at Henbury outside Bristol. Whereas his own house was large and somewhat sober, those that he got designed for his retired workers were tiny and explosively picturesque; nine cottages – grouped around an undulating green – that to this day have remained unaltered as the very pinnacle of the picturesque. With their myriad levels of roofs of either thatch, pantiles or stone slates, and their gables, porches and nooks in a dashing variation of building materials and design, they bulge and they soar off in every direction. Every one is different and every one a delight. All have over-tall and decorated brick polygonal and diagonal chimneys which seem like banners proclaiming their prettiness. Two of them were given the additional bonus of housing doves within their gables. In *The Buildings of England: North Somerset and Bristol*, Pevsner writes that 'Blaise Hamlet is ... responsible for some of the worst sentimentalities of England. Its progeny is legion and includes Christmas cards and tea pots. Why then are we not irritated but

enchanted by it?...its saving graces are its smallness, its seclusion from traffic and commerce, and the nicely maintained degree of artificiality throughout.'

Blaise Hamlet was an enormous influence on the Englishman's dream of his cottage in the country – a dream that has gone horribly wrong with so many of today's cottages now grotesquely enlarged, with thatched and plastic-doored garages to match.

## Bemerton, Wiltshire

This mid-19th-century dovecote was part of the exotic assembly of buildings of Bemerton Model Farm, created by the architect Samuel Clarke for the Russian Dowager Countess of Pembroke, born Ekaterina Semyonovna Vorontsova, who had married the 11th Earl of Pembroke in 1808. Their son was Sydney Herbert, who as Secretary of State for War during the Crimean War – being fought against his mother's people – sent Florence Nightingale to the Crimea.

With cloisters and colonnades, a tower and a myriad of architectural embellishments, the cote was in good company. The bottom half was built for poultry, the top for pigeons; today, white fantails make themselves at home throughout the building with particularly pleasing effect when peering through the arrow slits. Between 2002 and 2003 Bemerton Model Farm underwent an exemplary restoration and conversion into retirement homes by Arbuthnott Ladenburg Partnership, architects for Beechcroft Homes. The farmhouse, dairy, gatehouse and barns were all converted and with such sympathetic success that in 2004 they received the National Homebuilder Design Awards for the Best Retirement Development in the country.

Bemerton's cote is not alone in performing the role of an eye-catcher in an up-to-date development;

*Left: A circular dovecote on the Madresfield estate in Worcestershire.*

at Herringcote, near Dorchester-on-Thames in Oxfordshire, an ornamental brick cote by architect Sir Edwin Forbes – a building chosen by Gertrude Jekyll in her book *Garden Ornament* of 1918 – is the centre of attention surrounded by new retirement homes.

## Madresfield, Worcestershire

In 1867 the architect Richard Norman Shaw restored the old circular dovecote at the home farm on the Madresfield estate in Worcestershire, causing it to sprout forth with soaring grandeur. Seemingly double the height of an ordinary dovecote, it is built of flaming red brick with an elongated and elaborately carved stone dormer window frame that stretches up into the sky. From here the humans could look out while above them the doves could go in. Overall, emblazoned with heraldic devices, is the carving of a thumping great earl's coronet above the letter B – honouring the 6th Earl Beauchamp whose family had lived in the Tudor Madresfield since the day it was built. From 1863 he was making a series of medievalist additions throughout the house and when he died in 1872, his son was to commission Arts and Crafts decoration that has few equals in the country. The library, designed by the great C R Ashbee between 1902 and 1905, is rich with symbolic carvings created by his Guild of Handicraft of Chipping Campden. The staircase with its great balustrade has balusters of solid crystal. Then there is the chapel, created between 1902 and 1924, where a pin could not be pricked between frescoes, stained glass, enamel, metal and woodwork done by Birmingham Municipal School of Arts and Crafts. These are but a few of the architectural and decorative strands that enrich the many rooms at Madresfield. Today the house is particularly famed for being the inspiration for Evelyn Waugh's *Brideshead Revisited*.

# Adored & Adornment

*Previous page: The aviary at Waddesdon in Buckinghamshire.*

*Right: A late 18th- or early 19th-century birdcage from Ireland.*

Wʜɪᴄʜ of the umpteen architectural gems created for animals for the sheer delight of decoration should I alight upon? Perhaps some of the most extraordinary have been those built to house birds, ranging from delicate little structures of wood and wire to richly ornate giant cages. Birds have, of course, been held captive since ancient times. The Romans ensured that when their beloved songsters died, they would eventually be put in the same grave together – the bird had often cost more to buy than a slave. In England pet birds were caged from the 14th century onwards with trapped and wretched linnets, larks, nightingales, cuckoos, chaffinches and starlings all considered ideal companions for the ladies. Popinjays (the early name for parrots) were thought to be more suitable for the gents and were often allowed to fly free. The Tudor statesman Sir Thomas More had 12 parrots flying about his house.

Canaries, introduced into Europe from the Canary Islands as early as the 1400s, are arguably the sweetest songsters of all. As Johann Matthaeus Bechstein writes in his seminal work *The Natural History of Cage Birds* of 1845: 'The beauty of its form, its plumage, and its song, united with its great docility, soon gained it admittance into the most magnificent abodes where everyone delights in rearing and preserving it, whilst the fairest hands are often eager to present it with the most delicate food.' They were often kept in 'singing cages' – little domed or lanterned structures attached to a decorative cord and hung low in the room so that their occupants might be admired at close quarters. When hauled up to the ceiling the bird would burst into song. For nightingales, linnets and chaffinches there might have been vile fates in store – either having their tongues slit for a better trill or otherwise being blinded so as to prolong their song. Outraged at such cruelty, Thomas Hardy wrote *The Blinded Bird*:

> Who hath charity? This bird.
> Who suffereth long and is kind,
> Is not provoked, though blind
> And alive ensepulchred?
> Who hopeth, endureth all things?
> Who thinketh no evil, but sings?
> Who is divine? This bird.

The cages designed to house these and other birds from the 17th to the 20th century can be studied as exercises – in miniature – of all architectural styles. Indeed, Robert Wallace writing in *The Canary Book* of 1893 at the tail end of what had been a 300-year fashion of housing birds in the grand architectural manner states:

> In form, cages may be procured from that of a common fig-box to a miniature representation of the Crystal Palace at Sydenham. I have seen cages of almost every imaginable pattern, representing cottages, abbeys, castles, cathedrals and palaces, with fine fluted columns, porticos and pediments, stained glass windows &c., rich and varied in design, and in every known style of architecture, including Gothic, Doric and Ionic, and displaying great taste and marvellous mechanical skill.

Few pre-18th-century birdcages survive but it would appear these were heavily ornate – although somewhat half-hearted in their architectural ambitions. The rectangular shape was popular in the late 17th century with wood being used as much as metal. The cages often had panels, upright corner posts and crestings of carved oak, such as Nell Gwyn's cage for her canaries ('white sparrows') which still survives – as does a beauty in

County Wicklow. Architectural cages became popular in the 18th century and were to remain so until the 20th century – all too often more pleasing for the designer who had created them than for the birds forced to lurk behind their solidly ornamental façades. The virtuoso displays of the architectural designs meant birdcages started to take centre stage as important decorative features in the house. Great and small – and almost always wildly idiosyncratic – few of them could have been described as run of the mill. Take for example the 'Ornamental Water Cage' – illustrated in Bechstein's *The Natural History of Cage Birds*, it is a triumph of optical illusion whereby birds appeared to be perching on twigs amidst swimming fish. A wood-framed rectangular cage of fancy wire work supported the huge round fish-filled glass bowl, in which was a smaller glass bowl into which birds could fly from the cage below. As an added flourish, an enormous arrangement of flowers burst forth from the top of the fish bowl. What, too, about the Indian pavilions and Chinese pagodas for birds that were

elegantly wrought in wire and wood? On so small and affordable a scale, the variety of birdcage design knew no bounds – with lanterns and lattice work; with finials and feet of bone and ivory; with bodies that were gilded or even made of Sheffield plate – or otherwise japanned, lacquered or inlaid with mother-of-pearl or wood. In the early 1800s, John Hull of Oldham used 2,522 pieces of 21 different woods to create the Oldham coat of arms on the front of his cage, along with a façade of the Sailors' Home in Liverpool on the side. In the 1860s James Quin of Kidderminster was just as extravagant – as well as making reproductions of 18th-century mahogany Gothic birdhouses, he created a series of ornamental lantern cages with gilded bars and railings of tortoiseshell and pearl. And a late 18th- or early 19th-century birdcage from Ireland (*left*) was made of wood with fretwork gables, a dome, basketwork feeding troughs, an enamel clock face and small Gothic windows that were simply stuck onto the iron bars of the cage.

From such extreme extravagance, there was extreme modesty. In *A Regency Visitor*, Prince Pückler-Muskau records an 1827 letter written to his recently divorced wife: 'You know the English have stamped the day [Sunday] with a death like character; dancing, music and singing are forbidden. Indeed, the severely pious hang their canary birds in some remote corners, that no voice or song may offend their ears during the holy hours.' However, Bechstein's bible for caged birds was unabashed on that score:

> from my earliest youth I have delighted in being
> surrounded with birds, and am so accustomed to
> them that I cannot write at my desk with pleasure, or
> even with attention, unless animated by the warbling
> of the pleasing little creatures which enliven my
> room. My passion is carried so far that I always have

about thirty birds around me, and this has naturally led me to consider the best and easiest mode of procuring them... .

No European bird was exempt from his patient taming – the raven, hooded crow, hoopoe and five different types of woodpeckers, as well as 16 types of finches from Angola to Lapland. As for the sparrow, Bechstein wrote that 'no bird becomes more familiar, or testifies more attachment to his master. Its actions are lively, confiding and delicate.' He told of a soldier who had a 'sparrow which followed him every where and knew him in the midst of a regiment'. Bechstein's most earnest wish was that his book 'may contribute more and more to the love of that class of attractive creatures with which the Creator has adorned the earth and which sing His praises so melodiously and unceasingly!'

From the 19th and into the 20th century birdcages became lighter and simpler with wire taking over from wood – cheaper and more cheerful for the occupants. What a blessing for our benefit that sumptuous materials were once used to build some birdcages – their fragile counterparts of wicker, basket work and wire have now, for the most part, flown to the four winds.

Giant cages, known as aviaries, were also built to house birds. The aviary at Kenilworth, Warwickshire (*opposite*), was actually described as being brilliant with 'jewels' in 1575 by Robert Langham in a letter to a friend in London. He wrote that it was 'sumptuous and beautiful' and 'of a rare form of excellence'. Measuring 20ft high, 30ft long and 14ft deep, with eight great 'wyndoz', it was 'beautified with great Diamons, Emeraulds, Rubyes and Saphyres ... garnisht with their gold by skilfull hed and hand'. Today, if you can believe such a gloriously unbelievable thing, it has been recreated by English Heritage! Cages such as this were

to flourish for another 400 years; in 1806, the great Humphry Repton designed two sizzlers in the Indian style at Brighton for the Prince Regent. Few though, have been more elaborate than the aviary at Waddesdon in Buckinghamshire (*see* pp 152–3), which was built in 1889 for Baron Ferdinand de Rothschild by the architect Hippolyte Alexandre Gabriel Walter Destailleur – a name as fanciful as his creation. And in later years there have continued to be some extravagant creations, such as the small peacock house balancing atop two life-size iron palm trees that was built in the 1930s by the surrealist Edward James at Monkton House, West Sussex.

Menageries too, by their very nature, were showpiece buildings created as beautiful backdrops to the parade of exotic beasts on display. The allure of wild and unknown animals had once been the sole preserve of royalty, grandees and public exhibitions. For instance, Henry I amassed a private collection at Woodstock in the early 12th century with such creatures as lions, leopards and lynxes as well as camels and porcupines. The Menagerie in the Tower of London had its illustrious beginnings in 1235 when the Holy Roman Emperor Frederick II presented Henry III with three leopards. The Tower of London went on sheltering exhilaratingly exotic inmates until 1834, staking claims for such landmarks as England's first elephant to go on public display, arriving there in 1255 after it had been presented to Henry III by Louis IX of France. A John Bayely compiled a list of the animals in 1800, with useful notes of his own. 'Miss Howe' and 'Miss Fanny Howe' were two lions who had been born in the Tower on 1 June 1794, named, writes Bayely, 'after the gallant conquerer of the French on that day' (Admiral Howe's victory on 'The Glorious First of June' during the French Revolutionary Wars). Bayely also records 'A royal tiger – China' and writes too of the black leopard called Jack presented by Warren Hastings,

the first Governor General of India (who was unsuccessfully impeached by parliament for 'High Crimes and Misdemeanors' in 1786).

By the 18th century many and various menageries, both public and private, were being built all over the country; not merely built, but beautifully built, with an exotic or elegant extravaganza being the order of the day. A Major-General Loft came to Eagle in Lincolnshire in 1826 and wrote of seeing a bison and 'several very fine kangaroos' in front of a castle of burnt, blackened bricks. It was, though, the neoclassical that was thought to be a more suitable style for Northamptonshire, where two perfectly proportioned little temples of menageries were built within a stone's throw of each other in the mid-18th century – Horton and Castle Ashby. Both buildings are beauties and both are in tip-top order today.

Menageries were not only for show, they were also for the study of animals and their behaviour. Many private menageries, such as Wentworth Woodhouse in Yorkshire, were important for academic research, as were the public zoological gardens that soon developed. In Leeds there are the remains of a fancy castellated façade that once fronted the bear pit of the city's 19th-century zoo.

Some decorative architecture reflects the origins of the trade – such as the blacksmith's horseshoe-door surround that embraces you as you enter. A few can still be run to ground today – at Machynlleth in Powys a curiously flamboyant orange ceramic horseshoe, replete with pointed-head 'nails', surrounds the door of a blackened brick castle; while at Dunmore in Scotland a stone horseshoe was built around the door that now leads you into a private cottage. At Penshurst in Kent, the architect George Devy, as part of his 1850s intermingling of the old and the new, built a mock-Tudor saddler's and butcher's as well as a timber-framed blacksmith's with a huge wooden horseshoe around the door. It is now the village shop.

Then there are the oddities, the making-you-cheer-out-loud-with-excitement-at-their-very-existence oddities. Most extraordinary of all, in that it should ever have been built, must be the 19th-century stone temple for terrapins that still stands in the gardens of Wotton House in Surrey.

Below: An ornate oak birdcage from County Wicklow in Ireland.

Right: This castle-like birdcage from Beckley Park, Oxfordshire, is dated to 1749.

## County Wicklow

A rare survival. Although the exact date of this cage is not known, it would appear to be contemporary with late 17th-century descriptions of such birdhouses when the rectangular shape was popular and when wood was being used as much as metal. The highly decorated Wicklow beauty is made of oak with a display of craftsmanship that allowed its occupant but a meagre view of the outside world. A semblance of a building rather than an architectural model, it was painted green with dashes of decoration in brilliant scarlet. Bells once hung at the four corners and all was surrounded by a wealth of fretwork. Happily, such cages of the period often had a jutting bay of metal bars so that when put on the windowsill the bird could enjoy the breezes.

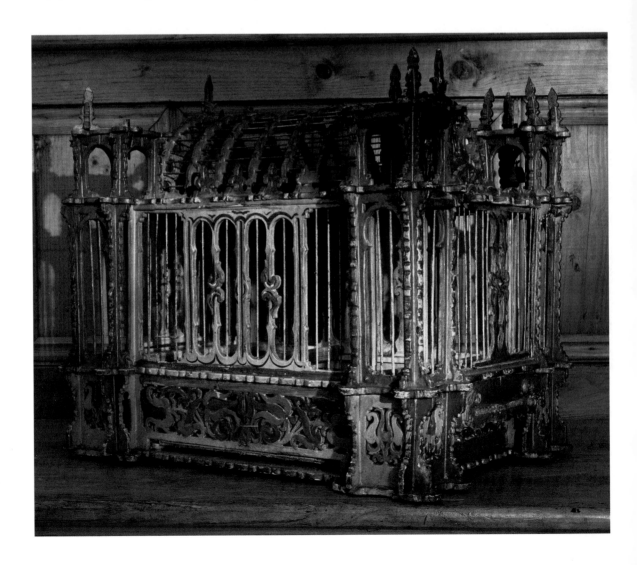

## Beckley, Oxfordshire

As fragile as the feathers it once housed, this grand 1749 castle for birds once stood at Beckley Park, looming forth in the lone narrow corridor that goes from end to end of the one-room deep, thrice-moated Tudor hunting lodge on Otmoor. Built by Lord Williams of Thame in the 1540s, Beckley had remained intact when Percy and Clotilde Fielding bought it in 1919. Their son Basil and his wife Peggy Fielding took it over in the 1930s and his daughter Amanda Fielding and her husband Jamie Neidpath live there today – all of them having nurtured and preserved its quite tremendous beauty.

## Biddick, County Durham

Built of beech with inlaid bands of ebony, rosewood
and yew, this 18th-century birdcage has as perfect an
architectural façade as could ever have been devised for
birds. A big bonus for its occupants is that it is bereft of
any building at the back. My mother came by it when I
was a child and thereafter it stood in her bedroom at
Biddick Hall, surrounded by birds on the 18th-century
Chinese wallpaper that she had also found.

Biddick was originally a pele tower to which was
added a Jacobean house. In 1610 it was bought by
Sir William Lambton who was steadily whittling away
his fortune having 29 children by two wives and by
taking the king's side in the Civil War. He was eventually
killed leading his regiment at Marston Moor. Cromwell
made his son, Thomas Lambton, governor of the
Leeward Islands and it was Thomas's grandson Freville
Lambton who in 1720 festively clad Biddick in 18th-
century pink dressed up with colossal Ionic pilasters,
corner stones, a central pediment and a multitude of
stone urns. There is an intriguing suggestion that Sir
John Vanbrugh had a hand in this. The monumentality
of these details – totally at odds with any local
architecture – suggest that the hand of the great man
could well have been at work, even before you discover
that Vanbrugh was employed for weeks on next door
Lumley Castle, finding, he wrote, 'a vast deal to do'. It
would have been the work of a moment for him to have
penned the Lambtons some helpful architectural advice.

These are the architectural periods that can be
spotted with ease as you step through the house – from
the light architectural gaiety of the exterior into the
sombre 4ft depth of the pele tower walls, then on
through what was the other exterior ancient wall and
out into the soaring 1720s stairwell with a baroque
ceiling fancying it up to the nines.

The birdcage is a handsome 18th-century edition, part
of the ongoing surge of splendours that would go on
being designed for birds for another hundred years. As
Robert Wallace would write in *The Canary Book* of 1893:

> The ingenuity and skill of men are so vast and varied,
> and the success which has been attained in the art of
> cage-making is so prodigious and wonderful, that it
> would be a task of no inconsiderable difficulty to any

person to attempt to give anything approximating to a full and lucid description of all the different patterns of cages that are to be met with in this country ... and whilst I admire them as works of art and masterpieces of workmanship, I cannot recommend them as fitting habitations for birds; for, with very few exceptions [Biddick's cage was one such exception] all such cages lack that most essential requirement – utility. Every consideration for comfort and convenience is sacrificed to carry out the design in its entirety, and hence many of those cages are, despite their external grandeur, mere dungeons for canaries and other birds. Nevertheless I am a great advocate for handsome cages; but what I admire most is artistic skill, combined with elegance of design, practical utility, and sound, substantial workmanship; for I consider a good bird worthy of a good cage, upon the same principle as I contend that a good picture is deserving of a good frame.

## Brighton, East Sussex

The architects Humphry Repton, John Nash and William Porden were three of the greats who drew up various and brilliant plans for the Prince of Wales's oriental schemes in Brighton. Some were built, others were not and many were neither acknowledged nor paid for. After both Henry Holland and James Wyatt had also attempted to design a palace for the prince, it was Nash who won the plum prize of the Pavilion, Porden built his stables (*see* pp 58–60) and poor old Repton got no commissions at all despite his exquisitely exotic efforts. He had produced a folio of 12 watercolours, including schemes for transforming the prince's Marine Pavilion into a Mughal palace, which was in fact so similar to Nash's that it is difficult to judge one as superior to the other. His watercolours,

as was Repton's habit, were displayed in one of his leather-bound Red Books (in this case his *Designs for the Pavillion at Brighton*). 'Before' paintings of scenes as he first saw them were painted on paper flaps which, when lifted, would reveal how it would be after he had carried out his plans.

What cries of 'Abracadabra!' would have greeted the sight of Repton's proposals for an aviary and pheasantry as part of an exotic garden walk. An ornate 'Flower Passage' would enable a royal progress to be made from the Pavilion through the gardens to the stables in the worst of weathers. Trellised, arched and writhed about with blooms, the glazed walls were to be decorated with arches in various Moorish styles, those that were scalloped giving a particularly festive air. With the occasional dome-topped tower and small pavilion, as well as a 50ft-long hothouse and an orangery that opened up as a draped 'chiosk' in the summer, Repton's most extreme dreams of the picturesque could be realised. Best and most exotic of all were the Indian aviary and pheasantry/dovecote that formed part of it. To cap it all, it was suggested that there should be an orchestra perpetually playing as the prince and his party progressed along their way; according to Repton this was an essential part of the state and pleasure of such a garden.

Both the pheasantry and the aviary were inspired, if not directly copied from, Thomas and William Daniell's six volumes of aquatints entitled *Oriental Scenery* published between 1795 and 1808. Uncle and nephew Daniells, aged 36 and 16, had gone to Calcutta in 1785 and for eight years produced what would, on their return to Britain, become electrifyingly influential watercolours and oil paintings of India's architecture. (Their Taj Mahal of 1791 has no one in sight for miles around, save for three men and two elephants.) Each

volume contained 24 aquatints of Indian scenes that were hand-coloured to look like the watercolour original. The technique was new and complex and William Daniell's experimentations and success with it made him one of the earliest pioneers of aquatint.

Repton's aviary in Brighton was undoubtedly inspired by the Daniell's watercolour of one of the *Hindoo Temples at Bindrabund on the River Jumna* – a somewhat risky allusion to the prince in Brighton, for legend has it that it was here that Krishna frolicked with milkmaids and stole their clothes while they were bathing. As for the pheasantry, the roofed lantern of its somewhat plain body – albeit flanked by the pillars of the floral walkway – was inspired by the Daniell's *View of the Palace at the Fort of Allahbad.* Both lattice works are identical.

The prince was delighted with the plans: 'Mr Repton, I consider the whole of this work as perfect, and will have every part of it carried into immediate

execution; not a little shall be altered.' He even paid the bill; but nine years later the folio was discovered to be still at the engravers. They had never been looked at again.

## Dropmore, Buckinghamshire

The delicately domed aviary at Dropmore is about to be full-whack restored, as is the adjoining assembly of wooden decoration – what *The Buildings of England: Buckinghamshire* describes as an 'orgy of trellis'. This is as idiosyncratic an assembly of buildings as you can imagine – always making you rub your eyes in disbelief. All dating from the early to mid-1800s, they march side by side along the red-brick garden wall and for years they have been in a perilously fragile state, hanging on for dear life by the spindliest of wire and wood as the various decimating fortunes of the estate crashed about their walls. Today, at last, their future is secure.

The survival of the countryside around Dropmore never fails to surprise (I have lived there for over 20 years and should know). It is only 25 miles from London, yet deeply rural. As in the olden days, there are whopping great houses still standing proud at every turn – albeit with new roles: Cliveden, Nashdom, Taplow Court and, today, the newly restored and perforce rebuilt, Grade I Dropmore joins this happy band. Designed initially by Samuel Wyatt in 1792–4 with additions by Charles Tatham in 1806, it was built for Lord Grenville who as prime minister to George III steered through the abolition of the slave trade. When it was passed he resigned exhausted, writing that: 'I could not bring myself to struggle much to get my chains on again', and determined to live at Dropmore for the rest of his life. He had loved the spot since walking there from school at Eton and, on the day he bought the

estate, he planted two cedars in celebration. They still stand on the lawn today. By the time he died in 1834, he had planted another 2,500 trees; thereafter his widow thundered on with the pinetum and, when she died in 1864, between them they had created the greatest collection of conifer species in Britain.

For the rise and fall of the fortunes of a house, Dropmore's story takes some beating. In 1939 it was requisitioned as a Canadian Army headquarters and over four years was reduced to a sorry state. In 1943 Grenville's great-great-nephew sold the house to Lord Kemsley, proprietor of *The Sunday Times*, whose major restoration of the place was hailed as a triumph. When he died in 1968, Dropmore was taken over by the University of San Diego, who allowed it to collapse once again, and sold off much of the land to boot. In 1972 it was bought by Mohamed Mahdi Altajir, billionaire Arab businessman, art collector and former United Arab Emirates ambassador to Britain and France. Determined that Dropmore be restored, he built an indoor swimming pool but barely ever went there. It was then that I first saw the aviary. Having written to Mr Mahdi Altajir and never receiving a reply, I was passing one day and somehow got past the guarded gates. WAM BAM! What an aviary! But what a reception too! Terrifying growling announced the arrival of a snarling, all-teeth-to-the-fore Alsatian dog hauling along a tattooed, bald and bearded man dressed from head to foot in black leather festooned with chains. At the end of one of those chains was the dog being goaded on to 'Get her!' By a whisker – literally – I failed to get into the car in time and was badly nipped in the calf but able to drive away at speed. In 1990 one of Wyatt's wings was destroyed by a conflagration and in 1997 the whole house was gutted by fire.

Today, at long last, all is set fair. The exemplary rebuilding and restoration of Dropmore is enabling it to become a series of dwellings, all designed under the strictest auspices of the rules applying to a Grade I building. Better still, 100 detailed drawings of the place by J C Buckler, commissioned in the late 1790s by Grenville, have survived in the British Library and they have been of huge value for this architectural tour de force. One terrific example is Grenville's double-height octagonal study, long since vanished in a later conversion, which has now been rebuilt to its original design. That is not all. In 1956 Gordon Nares wrote a blow-by-blow illustrated account of the building after Kemsley's restoration. With photographic records of all the fireplaces, curtains and staircases etc, nothing could have gone wrong. Gently domed and bayed on the south front, with a north front of square towers with pyamidial roofs and a Doric portico – all in its brilliant-as-originally conceived cream stucco, Dropmore is safe and sound. Developer Andre Meyers is its saviour.

Next in his sights are the garden buildings: a Chinese tea house, Grenville's dog's tomb, the trelliswork, and of course the aviary with its domed hexagonal lantern soaring tall over two domes. In its heyday all the wire work – seemingly as fine as a spider's web – was painted bright red and it was decorated throughout with two different sizes of – oddly heavy by comparison – green sculpted and pierced pottery tiles in the Chinese style. Many ran the full length of the building delineating its every architectural line. There were four caged 'rooms' each with a fountain embellished with shells. Soon it will be like a display of Chinese fireworks once again.

Left: The domed aviary at Dropmore, Buckinghamshire, is due to be restored.

Below: The recently revamped 19th-century aviary, built for Baron Ferdinand de Rothschild at Waddesdon in Buckinghamshire.

## Waddesdon, Buckinghamshire

Unmistakably a French fancy, the aviary built for Baron Ferdinand de Rothschild at Waddesdon was, I like to think, designed by the euphoniously named architect Hippolyte Alexandre Gabriel Walter Destailleur. Apart from the pleasure of writing his name, it was he who had already helped Rothschild whip up Waddesdon into a rich architectural concoction of all the great French châteaux – Azay-le-Rideau, Chambord, Chenonceau, Chaumont, Blois, all of them hollering out from the façade. Not only was this his specialty, but he had also done restoration work on châteaux in France. He was obviously a master of creating buildings inspired by others and Rothschild wanted this aviary to remind him of one that he had known as a child at the Villa

Grüneburg near Frankfurt in Germany. Not only that, the flamboyance of Waddesdon's cast-iron rococo trelliswork was inspired by pavilions at Versailles and Chantilly.

It was during the 40 years between 1850 and 1890 that the Rothschild family acquired great sweeps of the Vale of Aylesbury, on which they then built extraordinary houses. In the case of Waddesdon, this meant levelling the top of Lodge Hill to give their gargantuan 'Renaissance' house, with its acres of gardens, views to be reckoned with. All the stones to build it were from Bath, hauled halfway up the hill by a little railway, then pulled the rest of the way by a team of Percheron horses bought from Normandy for the job.

During the Second World War Waddesdon was given over to young evacuees from the Blitz. In 1957 it was bequeathed to the National Trust by James 'Jimmie' de Rothschild, although his widow Dorothy (known as 'Dollie'), a passionate and active Zionist, soldiered on there alone until she died at the age of 93.

Since then the whole estate has undergone a serious and scholarly restoration programme, with the house, the grounds and the gardens – a brave recreation of what was so often indelicate Victorian planting – all being brought back to vibrant life. In their midst, in active and useful pride of place, is the palace for birds. Repainted in its original colours, including a good deal of gleaming gold leaf, it remains unaltered except for the modernisation of the birds' hospital and kitchens at the back. The birds can escape from the public gaze through a hatch in the wall at the back of each flight cage and each of these internal shelters have glazed panels to give them light.

Curved wings sweep out from a central grotto in which reclines a statue of Minerva, with military trophies and two marble tritons, all surrounded by rocks, tufa, ferns, shells and trickling water. Water flowing from a fountain in each aviary is gravity fed from a tank on a hill nearby. Rearing out of the parterre in front is a statue of *The Infant Bacchus with a Goat* by Vittorio Barbieri, *c* 1740. That all of this is flourishing is thanks to the exemplary restoration masterminded by the hero of the day, Jacob Rothschild.

The building is considered perfect for ornithological purposes, and many and serious study and conservation programmes are on the go. Waddesdon Manor Aviary also supports worldwide conservation initiatives in the wild – such as in China's Jaingxi Province where they are trying to ensure the survival of the Blue Crowned Laughing Thrush. Even to read the names of the aviary's occupants is a delight: the Snowy-Crowned Robin Chat, the Yellow-Throated Laughing Thrush (critically endangered), the Fairy Bluebird from south-east Asia, all have been bred successfully at Waddesdon. Among the species bred for the first time in Britain are the White Bellied Go-Away bird and the White-Crested Laughing Thrush. New arrivals include the Hooded Pitta Sordida.

## Wentworth Woodhouse, South Yorkshire

In the Japanese sunken garden at Wentworth Woodhouse in South Yorkshire there stands a modest parade of arched stone niches for ducks. Remains of hinges show they once had doors and were no doubt inhabited by the collection assembled for Earl Fitzwilliam's menagerie in the mid-19th century, which included African coots, white-tail ducks, pintails, teal and widgeons, as well as a lone shelduck and one common teal.

The Japanese garden is all part of the sweep of ornamental gardens created by Maud, Countess Fitzwilliam, in the early 20th century when she gathered together and improved all the 18th-, 19th- and 20th-century plantings, as well as enhancing them with little buildings such as a tea house, along with a stone bridge and the 17th-century arched entrance to the former Bear Pit (*see* pp 178–9). So as to cheer her endeavours, her husband, the 7th Earl Fitzwilliam, had 'Come Into The Garden Maud' emblazoned over the arched entrance to her garden. Japanese gardens had become all the rage after the 1910 Japan-British Exhibition at White City, which celebrated the renewal of the Anglo-Japanese Alliance. Tatton Park in Cheshire and Compton Acres in Dorset were prime examples of the exotic influence. Here at Wentworth Woodhouse, a wooden Japanese bridge once arched high over the pond and the stone

bridge still survives. Sadly they did not follow the example of the 1910 exhibition when, to ensure authenticity, the stones for the garden bridge were brought specially from Japan. A few stone Japanese lanterns survive at Wentworth Woodhouse, as do the Japanese plantings of maples and cherries. Otherwise all have been writhed through with earlier and later plantings and the only proof of there once being a 19th-century garden here is the '1868' inscribed into the steps that lead out of this dell.

Sad beyond measure was the loss of the vast palm and plant house. Hearing of it gives a glimpse of the splendours that abounded in the gardens of Wentworth Woodhouse: 200ft long and 35ft wide, it had 14 'branches' of 40ft-long glasshouses – one a fernery, another for orchids, one for carnations, another for gardenias etc – each serviced by a 60-gallon Welsh slate rainwater cistern. In old photographs its glass gables seemed to march into infinity. The whole bang lot, along with a 188ft-long vinery, was demolished in 1954.

## West Dean, West Sussex

The life-size iron palm trees supporting a roof to shelter peacocks are but two of the many extraordinary elements that were assembled at Monkton House by Edward James, pioneer patron of surrealist art. With such plum players in the field as Salvador Dali, Leonora Carrington and Pavel Tchelitchev, the collection was generally acknowledged as being the best in the world of this oddest-of-all-movements. When the house and many of its contents were put up for sale in 1986, controversy raged as to whether or not it was worth preserving. As Alan Powers lamented in 'The Twentieth Century Society comes of age', Monkton was 'altogether too strongly flavoured' for the National Trust. No one came to the rescue, and when it was eventually sold, the surrealist one-offs in the auction catalogue filled five substantial volumes. As a shimmering surrealist fantasy – and how it did shimmer – it was seen as either a daring dream or a hideous nightmare but, as Britain's lone full-scale

Left: The extraordinary peacock shelter at Monkton House in West Sussex.

Opposite: The stairs and drawing room – animal-inspired and decorated in a distinctly surrealist style – of Monkton House.

The house was built in 1902 by Sir Edwin Lutyens for Edward James's parents, Mr and Mrs Willie James, as a bolt-hole from the grandeur of West Dean, their house some five miles away – now the Edward James Foundation for the promotion of the arts and crafts. Originally Monkton was somewhat conventionally clad in patterned brickwork with white wooden balconies and so on, but in the 1930s it was transmogrified into a screeching surrealist conceit. Dali advised Edward James on a good deal of the work and with the architect Christopher 'Kit' Nicholson – son of William, brother of Ben – assisted by Hugh Casson as well as Norris Wakefield in charge of the decoration, the house was brilliantly transformed.

At the sight of the exterior alone, Lutyens would have erupted in his grave. James had the walls painted purple over peacock blue and the pedimented front door painted sugar pink – flanked, furthermore, by two more life-size iron palm trees. Strangely fluorescent plaster 'linen' was 'hung' from the windows in imitation of sheets being aired. Plaster folds tied with 'rope' were looped around the bathroom window and draped over the clock on the roof – a clock, incidentally, which showed the days of the week rather than the hours. The drainpipes were fashioned to look like bamboo. Amidst all of this, Lutyens can be glimpsed with two central sections of his brickwork on display.

With the interior, though, the great architect has vanished without trace. Walk through the door and, as you would expect when stepping into a surrealist work of art, you are confounded. Up sweeps the 1930s staircase – designed by Nicholson – past a circular glass window that was designed so as to give you a clear view of a visitor sitting in the bath! There they would be, in all innocence, naked in the water behind

representative of the movement, it should undoubtedly have been saved, either for our delight or for our derision. I had the good fortune to be asked to photograph every inch of the place before it went under the hammer. So alone with my cameras in the drawing room with two of the sofas designed by Salvador Dali as Mae West's lips, I was well placed to relish the padded walls which Dali had proposed should have the appearance of 'the lining of an unhealthy dog's stomach' – padded and beige and mechanically contrived to 'breathe' in and out.

a one-way mirror – and with the extra bonus of appearing to be surrounded by the fish that James had arranged to be swimming between the mirror and the outer glass. All about you the violently patterned wallpaper was printed as the exact match (including the stitching) of the Italian material that covered the walls of the corridors. Star of the show, for our purposes, is the carpet woven with the paw-prints of James's Irish Wolfhound – no doubt a miserable symbol of his failed marriage to the dancer Tilly Losch, whose footprints Dali had woven into the stair carpet at West Dean.

No inch of the house was spared and every room was unique. No more elaborate examples of surrealist décor had ever been assembled in one place before – or since. Golden stars shone from the glass ceiling in the spare bedroom designed by Syrie Maugham (wife of Somerset); a golden sun and a silver moon, lit from behind, were cut through the pink alabaster walls of the circular bathroom with its dome of Styrian jade. I will never forget photographing James's bed, designed as Nelson's funeral carriage, which is in a room covered with moiré silk of palest turquoise laid over with shining chicken wire. I had stood my photographic lamps with their light-reflecting silver umbrellas – into which I had ripped holes to let the light through – side-by-side with a lamp by Giacometti. It was then that a moment of truth occurred, when into the room came an official group of adjudicators who were deciding whether or not the house should be saved. What was it that caught their fancy with cries of interest? My very own umbrellas! They clustered around: 'What could James have been thinking of here?' What a laugh; this was a surreal moment to my mind, of seeing through the surrealists. In the end though it was the adjudicators who had the last laugh of all. After they had long gone and I was taking my umbrellas down, there, unbelievably, hanging on the wall behind them was a painting – I think by Leonora Carrington – of silver umbrellas torn through with holes!

Monkton is now in safely sympathetic hands.

## Horton, Northamptonshire

A rarity if ever there was one: a tiny Palladian-rococo menagerie, designed in the 1750s by the genius architect and astronomer Thomas Wright of Durham to house Lord Halifax's exotic creatures. Some 225 years later it was saved from collapse by another genius, the architectural historian Gervase Jackson-Stops, for him to restore, embellish, live in and treasure.

By the middle of the 18th century, the number of private menageries was multiplying all over the country and, as exotic and exciting symbols of the wealth and dash of their owners, they were often exotically and excitingly designed. None more so than the Horton Menagerie. Originally conceived as an eye-catcher, it was in fact one of many buildings that were created to enhance the views from Horton Hall, the great porticoed Halifax house that was demolished between the wars. Today, the menagerie, marooned in the midst of great sweeps of Northamptonshire countryside, has all the appearance of a stone galleon adrift in an ocean of fields.

Seen from the outside, the main body of the little building with its richly rusticated – as curly as a

poodle's coat – window surrounds and its bulging bay, all topped by a split pediment, is delightful enough. But see inside and you scream. For here is the ornate banqueting hall created by Lord Halifax so that his guests could feast surrounded by exciting and exhilarating architecture. And to further their enjoyment, musicians would sit in the bay serenading the company in the lofty room, entered from the side pavilions through arched and columned aisles.

Most stupendous and surprising is the plasterwork, all created by Thomas Robinson of Oxford. Great medallions bearing signs of the zodiac hang heavy in the deep ceiling cove, with summer's symbols above the window and winter's above the fire. On the ceiling, Father Time lounges in billowing clouds, holding a great scythe as well as a ring as the symbol of eternity,

whilst all four corners are filled with the Four Winds and Apollo's head in a sunburst radiates over the bay. The room is encrusted with plasterwork – books burst forth from the walls and, as well as acanthus leaves and cornucopia, there are drums and all manner of musical instruments including a violin with a plaster musical score. Paget Toynbee's transcription of Horace Walpole's 'visits to country seats' records that he came here in 1763 and greatly admired the four urns in niches, describing them as 'representing the animals of the four parts of the world, made of plaster, painted to look like bronze'. He wrote too about the animals in their 2-acre circle of moated enclosures at the back of the building – of seeing a young tiger, a bear, two eagles and some storks, as well as 'many basons of gold fish ... several curious birds and beasts ... Racoons that breed there much ... two wart-hogs from Havannah with navals [scent glands] on their backs ... two uncommon Martins ... a kind of Ermine ... and doves from Guadaloupe ... with blue heads and a milk white streak crossing their cheeks'.

So much for the original beauty of the menagerie, which by the early 1970s had all but disappeared. Now it has been restored in full and fantastic measure. It was in 1972 that Gervase first heard tell of it and hacked his way through the undergrowth to discover an all but ruinous shell half-heartedly being used to store hay. Thereafter, until he died 23 years later, he masterminded the restoration of every precious inch of the place, including fine and funny flourishes of his own such as the restringing of the plaster violin with cat gut and the remoulding of its musical score with *Animal Crackers*. All the plasterwork was done by Christopher Hobbs and Lionel Stead and Son of Bradford.

As well as having the building restored, Gervase made his own and vastly enhancing additions, such as commissioning Hobbs to create a dripping-with-stalactites shell grotto in which a life-sized Orpheus plays his lyre to animals. Not only that – he got the architect Charles Morris to design what can only be described as magical manifestations of architecture: two little buildings with bulging mushroom-like roofs of thatch. One has a sturdy yet rough-hewn wooden classical portico, while the other – now a consecrated chapel – has two Gothic porches, one rough and ready, one refined. Between 1992 and 1994 Ian Kirby created a garden – incorporating four 18th-century fishponds – around both buildings. Today, with new owners, the menagerie's garden goes from strength to strength and is open to the public on various days throughout the year.

## Castle Ashby, Northamptonshire

The menagerie at Castle Ashby – in fact lived in mainly by birds, as well as a few other animals – was built in 1761 by Lancelot 'Capability' Brown as part of his work for the 7th and 8th Earls of Northampton. In 1757 the 7th Earl had met the architect Robert Adam in Padua and called upon him two years later to draw up the grand design for 'A Pleasure Ground, Kitchen garden ... Small Park for Deer ... [and] Court of stables'. Nothing though appears to have been built as Brown was soon ruling the roost and it is thought that Adam's only contribution to Castle Ashby was a modest helping hand with the design of the menagerie. And unfortunately the poor earl was never to see the fruits of his inspired patronage; having been made special ambassador to Venice, he had died of consumption having struggled through the pomp and ceremony of a formal entry into Venice literally on his last legs.

The 8th Earl succeeded his brother in 1763 when Brown's work at Castle Ashby was two years underway; it was to go on for another four, creating a romantic informality out of the existing rigidity of the 17th-century design. Marching avenues of trees were removed and 'pleasurable walks' meandering around through a 'natural' landscape were created; formal terraces were flattened and many a ha-ha was built to fling open a view. Brown had begun building at Castle Ashby in 1761 with an ice house, followed by the menagerie and then a dairy two years later. All were designed to enhance their surroundings. What is surprising is the modesty of the menagerie's inhabitants, kept in cages and pens at the back. Over 700 birds were listed in an account book, including 7 canaries, 1 red dove, 20 turtle doves, 3 'Paroquots', 2 widow birds, 2 blue birds, 2 wax bills, 3 oaterlins,

1 mistletoe thrush, 1 yellow bird, 7 green linnets, 8 chaffinches, 2 bullfinches, 1 blackbird, 5 goldfinches, 2 quails, 2 Cape geese, 7 Canada geese, 2 shell ducks, 2 sea pies, 1 Spanish cock, 3 gold, 2 white, 2 Chinese and 1 Canton cock pheasants, 1 grey curafsow, 2 nightingales, 7 turkeys, 77 turkey chicks, 2 parrots, 1 cockatoo, 3 eagles and 2 ducks. To cap it all, there were also white rabbits and a hare, a Newfoundland dog, a White Shag dog, two goats and two Angora goats, a squirrel and a mongoose in a box. Stuffed birds were also on display. Not quite as elegant an assembly as this elegant building deserves.

From the start of Brown's work, ponds and lakes were gouged out of the ground and a dam built to deal with them, and the longer he worked at Castle Ashby, the grander his schemes grew. So proud was he of his park, the menagerie and ponds for aquatic birds that, whilst gazing at his creations from his stone bridge, Brown is reputed to have cried out: 'Thames Thames, thou wilt never forgive me!'. It is a quote that has been attributed to Brown so freely and so often – for starters, at Chatsworth, Stowe and Blenheim – that it may well be a flight of fancy. Heaven alone knows what further schemes would have materialised had not his plans been brought to an abrupt halt by the wanton extravagance of the 8th Earl of Northampton. An inveterate gambler, he never paid his bills and in 1768 he was presented with a petition from Northampton people imploring him to pay the small amounts owed to them. But it was the notorious 'spendthrift election' of 1768 that was his final financial undoing, when both he and his neighbour Lord Halifax joined forces to prevent the local Lord Spencer from nominating a third man for Northampton's two parliamentary seats. By fair means and foul their extravagance was prodigious; it was reckoned that £160,000 had been

spent on both sides, with £6,000 of it on ribbons alone. The Lords Halifax and Northampton's cellars had been drunk dry by marauding electors and both men were ruined, although the even richer Spencer was not. Halifax was forced to sell his Horton estate, while Northampton had to sell all the contents of Castle Ashby, but was able to hang on to his great house set in its 10,000 acres.

## Eagle, Lincolnshire

To provide an exotic backdrop to his planned menagerie, Samuel Russell Collett clothed his 18th-century red-brick house in a somewhat alarming fancy dress of purple and black burnt bricks – and the rougher the brick the better. Oak was twisted into gnarled and Gothic frames around the doors and windows; a tiny pretence of a window was made from an old architectural fragment and there are three more Gothic windows, lofty and light, of more conventional elegance – mere glimmers of a smile on the otherwise scowling countenance of the building.

The sole glimpse of what the menagerie was like in its heyday comes from a chance account given by a visitor called Major-General J F Loft, who saw it only six years after it was built, appearing to take it calmly and on the chin that this fierce façade should be found in the fields of Lincolnshire. Although describing it as 'singular', he wrote that it was a 'tasty and handsome residence ... composed of overburnt Bricks until they are run together in large masses ... built ... in the manner of a castle and has a grotesque but not inelegant Appearance'. Hats off to the Major-General for such choice words and hats off again to him for having left us this description of the scene before him that day in 1826, a set piece of the animals against the unique backdrop that had been built for them:

It stands on the Edge but within an Inclosure of about 7 A[cres] in which are great numbers of Trees of different kinds of Timber, Thorns, several Deer of different Kinds are kept here, the American Axis, which has produced a Breed from with the Does; there are also several very fine Kangaroos, a Male & a Female Buffalo (I think) and their young Calf, all these running loose together; in one Corner of this inclosure a small piece is taken off in which there are several very fine Golden Pheasants; in another part of the Inclosure is a large Pond of water in which are kept a great Number of Gold & Silver fish, with the mixed Breed produced by them; the most singular Thing is they are never removed from the Pond in winter, and do not appear to suffer from the Cold.

Hats off too to Barbara Jones for quoting it in full in her encyclopaedic work *Follies and Grottoes* of 1953.

## Leeds

As you tackle the traffic along Cardigan Road in the Headingley district of Leeds, amid red-brick Victorian and Edwardian villas and squat 1960s blocks of flats, you suddenly see a surprising shaft from the past – a little stone castle that is, of all things, a bear pit. With its twin turrets and portcullis it is almost all that remains – some boundary walls survive – of the Zoological and Botanical Gardens which were opened with a blaze of fireworks, bands and a crowd of 2,000 on 8 July 1840.

In her book *Headingley: 'This Pleasant Rural Village'*, Eveleigh Bradford tells us, with enticing contemporary-to-the-opening quotes, that the trumpeted objective was to provide 'recreation for the people' and 'elevated pastimes for the operative classes, to wean them from the grosser pursuits ... an inducement to spend their hours of leisure in the pure breeze of the country air'. These were 'lofty aims' writes Bradford. The gardens were to be created by architect and civil engineer William Billington and Edward Davis, who was a botanist and landscape gardener. The initial schemes were 'astonishingly grandiose'. Bradford even goes so far as to say that 'if these ambitious schemes had been realised, Leeds would have had public gardens to match the finest in the land'. Plans were drawn up for an immense and multi-domed conservatory, as well as a neoclassical entrance with sweeps of colonnades – and, believe it or not, there were plans for what can only be described as an Italianate palace to house the stoves that warmed the hothouses. Eventually there was not enough money to build these extravaganzas, but the more modest greenhouses that did materialise were soon to flourish with exotic plants. Picturesque walks were laid between the already established trees and there were ornamental gardens, parterres, grottoes, fountains, statues and crinkle-crankle walls espaliered with fruit trees. Two great ponds for swans and other waterfowl had islands which you could stroll to over rustic bridges, and, according to our chronicler-in-chief Bradford, 'the habitation of the bear' was built in 1841.

From all accounts it would seem that a sad-sounding lone brown bear was the garden's most exotic exhibit. It was on display in a round brick pit dug into the hill behind the fancy façade and looked down on from on high by the crowds who had climbed up the stone circular staircases in the turrets. In European zoos and menageries, brown bears – whether from Russia, the Carpathians or Finland – were habitually housed in pits disguised as castles. A particularly fine one survives in Berne, Switzerland, where a bear was still disporting beneath its towers and crenellations as late as 2009.

In Leeds there were also monkeys, as well as an eagle, a raccoon and tortoises – along with the extra grim attraction of live jackdaws being let loose in the hawk's cage, all ghoulishly recorded by the *Leeds Intelligencier* on 11 July 1840, three days after the grand opening.

Altogether the Zoological and Botanical Gardens had cost £11,000 and were thought to be the most refined success, attended by 'the largest and most respectable company ever known ... including many of the principal families in the town'. Such snobbery though – so far removed from the zoo's original and improving ideals – was the start of their downfall. What with charging the then hefty entrance fee of 6d, as well as being closed until late afternoon on Sundays so as not to distract the

public from church or chapel, the gardens were not a success. Desperate moves were called for and in 1841 it was agreed to have Sunday openings, masking the moral objections with the announcement that such contact with nature would in fact 'advance the moral and religious feeling of the humbler classes'. All to no avail – despite such valiant efforts as the 'Display of Fireworks' on 1 September 1841, given by 'Mr BYWATER, the unrivalled pyrotechnic artist', and with such dazzling attractions as 'the grand Napoleonic Piece, introducing the WEEPING WILLOW, as drooping over the Tomb of the departed Emperor at St Helena &c &c &c...', within eight years the gardens were sold to entrepreneur Thomas Clapton. After ten more declining years – despite such alluring announcements in *White's Directory of Leeds* of 1853 that 'These 'MAGNIFICENT and PRINCELY Gardens are the most beautiful Public Gardens in England' – in 1858 the land was eventually sold off for building 'villa residences'.

By the mid-1900s the bear pit, still surviving amidst its suburban surroundings (albeit very leafy thanks to whatever lavish planting remained), was in ruins. Exactly 110 years after the sorry selling-off of the land, this strange little building was given new life when it was restored by the Civic Trust in 1968.

## Wentworth Woodhouse, South Yorkshire

'If you lay out your money in improving your seat, land, gardens, etc, you beautifye the country and do the work ordered by God himself.' So wrote Sir Thomas Watson Wentworth, 1st Marquess of Rockingham, in the 1730s as he was starting to build the vast double-fronted Wentworth Woodhouse, which with its east façade of 600ft is the longest domestic façade in England. Eventually, thanks to the building of subsequent generations, this great pile was to rule the roost over an assembly of follies that for beauty and variety have few equals.

The Bear Pit is one of them, but its history is by no means straightforward. Its entrance is a wildly grandiose doorway that predates all the early 20th-century garden buildings around it by some 300 years. With stone scrolls, shields and swags surmounted by a draped urn, it is a surviving fragment of an earlier house built around 1630 by Sir Thomas Wentworth, later Earl of Strafford. 'Black Tom Tyrant', as he was known, was one of Charles I's loyalest supporters but he was thrown to the wolves by the king and beheaded before a crowd of 200,000 on Tower Hill in 1641. (When Charles I was executed eight years later, amongst his last words were that God had allowed his execution as punishment for him having allowing Strafford's.) The Bear Pit was part of Thomas Watson Wentworth's enthusiastic development of an extensive 'menagery' in 1738. Ten years later an anonymous visitor wrote of the 'prodigious number of foreign birds, particularly, gold and pencil pheasants, cockatoos, mollarca doves, etc, etc'.

By 1850 the estate had been taken over by Earl Fitzwilliam, who, as well as amassing a collection of rare beasts, was determined – well before his time – to make records of his private zoo. Many of his animals came from English zoological gardens, while others were imported – and he carefully detailed their arrivals at the ports of London, Liverpool and Hull. In 1851 it is recorded that £31 9s 1d was spent on four llamas from Arica in North Chile and that it cost £20 15s to ship them to Liverpool, making the grand total of £52 4s 1d –

Below: This 17th-century doorway was used as the entrance to a later Bear Pit at Wentworth Woodhouse in South Yorkshire.

a vast sum in those days. Like Noah's Ark – except sadly hardly ever two by two – they trooped in from all over the world: as well as the llamas and agoutis from South America, there was an alpaca, a tapir and a tiger cat; from Africa there were mongoose rats, as well as 'Ringtailed and Red and Black Fronted lemurs', a chimpanzee and a goat; an Indian antelope, axis deer,

a java hare and four Cashmere goats came from Asia; a wombat, an emu and a pair of kangaroos – with a baby in the pouch – were from Australia. It also held Chinese monkeys and armadillos – I could go on until the cows, or rather the capercalli come home.

All these animals required feeding. We can read of the enormous consignment of food that was delivered on 24 June 1850, including four stones of fish and three of grapes – '...along with a bottle of port wine for the emu'. 'Fallen sheep' and 'fallen lambs' are less appealing. There were weekly bills for the 'carriage of rabbits' as well as for ants and their 'gathering'. In the account book of 1850, three pennies were charged by 'a boy for bringing a basketful of mice'.

In the 19th century when a private zoo was often a place for serious enquiry, the menagerie at Wentworth Woodhouse was one of the most serious of them all. As in life, so too in death the animals were studied – and afterwards preserved for posterity in a private museum. The most important creature, for our purposes, was the female American bear 'from Greenhouse Court'. I fear that no words would be adequate to describe the dank, dark and wretchedly cramped confines in which she was forced to live, gazed at from on high by those who had climbed the stone spiral stairs around the wall leading up to a platform, or otherwise peered down at from the garden above. It must have been a sad sight.

## Culzean, Ayrshire

The monkey pagoda is in my view the most surprising of all Culzean's buildings for animals, even outstripping Robert Adam's design for the Home Farm of 1775 (see pp 97–9). It is thought by some to be by Robert Lugar and to have been built with the sweeping changes of around 1814, along with the swan pond, the duck house, the aviary and three Gothic lodges. Others

*Opposite: The monkey pagoda at Culzean, Ayrshire, in ruins (top) and after its restoration in 1997 (bottom).*

*Below: The entrance of the smithy at Gonalston, Nottinghamshire, is adorned by a brick horseshoe.*

believe, somewhat surprisingly, that it was built in 1860 when the 2nd Marquess of Ailsa was at the helm – a man whose greatest passions were to go hunting throughout the winter and yachting throughout the summer, although true to say, he also drained Culzean's coffers with various extravagant improvements.

By the 1930s the monkey pagoda had become roofless and when photographed in 1985 appeared for all the world to be a Gothic ruin. Accounts of it having been a Chinese pagoda for monkeys seemed fantastical – or so I thought. In 1997 it was restored to its full measure of original idiosyncrasy revealing a tiered tower with multiple eaves, in which the Cassillis family would have taken tea at the top, while various creatures were given quarters below. At one time it was an aviary, at others it was lived in by swans, but the most suitably exotic tenant was a monkey – it is known locally as the Monkey House – and the new balustrades of the outer stairs have been designed with monkeys' tails. The weathervane too is a monkey, cavorting into the sky. Few places in the British Isles have served animals so well with good architecture as has Culzean.

## Gonalston, Nottinghamshire

Built to entice you in, the horseshoe entrance of the old smithy at Gonalston is built entirely of brick – those that project to form the 'fullered' (grooved) shoe are painted black with white 'nails' against the red clay. The sign above the door reads 'GENTLEMEN, AS YOU PASS BY, PRAY ON THIS SHOE CAST YOUR EYE IF IT'S TOO STRAIT WE'LL MAKE IT WIDER T'WILL EASE THE HORSE AND PLEASE THE RIDER IF LAME BY SHOEING (AS THEY SOMETIMES ARE) YOU CAN HAVE THEM EASED WITH THE GREATEST CARE'– all written around little paintings of an anvil, a horseshoe, a hammer and blacksmith's tongs. Crisp and bright and un-Victorian, it would

appear to be a later addition to this building with its datestone of 1845. The initials J F carved above the date record that the smithy was created by Sir John Franklin of nearby Gonalston Hall, who built and improved several buildings on his estate.

Some 20 miles from Gonalston at Carlton-on-Trent, the smithy has a much earlier sign – roughly written and without the tools – over the door.

## Ford, Northumberland

'An outstanding event is coming off tomorrow' –
so, according to Claire Brisby, wrote Dante Gabriel
Rossetti to his mother in 1855. He continued: 'The
Marchioness of Waterford has expressed a wish to
Ruskin to see me paint in watercolours, as she says my
method is inscrutable to her. She is herself an
excellent artist and would have been really great, I
believe, if not born such a swell and such a stunner.'

Lady Waterford was a beauty and we must rejoice
that she was also a swell, for it was she who was
responsible for the building of the blacksmith's forge,
and much more, when in an act of characteristic
philanthropy, she created the model village of Ford
next to her home at Ford Castle. She had already been
publicly acknowledged in Parliament for her work in
the great famine in Ireland, where she had established
a factory and built a school and two churches. At Ford

she decreed that the village should be built entirely of golden stone, with wooden bargeboards and red-tile roofs on all the cottages. A handsome schoolhouse was to be built, as well as a tall pillar of polished Aberdeen granite supporting a stone angel commemorating her husband. Finally, there is the blacksmith's; with its satisfyingly substantial stone horseshoe – complete with stone nails – around the door, it is the most beguiling of all the exteriors.

As well as creating these buildings, it was her work on the schoolhouse interior that brought her national renown. With a series of biblical frescoes – in fact watercolours stretched on frames and stiffened with distemper – she attracted the great and the good to Ford, including W E Gladstone, G F Watts and John Ruskin, all of them beating a path to the Northumbrian schoolhouse door. They were Old Testament scenes, conceived on the grand scale with life-sized figures enclosed in Gothic arches inscribed with the relevant biblical passages and surrounded by plants, flowers, birds and beasts. Defying the 19th-century death-knell dilemma doled out to women artists and architects that they could not be taken seriously, this assembly of paintings in their soaring timber-roofed setting became an important stepping stone towards their recognition. Nor had that been the only obstacle to Lady Waterford's popularity – as well as being a woman, she was also a woman of means. According to Brisby, Ruskin, who particularly admired her soft 'Venetian colouring', wrote that 'she might have been a Paolo Veronese, had she been poor, but I suppose it is all right that she should be great and rich'.

A particularly appealing aspect of the 'frescoes' was that all the figures were painted from life and depicted the villagers at Ford, especially those who worked on Lady Waterford's estate. Thus Jimmy Locke, the joiner's son, is Jesus; Dickie Dunn, the head gamekeeper, is the venerable and bearded St Paul; and Peter Roule, the butcher's boy, appears as David the Shepherd. Lady Waterford's personal maid 'Miss Boardman' takes her child up to Christ to be blessed, as does the beautiful Bessie Thompson, whose husband was the Waterford's coachman. Mrs Mary Heslop, Lady Waterford's housekeeper until she was 93, appears both as Rebecca and Lois, almost spanning the 21 years (1861–82) that it took Lady Waterford to do her great work.

Beatrix Potter came to Ford in the 1890s and intensely disliked its perfection: 'No cocks or hens allowed ... a peacock strutting about ... If I had lived there I should have let loose a parcel of sighs.'

## Biddick, County Durham

There are four arched lairs for dogs – in daily and delighted-to-get-out-of-the-way use – in the dining room of Biddick Hall. Each with a brass nameplate hanging on chains, they were designed by my mother and father as part of their improvements to the house in the 1950s.

When my parents moved here in 1948, they found that the remnants of the Jacobean house – I have a grim memory of its beige pebble-dash – was about to fall down. Between 1954 and 1955 E M Lawson and Partners were employed on its rebuilding and the results are entirely satisfactory, with a new wing of 18th-century bricks topped with pyramidal finials and a large wooden dovecote built onto the end wall. The dining room was refashioned at the same time by Trenwith Wills with a plasterwork ceiling and, in every corner, an arched niche of a china cupboard above a dog lair.

Hops (of Hereford – born in Hereford at harvest time) posed for the picture, sitting absolutely still for a full 60-second exposure. A black, grey, chestnut and white long-haired dachshund with white eyelashes and blue eyes, she belonged to my son Huckleberry Harrod.

## Charles Lamb's Cabbage Castle

In 1823 Charles Lamb, aged 7, announced to his mother that he was going to write the life and adventures of his guinea pigs; that he would call it *The History of the Kingdom of Winnipeg from the Foundation to the Present Time BY ROYAL COMMAND*; and that a kingdom would be built in which they would live. As he grew older, so his plans grew greater, resulting in

eight miniature hand-written and illustrated books bound in red and green leather as well as about 40 watercolours of his many hundreds of guinea pigs, all of them running free in their kingdom of little buildings. Furthermore, he decided his 'peeks' should all be heroes of old-world chivalry. Lamb's family was imbued with such romantic notions. His father and grandfather had both been Knight Marshals to the royal household; his father had married the widow of the Earl of Eglinton and his half-brother was the earl who inspired a group of young aristocrats to stage the famed Eglinton Tournament of 1839. This was a doomed attempt to revive the ideals of chivalry – an uphill task to undertake in the midst of the Industrial Revolution – with the full panoply of parades, jousting and revelry,

banners and banquets, operas, theatricals and entertainment on the grand scale, all enjoyed in full suits of armour and medieval dress. It had taken four years to plan and cost a vast amount of money; in the event it poured with rain and was a symbolically sodden washout with the Marquess of Londonderry being much mocked in his medieval attire carrying a giant green umbrella.

Meanwhile, in the background, Charles Lamb had been working for a full 16 years on his own chivalrous schemes for guinea pigs, creating them kings and queens, princes and princesses, knights, counts and dukes and giving them coats of arms and castellated homes. His map of Winnipeg showed a mainly walled city with six pyramid tombs and a columned monument; then there were the two smaller cities of Farai and Lelia. The estate carpenter made a Camelot of miniature castellated buildings, with Guinea Pig Castle – or Cabbage Castle as it was also called – being given pride of place.

In his book, the original King Geeny and Queen Cavia had had two 'blameless children', Limpy and Loidowiskea; then 'poor Cavy, dear Cavia' died of consumption. Loidowiskea, now queen, bore her father five children, then seven more guinea pigs arrived in the kingdom and the story began – all written in Charles' quaint hand. He lamented that plagues of 'dusyintery', then consumption, carried off many of the bucks, does and 'cheeldren', 'and thus did ten thousand griefs happen to the Winnipegs'. The 'Rarribuns' (rabbits) were troublesome neighbours: 'whenever there was panionium in came those gaulking ambassadors ... bullying the inhabitants, these horrid pests'. They were illustrated as arms bearers along with the 'peeks'. In one of his pen-and-ink drawings a guinea pig stands below his coat of arms while his

sword and feathered hat lie on a Gothic chest. Below is written 'Sir Ino Redais of Wittaken, K.W.R. Sherriff of the border. A.P 12–13. From the original picture in the possession of The Rt Hon Coccineus Hector. Earl of Wittaken, &c &c at Wittaken Castle.' There was also a Sir Coccineus Wallai, as well as the Knight of Killinger, the Prince of Rarribu and Turkine de Newton. There were also drawings of fierce battles. Could it be that it was this medieval kingdom for guinea pigs that sowed the seeds of the Eglinton Tournament?

## Wotton, Surrey

A temple for terrapins, no less, was built in the 1800s by William John Evelyn – kinsman of John Evelyn – in a small garden at Wotton House. Originally with an Ionic portico of four bays on the ground floor and with an open upper floor, embellished with Corinthian pilasters, from which to 'view' the tiny creatures disporting themselves in the pool below, this little building has undergone fierce changes. In the 19th century a refined spot for taking tea, by the 20th a rotting ruin and at the turn of the 21st restored to its temple state, although only half its original height. This is all thanks to Hayley Conference Centres who leased the house and grounds in 2000. Here you see two photographs: one of the wrecked temple in 1984 (*right*) when Wotton was leased to the Home Office as the Fire Service College, another showing its exemplary restoration some 20 years later (*see* pp 188–9). In the 1980s there were niches containing mere fragments of statuary, which are no longer in place, although a black-and-white marble floor has remained intact. It is now known as The Turtle House.

The great polymath John Evelyn – horticulturist, scholar, connoisseur, town planner, bibliophile, diarist and much more besides, who was writing of air

*Below: The ruined 19th-century temple for terrapins at Wotton House in Surrey.*

pollution in the 17th century – was born in Wotton in 1620 and lived there as a young child. However, he wrote in the first volume of his *Diary* that, 'in regard of my Mother's weakness or rather custom of persons of quality', he had been sent to live with a wet nurse until he was 14 months old. In 1694, as his aging elder brother had no heirs, the septuagenarian John Evelyn moved back into his beloved birthplace and lived there until he died in 1706. The house, he wrote in his *Diary*, 'is large and ancient', and 'so sweetly environed with those delicious streams and venerable woods, as in the judgement of strangers as well as Englishmen it may be compared to one of the most pleasant seats in the nation, and most tempting for a great person and a

wanton purse to render it conspicuous'. Of his library of some 4,000 books he wrote that he looked upon it 'with the reverence of a temple'. '*Omnia explorate meliora retinete*' was his motto – 'Explore all things, retain the better.'

He had applied his gardening genius to the place, at one point removing or 'digging down' a mountain 'with huge trees and thicket, with a moat' as he wrote in his *Diary*; he later created an artificially terraced hill that survives to this day. The pool that would later be used by the terrapins was fed by one of the tributaries of the River Tillingbourne; all part of Wotton's 'water in abundance' in the garden that was probably the first in England to be designed in the Italian style. His pride in the place knew no bounds – in his *Diary* he states: 'I should speak much of the gardens, fountains and groves that adorn it, were they not as generally known to be among the most natural, and ... the most magnificent that England afforded; and which indeed gave one of the first examples of that elegancy, since so much in vogue, and followed in the managing of their waters, and other elegancies of that nature.' John Dixon Hunt and Peter Willis record the stirring summary of his gardening sensibilities from a letter to Sir Thomas Browne in 1657:

> We will endeavour to shew how the aire and genious of Gardens operat upon humane spirits towards virtue and sanctitie, I meane in a remote, preparatory and instrumentall working. How Caves, Grotts, Mounts, and irregular ornaments of Gardens do contribute to contemplative and philosophicall Enthusiasms ... do influence the soule and spirits of man, and prepare them for converse with good Angells; besides which, they contribute to the lesse abstracted pleasures, phylosophy naturall and longevitie...

It is, though, William John Evelyn with his inordinate love of animals who is the hero of the hour for our purposes. In 1830 his father George Evelyn had died from a wound received 15 years before at the Battle of Waterloo, leaving his 26-year-old wife a widow with six boys, aged between six years and six weeks, to bring up by herself at Wotton. The eldest William John was to live there all his life. An idealistic, poetical and painfully shy

figure who delighted in natural history, he assembled animals by the score, as is recorded in Helen Evelyn's *The History of the Evelyn Family*: 'There were wild boars, Indian cattle, kangaroos, a zebra, a vulture, chameleons, a seagull and various tortoises.' This surely confirms him as the hitherto uncredited creator of this terrapin temple. 'The kangaroos', we further read, 'were once let loose on to Leith Hill where they flourished for years until

Left: The temple for terrapins at Wotton House has now been restored to its former glory, although at only half its original height.

a place called the Duke of Norfolk's Copse, but was flushed out and cornered at Abinger Rectory.' Trumble noted that the report of the incident – sadly anonymous – was worth quoting:

> Here the animal's peculiar mode of progression was exhibited in a style which astonished the field – a singular succession of leaps carrying it over the ground at a rate perfectly startling. Those who were well mounted alone were enabled to go the pace, and they speedily found themselves at the top of Leith Hill, where the kangaroo took to the road, and for about a mile and a half they all dashed along, 'the field' rapidly augmenting in numbers as they proceeded in their novel chase.

In 1856 Nathaniel Hawthorne went to Wotton. An extract from his English Notebooks, reproduced in *The History of the Evelyn Family*, records his curious impression of William John Evelyn as he was showing off the blood-stained prayer book used by Charles I at his execution:

> ...though he has the manners of a man who has seen the world, it evidently requires an effort in him to speak to anybody; and I could see his whole person slightly writhing itself, as it were, while he addressed me. This is strange in a man of his public position, member [of Parliament] for the county, necessarily mixed up with life in many forms, the possessor of sixteen thousand pounds a year, and the representative of an ancient name. Nevertheless, I liked him, and felt as if I could become intimately acquainted with him if circumstances were favourable; but, at a brief interview like this, it was hopeless... .

gradually exterminated by ruthless individuals.' There was a very funny account of a recaptured escapee kangaroo – given in a lecture in 2003 by Angus Trumble, most suitably in the National Library of Australia. He described how William John raised the alarm to catch the creature: 'Evelyn called out the local hunt, replete with huntsmen, a pack of beagles, whippers-in and so forth. The kangaroo sought refuge in

William John Evelyn should, however, henceforward be credited for building what is unique the world over – a temple for terrapins.

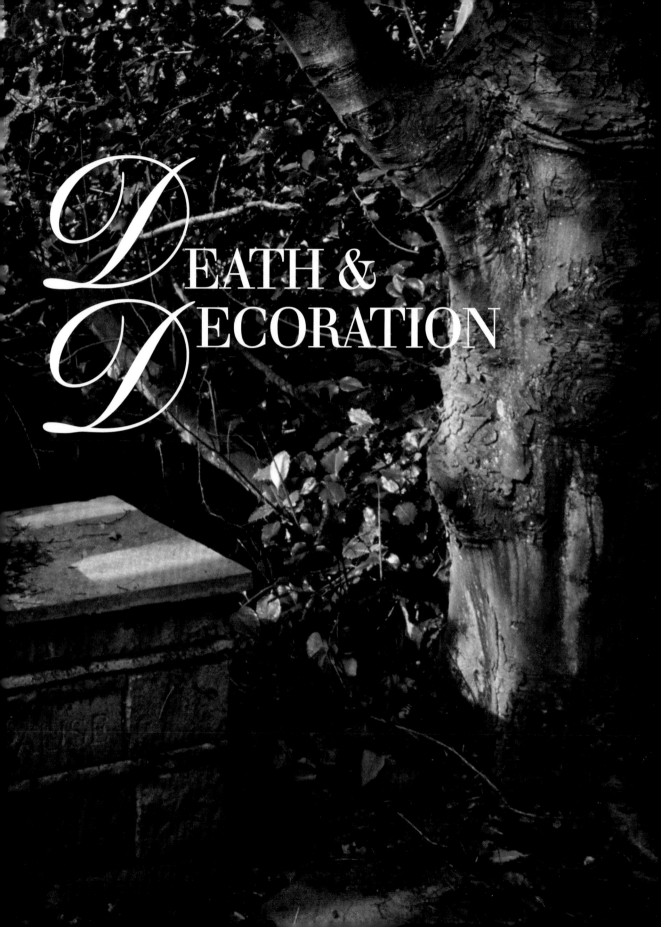

# DEATH &
# DECORATION

HIS CHAPTER reveals some of the glittering array of monuments and memorials remembering what seems to be every creature under the sky. Of course, dogs have been unashamedly commemorated throughout the British Isles – for instance, an interesting dog memorial at Dyneley, Lancashire, was cast from a Roman statue of two dogs at play from the British Museum (*see* pp 190–1). This memorial was commissioned by my husband's brother, Simon Townley; it was his great-great-great-uncle, Charles Townley, who had bought the statue for the museum in 1774. The dogs had been discovered on Monte Cagnolo (Dog Mountain) near Lanuvio, Italy; their counterparts stand – or rather sit – in Dyneley's garden, commemorating 60 years of canine companionship. However, it's not just dogs that are memorialised in Britain – there are also tombs for tortoises, monkeys, wombats, pigs, pigeons, rabbits and robins. There is even a memorial to a trout, as well as one to a cow – and who could not be surprised by the sight of two 20th-century gravestones to 'GLADSTONE A KIND RAT' and 'DISRAELI A LOVING RAT'?

Such proof of the mutual affection between man and beast abounds throughout the country. At Easton Neston in Northamptonshire, there is a stone slab of 1641 incised with uncommonly beautiful lettering which states: 'TO THE MEMORY OF A PUG: NOT UNLAMENTED NOW SHE DIES:/BESPRINKLED HERE THIS TRIBUTE LIES/WITH HEAVENLY TEARS FROM ANGELS' EYES.' And high on a hill in Herefordshire, I came upon a fluted urn which I had been told commemorated a racehorse (*opposite*). The inscription was oddly vague considering that it had been so carefully carved in stone: 'SUPPOSED DATE ABOUT 1800. RESTORED 1900 BY W. HENRY BARNEBY OF LONGWORTH'. In 1820 Sir John Soane gave his old dog a memorial monument of

peculiar splendour. A tiny chihuahua called Fanny, who had belonged to Mrs Soane, had outlived her mistress by five years and became Soane's most faithful companion, causing him to write in his *Description of the House and Museum* of 1835, that she was 'the delight, the solace of his leisure hours'. She died on Christmas Day 1820; 'Alas poor Fanny', Soane had straightaway lamented in his diary, 'faithful, affectionate, disinterested friend. Farewell.' In the basement courtyard of his remarkable house in Lincoln's Inn – built as a monument to inspire and instruct through the magic of architecture, which for him was always the Queen of the Fine Arts – there stands a vast assembly of neoclassical architectural fragments, piled high amid the recreated Gothic ruins of a monastery. It was under this towering – if designed by any other hand, teetering – edifice that the tiny dog was laid, with Soane's sentiments, 'ALAS – POOR FANNY', carved into the stone. And at Wrest Park in Bedfordshire, there is a late 19th-century dogs' cemetery, including a monument bearing the statue of a particularly mournful looking dog (*see* pp 194–5).

Nor are such memorials relegated to our past – far from it. Today, with the founding of ever more pet cemeteries, they are multiplying on a vast scale. Many too have been restored; by the turn of the last century, the PDSA cemetery at Ilford in Essex, for example, was in a sorry state of disrepair. Such sights as the gravestone of Tich – the canine 'Desert Rat' – being split in half by a tree could no longer be tolerated. Tich had stayed with her master in North Africa, as well as on the front line throughout his fighting in Italy, riding on the Bren gun carrier and on the bonnet of his jeep, and despite suffering several and terrible wounds would never leave her post even when under heavy fire.

*Right: A sorrowful monument in the dogs' cemetery at Wrest Park, Bedfordshire.*

'SLEEP WELL LITTLE GIRL' is once again written on her newly restored stone. On Punch's memorial, we read that he 'SAVED THE LIVES OF TWO BRITISH OFFICERS IN ISRAEL BY ATTACKING AN ARMED TERRORIST' in 1946. With the final resting-place of such heroes in danger of disappearing, the PDSA applied for and got a grant of lottery money, specifically for the restoration of their graves. A grand reopening took place on 18 December 2007. A new Garden of Remembrance has been planted and a new Memorial Wall 'TO HONOUR PETS LOVED AND LOST' is planned. Guest of honour at the reopening ceremony was the black Labrador Sadie – 'The Heroine of Kabul' – who in 2005 won the Dickin Medal for saving hundreds of lives; she had discovered an unexploded bomb under sandbags outside the United Nations Headquarters – maintaining a heroic canine tradition in Afghanistan going back to Cruiser, a dog commemorated in Rosshire. There on the Seaforth Estate, in a dog cemetery in an arboretum, we read that he was the 'FAITHFUL FRIEND AND COMPANION OF COL F. A. STEWART MACKENZIE OF SEAFORTH FOR 15 YEARS, WHO ACCOMPANIED HIM ON MANY OF HIS CAMPAIGNS INCLUDING THE GREAT MARCH FROM KABUL TO KANDAHAR.'

Finally we come to the great question of whether animals have souls – obviously not merely an academic question when it comes to determining how they should be honoured in death as well as in life. Keith Thomas tells us, in *Man and the Natural World*, of Samuel Clarke in the late 17th century who thought it probable 'that the souls of brutes would eventually be resurrected and lodged in Mars, Saturn or some other Planet'. And the Reverend Augustus Toplady, author of the hymn *Rock of Ages*, when seeing boys baiting a bull declared 'who could bear to see that sight if there were not to be some compensation for these poor suffering

animals in a future state?'. In his memoirs of 1794 he wrote: 'I firmly believe that beasts have souls; souls, truly and properly so called: which if true, entitles them not only to all due tenderness, but even to a higher degree of respect than is usually shewn them.' Asked if he believed that all the animal creation went to Heaven, 'Yes' replied Toplady, with great emphasis, 'all, all!' There was an unnamed 'Divine' who thought otherwise; allowing vermin to bite him without hindrance: 'We shall have Heaven to reward us for all our sufferings, but these poor creatures have nothing but the enjoyment of this present life.' This was recorded in *Man and Beast Here and Hereafter* (1874) by the Reverend J G Wood – a man after my own heart, author of some 59 books on animals, including one about a frog who 'took up permanent residence on his mistress' nose'. His heftiest volumes were those arguing for animal immortality and he had many letters

of abuse. One enraged critic wrote an attack of 12 pages of 'full-sized letter paper' telling him that 'anyone who cherished the hope that animals could live after death was unworthy of his position as a clergyman, ought to be deprived of his university degrees, and expelled from the learned societies to which he belonged'. Wood was scornful: 'This argument was so unanswerable that I did not venture to reply to it.' He was less reticent with another correspondent who wrote that 'he would never condescend to share immortality with a cheese-mite'. Wood was ready: 'I replied that, in the first place, it was not likely that he would be consulted on the subject; and that, in the second place, as he did condescend to share mortality with a good many cheese-mites, there could be no great harm in extending his condescension a step further.'

Such arguments still rage. But one thing is certain: in today's western and Christian world, at least, the status of animals is on the rise. I never cease to marvel that in the modern foyer – next to the cash machine – of Lloyd's Bank in Kingston-upon-Thames there is a steel plaque informing the busy customers that Nipper (the dog listening to 'His Master's Voice') is buried in the backyard! Beneath a small outline of the terrier, with his ear to the horn, are the words: 'At the rear of Lloyd's Bank is the last known resting place of Nipper, the famous HMV dog. This commemorative plaque was unveiled by Mr D F Johnson Chairman of HMV Shops Ltd on the 15th August 1984.' Incidentally Nipper was painted on his left side, as he had lost his right eye during a tussle with a rat!

Most wondrous of all is that many millions of pounds have been raised to build, in the middle of London, a great memorial to animals, albeit 'Animals in War', which shows that at long last officialdom is giving animals the status they deserve.

## Farley Mount, Hampshire

Suitably built atop an ancient burial mound, a 30ft-high pyramidal monument to a horse spikes high into the sky over Hampshire. It was built in the 1740s to commemorate the brave dexterity of the creature that had saved his master's life, as well as his own, by managing to jump safely and sure-footedly into a 25ft-deep chalk pit come upon unexpectedly while out hunting. Local squire Sir Paulet St John had lived to tell the harrowing tale; so too the horse, who was straightaway renamed Beware Chalk Pit and went on to win the Hunter's Plate at Worthy Down Races. Such was the squire's gratitude that when his horse died, he arranged for this memorial to be put up over his saviour's remains. Built of brick and rendered, the pyramid's regular restoration and repainting in either bright white or cream ensures that the horse is still honoured to this day. Inside there are seats set into the walls. Four roofed porches once sheltered four arched openings giving Gothic-framed views of Hampshire, Sussex, Surrey and Berkshire. Now three of those arches are bricked up, while in the fourth hangs an iron plaque on which we can read the whole story:

UNDERNEATH LIES BURIED
A HORSE
THE PROPERTY OF
PAULET ST JOHN ESQ
THAT IN THE MONTH
OF SEPTEMBER 1733 LEAPED
INTO A CHALK PIT TWENTY FIVE
FEET DEEP A FOXHUNTING
WITH HIS MASTER ON HIS BACK
AND IN OCTOBER 1734 HE WON THE
HUNTERS PLATE ON WORTHY DOWNS
AND WAS RODE BY HIS OWNER
AND ENTERED IN THE NAME OF
"BEWARE CHALK PIT"

THE ABOVE BEING THE WORDS OF

THE ORIGINAL INSCRIPTION

WERE RESTORED BY THE RT HON

SIR WILLIAM HEATHCOTE BARONET

SEP A.D. 1870

The squire and his horse made a robust pairing in 18th- and 19th-century England with characters such as Squire Mytton from Shropshire who it is doubtful we will ever see the like of again. 'Mad Jack Mytton', as he was known, delighted in performing death-defying feats. He once rode his horse up the grand staircase of the Midland Hotel in Leamington Spa, then onto a balcony above the restaurant from which he leapt over the diners below; then, with a final flourish, out through the window. Most famously, he urged his horse to jump a five-bar gate whilst it was still harnessed to the gig in which Mytton was standing cracking his encouraging whip. The horse jumped clear but only with his front legs, while his back legs and the gig did not – as Edith Sitwell tells us in *English Eccentrics*, '...carriage accidents were Squire Mytton's strongest point'.

## Stratfield Saye, Hampshire

Copenhagen was the little horse that carried the Duke of Wellington for a full 18 hours through the Battle of Waterloo – both their strength and spirits on fire to the end. Indeed, as Wellington dismounted with a grateful pat, Copenhagen lashed out with a kick so vicious that it could have succeeded where the might of Napoleon had failed.

The duke had had a horse shot from under him the morning of the day before the battle and he had ridden Copenhagen for the whole of that day too. As Archibald Forbes recorded, the duke later said that this meant his horse 'never had a morsel in his mouth until 8 p.m ...

COPENHAGEN.
*Cheval monté par le Duc de Wellington à la bataille de Waterloo.*

Copenhagen.
*Pferd so der Herzog von Wellington in der Schlacht von Waterloo ritt.*

The poor beast I saw, myself, stabled and fed. I told my groom to give him no hay, but, after a few go-downs of chilled water, as much corn and beans as he had a mind for. I impressed upon him the necessity of strewing them well over the manger first.' Later that night on the eve of the battle, they were off again on a secret meeting to see the Prussian Marshal Blücher, 30 miles there and 30 miles back, when they came perilously close to a potentially history-changing disaster when the duke and Copenhagen fell into a deep dyke. 'Thank God', wrote Wellington, 'there was no harm done to horse or man.' The duke had had a string of eight other chargers in waiting – but only Copenhagen was to see service at Waterloo.

At 15 hands high, barely bigger than a pony, the little chestnut was called Copenhagen after the siege of Copenhagen in 1807 – his mother Lady Catherine had been mistakenly sent there whilst in foal to the famed racehorse Meteor. The sire of Meteor was none other than Eclipse, one of the greatest racehorses of all time. On his mother's side, Copenhagen's grandmother was

The Duke of Wellington and Copenhagen became synonymous; paintings were painted and statues were sculpted, honouring the horse as well as the man – for instance Edinburgh sculptor Sir John Steele's statue of the duo was known as *The Iron Duke in Bronze by Steele*. In 1828, when Wellington was made Prime Minister, he rode up Downing Street on Copenhagen.

His old equine friend was retired to Stratfield Saye, the duke's house in Hampshire, where he was ridden by children and friends – obviously having mellowed over the years. In 1815 at Malmaison, just after the Battle of Waterloo, Lady Shelley – cousin of the poet and friend of the duke – wrote in her diaries that Wellington had 'offered to mount me on Copenhagen … A charming ride of two hours. But I found Copenhagen the most difficult horse to sit on of any that I have ever ridden. If the Duke had not been there, I should have been frightened. He said: "I believe that you think the glory greater than the pleasure in riding him!"'

When Copenhagen died at the great age of 29 in 1836 he was given a funeral with full military honours. A grim detail that enraged the duke was that one of the horse's hooves had been cut off as a souvenir. It was returned years later to the second duke, who made it into an inkwell; this was the same duke who arranged that Copenhagen's grave should have a tombstone that is inscribed with 'HERE LIES COPENHAGEN. THE CHARGER RIDDEN BY THE DUKE OF WELLINGTON THE ENTIRE DAY AT THE BATTLE OF WATERLOO. BORN 1808. DIED 1836.' In 1943 Mrs Apostles, the housekeeper at Stratfield Saye, planted an acorn by the grave which has now grown into an enormous turkey oak tree.

And a final note on Copenhagen's fame: one of the largest 21st-century office developments in Glasgow is the Copenhagen Building named after the little horse.

an Arab mare and his grandfather an English thoroughbred called John Bull.

After Copenhagen proved useless at racing, it was realised that he might do well in battle and so he was taken over by the Duke of Wellington, under whom he excelled. He once carried the duke into a square of infantrymen under cannon fire, where they unflinchingly remained as the duke encouraged his men. 'There have been many faster horses, no doubt many handsomer', the duke had told Henry Pierrepoint, the father of his son Charles's wife, 'but for bottom and endurance I never saw his fellow.'

## Gaddesby, Leicestershire

St Luke's Church, dating from the 1300s, is described in Pevsner's *The Buildings of England: Leicestershire and Rutland* as '[o]ne of the largest and most beautiful of the village churches of Leicestershire'. In its chancel stands the Cheney Memorial of 1848, surely one of the most dramatic monuments in all the country: Colonel Edward Hawkins Cheney of the Scots Greys astride the death agonies of his mount Tanner – one of the five horses that were shot under him at the Battle of Waterloo. Four of them died and the fifth was injured.

The monument, although it seems somewhat small, is probably life-size, as the colonel leans forwards at 5ft 3in high. It is sculpted in a grey marble that so suitably gleams on the flanks of a horse from the Scots Greys. Every detail should be studied, if only for the 'straight from the horse's mouth' documentary evidence of what a colonel of the Scots Greys at Waterloo would have looked like. His uniform has been sculpted in its every detail – his bearskin lies with its strap broken by the horse's hoof and the scabbard sling hangs from the colonel's waist, as does the many strapped and elaborately 'embroidered' sabretache (the flat shoulder bag for documents with a writing surface on which mounted officers and cavalry wrote messages and orders). Colonel Cheney's trousers would have been grey, his jacket scarlet with 'garter blue' facings, trimmed with gold lace. He has one hand on the reins, the other with sword aloft still manages to point forward, urging on his men as his mount sinks into a flattening field of wheat with its bridle, bit and martingale disordered in the death throes. '*Ces terribles chevaux gris! Comme ils travaillent!*' – 'Those terrible grey horses! How they strive!' – was Napoleon's still famed remark as 416 were killed that day.

On the base it is Sergeant Charles Ewart who is sculpted as the hero – capturing the colours from the French after the famed charge at Waterloo by the Royal Dragoons, the Scots Greys and the Inniskilling Dragoons. Their stirrups were hung onto by the musket-carrying and kilted Gordon Highlanders yelling 'Scotland Forever!' as they pressed together into the French ranks – not at the gallop as has been so popularly painted but at a relentless walk. David Hamilton-Williams records the words of a French Captain Duthilt, who wrote an account of the Scots Greys that day:

> Just as I was pushing one of our men back into the ranks I saw him fall at my feet from a sabre slash. I turned round instantly – to see English cavalry forcing their way into our midst and hacking us to pieces. Just as it is difficult, if not impossible, for the best cavalry to break into infantry who are formed into squares and who defend themselves with coolness and daring, so it is true that once the ranks have been penetrated, then resistance is useless and nothing remains for the cavalry to do but to slaughter at almost no risk to themselves. This is what happened, in vain our poor fellows stood up and stretched out their arms; they could not reach far enough to bayonet these cavalrymen mounted on powerful horses, and the few shots fired in chaotic mêlée were just as fatal to our own men as to the English. And so we found ourselves defenceless against a relentless enemy who, in the intoxication of battle, sabred even our drummers and fifers without mercy.

Sergeant Ewart later wrote of battling with the standard's escorts and bearer as he captured the eagle of the French 45th Infantry. His grim story was

published under the heading 'Deeds that won the Empire' in the *Evening Post* in Putanga, New Zealand, in 1896. He had overtaken the officer carrying the colours, and, to quote his own story,

> he and I had a hard contest for it. He made a thrust at my groin, I parried it off and cut him down through the head. After this a lancer came at me. I threw the lance off my right side and cut him through the chin upwards through the teeth. Next a foot soldier fired at me, and then charged me with his bayonet, which I also had the good luck to parry, and then I cut him down through the head.

He had single-handedly taken the standard of the French 'Invincibles'. Crossed flags are carved in relief on both semicircular ends of the pedestal – the French eagle to the right, Cheney's regimental standards to the left.

Incised into the base is 'J GOTT FT' ('Joseph Gott fecit'), which tells us that it was sculpted by Joseph Gott (1785–1860), who was particularly admired for his animal and neoclassical sculptures. He won the Royal Academy's silver medal aged only 20 as well as the gold aged 34 and his body of work was enormous – it is claimed by the *DNB* that '[h]is prolific output and repertory of subjects were unequalled in the history of British sculpture'. Much of it is to be found in the north of England, although he lived most of his life in Rome, where he was much admired by Canova.

The backs of Tanner's marble teeth are black, thanks to an apple having been put in his mouth at every harvest festival.

## Latimer, Buckinghamshire

Within the tiny and picturesque confines of Latimer's village green, a palpable sense of the battles of the second Boer War – most particularly the Battle of Boshof – will forever linger in the air. Here under the auspices of Brigadier General Lord Chesham – the village was part of his Latimer House estate – an obelisk was built commemorating the 126 Buckinghamshire men and women who served, as well as fell, in the South African war between 1899 and 1902. Thus we read that Lord Chesham's wife Beatrice and his daughter Lilah Cavendish both worked in the Imperial Yeomanry Hospital – founded by Lady Chesham; this was to become one of the largest private hospitals set up in South Africa during the war. We see too that Private Biggs was 'WOUNDED AT COLENSO'; Sergeant Atkings '...AT MODDER RIVER'; Sergeant Marchant '...AT KOOMATI PORT'; Private Birch '...AT PAARDEBERGEN' and that Sergeant Priest was 'DROWNED IN VAAL RIVER'. Saddest of all for Lord Chesham was the death of his only son Charles Cavendish – 'KILLED AT DIAMOND HILL' in 1900.

It is, though, the other and more modest monument that gives the Boer War's Battle of Boshof a strangely ever-present and poignant life in Buckinghamshire: the memorial under which is buried the heart of the horse ridden by the vanquished hero and French mercenary, George Henri Anne-Marie Victor de Villebois-Mareuil, who was beaten in brave battle by Lord Chesham in 1900. So great had been his courage – after three hours under Maxim gun fire and left with 30 men from 300 – that when he was killed he was given a funeral with full military honours by the English. His horse, a small dark Arab, had been wounded and Lord Chesham determined that it should be nursed back to health; so it was, in Buckinghamshire. Renamed Villebois, it was to live at Latimer for another 11 years. When the horse died, its heart, along with its ceremonial trappings, was buried here on the village green.

Below: Two views of the village green at Latimer,
Buckinghamshire – the smaller memorial commemorates a
French horse who served at the Battle of Boshof.

Right: An 18th-century obelisk to a pig at Mount Edgecumbe,
Cornwall.

On its west side the memorial stone is inscribed:
'VILLEBOIS BROUGHT TO ENGLAND BY MAJOR GENERAL
LORD CHESHAM KCB., IN 1900 DIED 5TH FEBRUARY
1911'; on the east: 'THE HORSE RIDDEN BY GENERAL DE
VILLEBOIS-MAREUIL AT THE BATTLE OF BOSHOF, SOUTH
AFRICA 5TH APRIL 1900 IN WHICH THE GENERAL WAS
KILLED AND THE HORSE WOUNDED.'

As if that was not enough – which it most certainly is
– there is an iron fence encircling the green on which
all the spikes have been covered by a narrow strip of
white painted wood, another legacy of Lord Chesham's
admirable attitude to animals. In the early 1900s one of
his greyhounds had tried to jump the fence and was
impaled, so Lord Chesham arranged for the board to be
put up to make the spikes harmless and painted white
to make sure it was seen. This beguiling arrangement
has since been kept in good order for over 100 years.

## Mount Edgecumbe, Cornwall

An 18th-century obelisk built in honour of a pig soars high on the Rame Peninsular overlooking Plymouth Sound, where the River Tamar joins the English Channel. Stately, substantial and some 30ft high, it was put there in 1768 by Emma Gilbert, the Countess of Mount Edgecumbe, to commemorate Cupid, her porcine pal and most faithful companion. Always by her side, the pig was in the dining room at mealtimes and even accompanied his mistress on jaunts to London – picture them please, together in the coach on their long jolting journey! When the pig died, according to *The Exeter Evening-Post or Plymouth and Cornish Advertiser* (a newspaper produced between 18 September 1767 and 21 April 1769), he was '...buried in a gold casket, the spot being marked at the obelisk on the instruction of the Countess'.

Her grief was satirised by the poet Dr John Wolcot, a Devon man who versified in a brilliant and satirical vein – most particularly targeting the royal family – under the name of Peter Pindar:

> O dry that tear so round and big
> Nor waste in sighs your precious wind,
> Death only takes a single pig –
> Your Lord and son are left behind.

Pindar also writes of George III who was 'at Mount Edgecumbe, happening to be gravely pondering' near the monument when Queen Charlotte asked him what he was looking at so seriously. 'His Majesty', wrote Pindar, 'with a great deal of humour, immediately replied, "The family vault Charly family vault, family vault."'

In appreciation for their animals the Mount Edgecumbes had scored another hit when Sir Richard, 1st Baron Edgecumbe, commissioned Sir Joshua Reynolds to paint him with his dog; furthermore, when the dog died, he had it stuffed and on show in a glass case. Many were the times he was heard talking to his old friend. It was later buried in Mount Edgecumbe's dog cemetery at Fern Dell.

According to a piece from 1806 in *Early History 1799–1816. Extracts from the Naval Chronicle,* on a

> Sunday Morning, 12 October, a duel was fought near the obelisk, Mount Edgecombe, by a Mr Armstrong, Midshipman of His Majesty's ship PRINCE OF WALES and a Mr Long of the RESISTANCE frigate ... His antagonist's ball entered Mr Long's right side ... and he was found lying on his back, his hat on, his pockets turned out, and a cane lying across his arm ... The dispute originated in a common hop ... where Armstrong wanted to put out the lights while the deceased was dancing with his girl. High words arose, and they immediately adjourned to an inn where the challenge was settled. Mr Long was a youth of engaging manners, about 18 years old, and, it is said, related to the Duke of Montrose.

There are those spoilsports who claim that this obelisk was merely built as a navigational eye-catcher; there was in fact another nearby that was said to be demolished in 1747 and replaced by a 'picturesque' ruin. Whatever the case, no one denies that Cupid was buried in his golden casket beneath this great stone monument.

The countess was not alone in having a pet pig as a companion. The Reverend Stephen Hawker, who between 1834 and 1875 was the parson poet to smugglers both dead and alive at Morwenstow in Cornwall, had a black pig with him at all times. His biographer, the Reverend Sabine Baring-Gould – author of the hymn *Onward Christian Soldiers* – takes up the tale in his *The Vicar of Morwenstow* of 1876:

> He had a favourite rough pony which he rode, and a black pig of Berkshire breed, well cared for, washed and curry-combed, which ran beside him when he went out for walks and paid visits. Indeed, the pig followed him into ladies' drawing-rooms, not always to their satisfaction. The pig was called Gyp, and was intelligent and obedient. If Mr Hawker saw that those whom he visited were annoyed at the intrusion of the pig, he would order it out, and the black creature slunk out of the door with its tail out of curl.

## Blockley, Gloucestershire

A wooden memorial to a trout – no less – was carved in 1855 by the son of the man who had tamed it; after which it stood for some 100 years in the garden of what was to become known as Fish Cottage in Blockley.

MEMORY
OF THE
OLD FISH

UNDER THE SOIL
THE OLD FISH DO, LIE
20, YEARS HE LIVED
AND THEN DID, DIE.
HE, WAS SO TAME
YOU, UNDERSTAND
HE, WOULD, COME, AND
EAT, OUT OF OUR HAND
DIED April the 20th 1855
Aged 20 YEARS

The trout had belonged to William Keyte, a wheelwright; there were also funeral directors in the family, which may explain this fine flight of fancy. In a surviving photograph Keyte appears as a distinguished Gladstonian figure in a stove-pipe hat. His son Charles had inscribed the memorial – with its definite but indiscriminate commas – to honour the affection that had existed between his father and the fish, which would rise to the surface whenever the old man went near the pond. It was seen as a cruel blow to the old gentleman when his piscatorial pal was murdered – bashed on the head by a vengeful neighbour.

That this frail memorial has survived is miraculous.

By the mid-1900s it was 'rotting' away but was restored by Donald Charles Keyte – a later member of the family – when it was protected by an elegantly framed glass case that was hung out of harm's way on the outside wall of the house. It has since been brought indoors to a shrine-like setting surrounded by old photographs – one of them of the memorial in its original garden setting – assembled by Alan Rusbridger, editor of *The Guardian*, who now lives in Fish Cottage. Thanks to him and members of the Keyte family, this memorial to a trout has now survived for over 150 years.

On 23 April 1955 the *Evesham Journal* had marked the centenary of the trout's demise:

No guns sound in Blockley; no flags fly or diplomats walk; no civic heads pay friendly compliments. Yet in this Cotswold village, exactly 100 years ago, died he whose fame has spread all over the world and whose graveside is visited over the years by hosts of eager pilgrims. He did no great deeds, nor did he change the world for the better or for the worse ... During the century that has passed since his death the Old Fish has been sung of far and wide. I have seen him eulogised in journals appearing as far apart as Pennsylvania, Rhodesia and the Antipodes. And the marvel is that the tradition he began lives on in that quiet pool where, during his short life span, he swam into the shoals of fame! ...Though the guns are silent and the flags unhoisted, let us now acclaim him who in a century of change and violence has occasionally reminded men of tenderer things! Perhaps from those secret depths where good fish go when their swimming days are o'er, the Old Fish gazes up at us today, a gleam of pride in his cold unblinking eye. Old Fish we salute you! May your fame endure forever.

Those who doubt the truth of the Blockley trout should know that similar stories are vouched for by illustrious company. For Francis Bacon, in his *Natural History* of 1622, wrote of seeing carp who would come at the ringing of a bell; Dr Hakewell in his *Apology of God's Power and Providence* of 1627 quotes Pliny, who records an emperor calling his fish individually and by name; while Izaak Walton, in *The Compleat Angler* of 1653, quotes Pliny's description of Antonia, wife of Darsus, who 'had a lamprey, at whose gills she hung jewels or ear-rings; and that others have been so tender-hearted as to shed tears at the death of fishes which they have kept and loved'. Walton wrote too of

St Ambrose, the Bishop of Milan who 'was so far in love with him [a type of fish he called flower-fish] that he would not let him pass without the honour of a long discourse'. And finally, Walton tells us that 'these observations, which will to most hearers seem wonderful, seem to have further confirmation from Martial (lib 4, Epigr. 30), who writes thus:

*PISCATOR, FUGE; NE NOCENS, ETC.*
*Angler! wouldst though be guiltless? then forbear,*
*For these are sacred fishes that swim here,*
*Who know their sovereign, and will lick his hand;*
*Than which none's greater in the world's command:*
*Nay more, they've names, and, when they called are,*
*Do their several owners' call repair.*

## Henley, Oxfordshire

JIMMY

A TINY MARMOSET

AUGUST 16TH 1937

THERE ISN'T ENOUGH

DARKNESS IN THE WORLD

TO QUENCH THE LIGHT

OF ONE SMALL CANDLE

So reads a tiny memorial stone that stands at the foot of a tree and facing a large block of flats on the busy Henley to Oxford Road – barely noticeable to those who walk and drive by. On first running it to ground I had the great good fortune to meet a man who had actually known the little creature, although never loved him. Wrapped round his mistress's neck like a fox fur, he always appeared a charming sight but woe betide those who tried to stroke him; fiercely gnashing out with ferocious teeth to the fore, he would bite any friendly hand to the bone.

The roll call of pet monkeys is a rich one. The explorer Richard Burton had 40 when serving in the East India Army between 1842 and 1853 and, according to his wife Isobel in her biography of her husband, *The Life of Captain Sir Richard F Burton* of 1893, he did much in order to learn their habits, manners and customs:

His great amusement was to keep a kind of refectory for them, where they all sat down on chairs at meals and the servant waited on them, and each had its bowl and plate ... He sat at the head of the table, and the pretty little monkey sat by him ... He had a little whip on the table ... as they frequently used to get jealous of the little monkey and try to claw her. He did this for the sake ... of ascertaining and studying

the language of monkeys, so that he used regularly to talk to them, and pronounce their sounds afterwards, till he and the monkeys at last got quite to understand each other. He obtained as many as sixty words... .'

In 1599 there was one pet monkey who by his actions could have changed the course of our history. It belonged to Sir Henry Cromwell, grandfather of the future Lord Protector, and out of the many accounts of what happened, Michael Russell's *Life of Oliver Cromwell* (from *Constable's Miscellany*) of 1829 is irresistible:

Right: Dante Gabriel Rossetti weeps over his wombat in this drawing.

If we may trust to the gossip of his more ancient biographers, his childhood did not pass without many remarkable occurrences, which seemed to indicate that an uncommon fortune awaited his riper years. For example, they say that his grandfather, Sir Henry Cromwell, having sent for him when an infant in his nurse's arms, to Hinchinbrooke, a monkey took him from the cradle, and bolting from a window, ran with him upon the leads which covered part of the roof. Alarmed at the danger to which the young visitor was exposed, the family brought beds upon which to receive him, supposing that the creature would drop him from his paws; but, it is added, the sagacious animal, appreciating the value of its treasure, brought the 'Fortune of England' down to safety, and replaced him in his bed.

## Rossetti's wombat

I never reared a young Wombat
To glad me with his pin-hole eye,
But when he most was sweet & fat
And tail-less, he was sure to die!*

So lamented Dante Gabriel Rossetti, on a drawing (held by the British Museum) commemorating the death of Top, his pet wombat, in 1869.

In 1862, after the suicide of his wife Elizabeth Siddal, Rossetti had moved to 16 Cheyne Walk in London, where he lived for the rest of his life, keeping company with a menagerie of creatures great and small. There was almost an acre of overgrown garden,

allowed to get ever more so by the day, and it was here that they all roamed together – to the despair of the neighbours. The cook of a nearby household had words about an armadillo burrowing through the floor of her kitchen and another nearby cook was enraged when the raccoon made off with her eggs. Thomas Carlyle, also a neighbour, was driven mad by the noise. Rossetti had two wombats in succession, a chameleon, a wallaby, a marmot, two jackasses, a raccoon, a woodchuck and a deer, as well as zebus, salamanders and armadillos. There were two kangaroos (the mother was killed by her son) and there were peacocks (one had its tail stamped off by the deer). He had green lizards, as well as innumerable little creatures such as dormice, hedgehogs and a mole. His Brahmin bull – whose eyes he always likened to the eyes of William Morris's wife Jane – caused many a rumpus. It chased Rossetti at speed through the house and out into the garden on

---

* A parody of Thomas Moore's *Lalla Rookh* of 1817: 'I never nurs'd a dear gazelle/To glad me with its soft black eye/But when it came to know me well/And love me, it was sure to die!'

the first day, then back through the house and out to the street on the second. With nowhere else to go, it regularly chased him round the garden. Rossetti conceived of an excellent plan to buy an elephant to clean the windows; the passing public would be interested, stop to ask who lived there and be enticed in to buy his pictures.

Wombats though were his favourite animals – he would often spend hours alone with them at what he called 'The Wombat's Lair' in London Zoo. When the first one arrived in Cheyne Walk, he was away in Scotland and, as Angus Trumble records, was moved to a pitch of anticipatory excitement:

> Oh! How the family affections combat
> Within this heart; and each hour flings a bomb at
> My burning soul; neither from owl nor from bat
> Can peace be gained until I clasp my wombat!

Returning home at last, he wrote in ecstasy to his brother William Michael that the wombat was 'a Joy, a Triumph, a Delight, a Madness'. In an earlier letter he had given us a tantalising glimpse of architecture for animals with his mention of 'a shrine in the Italian taste' for the wombat, which he thanks his sister Christina Rossetti for having 'reared'; however, he also wrote 'I fear his habits tend inveterately to drain architecture'. She too had been enraptured by the creatures, calling them *agil, giocondo* (nimble, cheerful), as well as *irsuto e tondo* (hairy and round).

The creature slept a lot, either in the bowls of hanging lamps or in the épergne on the dining room table. James McNeill Whistler wrote of having dinner with Rossetti in Cheyne Walk with, among others, George Meredith and Algernon Charles Swinburne, with the somnolent wombat curled up in the épergne throughout the evening. Ford Maddox Brown always claimed that the sight of the sleeping wombat inspired Charles Dodgson (Lewis Carroll) to write of the dormouse in the teapot in *Alice in Wonderland*. There were many stories: throughout a long monologue by John Ruskin, his dignity was somewhat disordered by one of the wombats persistently and patiently burrowing between his jacket and waistcoat. Then, when a solicitor's wife called Mrs Virtue Tebbs came to be painted, she was less charmed by the creature – it ate her straw hat. 'Oh poor wombat', wailed Rossetti, 'It is so indigestible!' Lamentably, Top died within two months, and seeing that he spent so much time in the dining room, Whistler wrote a satire on his demise – that when munching his way through a box of cigars, the lid closed and the wombat had perished inside, and that Rossetti later found the skeleton in the empty box.

The great man applied himself with due reverence, drawing a mournful scene with him kneeling over his little pal beneath a weeping willow and beside a handsome memorial, carved with an angel and topped with an urn. It was a monument that sadly never materialised; instead the creature was stuffed and put on display in the front hall of 16 Cheyne Walk. A second wombat was soon on its way.

## Wimborne St Giles, Dorset

In 1887 Hannah Augusta Anna Seymourina Ashley Cooper – the newly widowed daughter-in-law of the great philanthropist, the 7th Earl of Shaftesbury – called in the architect G F Bodley to Gothicize the Georgian church of St Giles at Wimborne St Giles. In the midst of the work, with the building open to the skies, two robins nested south of the high altar. All activity around them stopped and for weeks the

workmen took care not to disturb the birds, taking up their work again only when the fledglings had flown.

The robin, with the blood of Christ on his breast from having plucked at the crown of thorns on the road to Calvary, has always been thought of as a sacred bird and the nesting was seen as a good omen for this rebuilding of the church.

The workmen put the nest in a jar, along with an account of what had happened and built them into the wall. Twenty years later there was a fire and Bodley's pupil, the architect Sir Ninian Comper, was called in to repair the damage and make various additions of his own. Once again two robins nested south of the altar, once again they were left undisturbed, once again it was decided to build the nest into the church walls. It was only then, when concealing the second nest, that they found the first, having known nothing of what had gone on before. A painting celebrates this odd coincidence in flamboyant Gothic script: 'Here while the respond to the arcade of A.D. 1887 was building a robin nested + again during the building of the new arcade after the fire of 1908.'

Although so far uncredited, judging from the quality of the decoration and the fact that it is dated 1908, when Comper was working on the church, this wall painting to robins might well have been designed by the great architect himself. Most particularly as gilding was his great forte. Builder of 15 churches and restorer of countless others with purist medieval methods, his depth of research made him the designer par excellence of church furnishings, as well as of stained-glass windows – most particularly those of abbots and kings in the north aisle of Westminster Abbey. Later, passionately believing that 20th-century church architecture should reach 'unity by inclusion', he strove to create a fusion of styles – first tried out in St Giles, where influence from the French Renaissance was built into the early 17th-century amalgam of the Gothic and the classical. The wall painting to the robins, with its frame of gilded Jacobethan strapwork around the elaborate Gothic lettering, was the plum in this rich architectural pie.

## Larchill, County Kildare

In addition to its architecture for goats, pigs and ducks (*see* pp 100–2), Larchill boasts another building for beasts that must beat most in the world into a cocked hat – but it was designed not for this life but the next. An early 20th-century classical temple standing atop a mound built to resemble a fox's earth, it was designed as a safe bolt-hole for a master of foxhounds, who having hunted so much throughout his life, was convinced he would be reincarnated as a fox. Here, if pursued by hounds in the afterlife, he could escape. With its arched Gothic entrances opening into tapering tunnels large enough for a fox, but too small for a hound, Robert Watson, master of the Carlow and Island Hunt, would be safe. Furthermore, he left it in his will that hunting on his land be banned in perpetuity

There was much to make up for – his father had been master of the Tallow Hunt for 62 years; his grandfather was credited with killing the last wolf in Ireland; his son was master of the Meath Hounds; his uncle William was master of the Cotswolds, and his brother George founded the Melbourne Kennel Club and had the best pack of hounds in Australia – often, I fear, hunting emu and kangaroo. Robert Watson himself was master of the Carlow and Island Hunt for 32 years. When he died aged 86 in 1908, the mourners at his funeral were in full cry 'Gone-away gone-away.'

## Cobham, Surrey

'There is a necklace of jewels that is strung around London, otherwise known as the M25.' This is always my rallying cry, huzzahing the realisation that the motorway that causes misery and mayhem to so many is in fact surrounded by a wealth of historic and architectural diversions which should provide the richest ruminations to all those stuck in the traffic, knowing that they are only yards – albeit often tantalising yards – away from some tremendous treat or treasure. From hell to heaven within a few yards – there are hundreds of such diversions to be made.

None better than to Silvermere Haven Pet Cemetery, Byfleet Road, near Cobham – what livelier discoveries could there be than to come upon the gravestones of 'GLADSTONE A LOVING RAT' and 'DISRAELI A KIND RAT'? They are but two of the many hundreds of memorials set in idyllic undulating woodland of marching silver birches, as well as bulging shrubs and open fields. Established in 1977 by the Gilbert family, who still run it today, Silvermere Haven has undoubtedly brought solace to grieving pet owners who do not want their old pals simply to vanish without trace. I once saw a cat's funeral at Silvermere Haven, with a tiny coffin arriving in a full-size hearse which had been driven at walking pace from Kingston 7½ miles away. A small and solemn procession of black-coated undertakers – one of them with a top hat – bore the little body to its grave. As for canine care, I met a couple who feel bound to come here for two days every week from Bournemouth so as to tend to as well as sit by their poodle's grave. Another dog memorial, inscribed 'GONE FOR LONG WALKIES', must have inspired many a sad smile.

Among the other animals buried or cremated here are a 12ft-long python, two goldfish, two pigeons and a dog and a rabbit in the same coffin. The tiniest internment was a cremation casket for a budgerigar and the largest was for Andy Parker, a 17-stone Irish Wolfhound, who was so enormous that an MFI wardrobe had to be bought to bury him in. His stone reads 'ANDY PARKER WOLFHOUND. A TRUE FRIEND AND A KIND AND LOVEABLE GENTLEMAN'. There is a terrapin too – 'SHELLY. A LOVELY REPTILE' – buried in these Elysian Fields, and not far away is the marble memorial to 'MONTY THE AMAZING ALLIGATOR'.

Particularly welcome is Silvermere Haven's announcement on their website: 'When it comes to memorials at pet cemeteries, we are not under the strict regulations governing the human world. You can inscribe any message, names or nicknames on a wide variety of tributes ranging from a simple plaque right through to ornamental headstones...'. Hurray! What a blessed relief from the blighting blank blocks of human memorials of today, which, thanks to bureaucratic ecclesiastical regulations have transformed great tracts of our consecrated land countrywide into what look like soulless modernistic cities in miniature. A mere glance at the diocesan rules will show you just how grim. As well as the demands for a uniform height and width of all the stones, there are other equally detailed restrictions, such as crosses being frowned upon, along with statues and other innocent images such as hearts and books. As if that were not enough (which it is) to choke all spirit out of 'God's Acre', there are many stringent strictures such as those that were laid down by the Diocese of Birmingham, with the chilling dictum that inscriptions 'be neither presumptuous or laudatory'.

Not so with Silvermere Haven Pet Cemetery; here we can be touched by individuality: 'WILLIAM: WILLY'S LIFE WENT RUSHING BY/TWO YEARS OLD WHEN HE DIED/

I HOPE MY WILL'S IS/SOMEWHERE AROUND/CHASING RABBITS UNDERGROUND.' Recorded in gold letters on grey slate is '"MISTER" DOUGLAS. MY BIG BABY. WE MISS YOU LIKE THE DESERTS MISS THE RAIN'. On a brown marble heart, we read of 'BINKIE OUR LIFE OUR LOVE', while gold letters with gold hearts on brown marble tell us of 'SILKY GRACIOUS BEAUTIFUL WONDERFUL FRIEND'. Strangely old-world are the words 'BUTTERKISS 1977–1990 A WONDROUS CREATURE. FOREVER FRIEND AND COMPANION OF T. F. DARNWOOD ESQ.' Recently rendered neat as a pin is a white marble headstone inscribed 'BASIL 1980–1999 GOODBYE MY LITTLE MAN. THANKS FOR EVERYTHING.'

I defy any traveller to return unmoved from the M25.

## Park Lane, London

The Animals in War Memorial in Park Lane is as moving as it is momentous – shamefully the first to be built in Britain. Gently traditional, yet slicing edge modern, it moves you to the roots of your boots. It was Jilly Cooper – with her book *Animals in War* – who inspired its creation and it was Leo Cooper, her military historian husband, who thought up the all-important

words incised into the wall – 'THEY HAD NO CHOICE'.

The sculptor David Backhouse was the genius behind its design, and it was he who sculpted the bronze animals. Richard Holliday and Harry Gray, also geniuses both, sculpted the stone animals. All the names of those who brought it into being are incised into the back of the wall. The monument was commissioned by the Imperial War Museum. A 58ft (17.68m) sweep of curved Portland stone wall designed as 'the arena of war' seems to enclose you along with all the warrior creatures – carved in bas relief – as they thunder by. Carrier pigeons fly ahead; two million were used in the Second World War and of the 17,000 parachuted into enemy territory only one in eight returned. An elephant – considered a 'skilled sapper' in Burma – leads the charge on the ground. There are horses – eight million of them perished during the First World War – and there are dromedaries and camels, as well as a chicken, a dolphin, a donkey, a cat and a goat. A mule, at the gallop, with its head thrown back, is enjoying the last of his food in his 'leather' nosebag. Even a glowworm is to be seen – the little creatures would provide light for the 'boys' to read

maps and letters in the trenches. The wall, curving on round, is incised with the ennobling words: 'THIS MONUMENT IS DEDICATED TO ALL THE ANIMALS THAT SERVED AND DIED ALONGSIDE BRITISH AND ALLIED FORCES IN WARS AND CAMPAIGNS THROUGHOUT TIME'.

Bronze mules, life-sized and heavily laden, toil up to an opening in the wall, through which you walk. This enables you to look back at the empty silhouettes of the animals on the other side, all of them wraith-like, representing ghosts of these victims of war. There are two bronze animals walking away from conflict into the future: a 10ft-tall stallion, front leg up and on his way, and a dog wistfully looking back over his shoulder. Never have I gone past that dog – and I pass it very often – without being pierced through by the poignancy of its attitude. Never, indeed, can I see the memorial without wailing in sad delight.

Some of the most exhilarating hours of my working life were spent photographing this memorial; every second of it was intoxicating. The sun was out, Park Lane's traffic roared past on either side, people poured by, and in the midst of this mayhem was this great modern masterpiece – looked at and loved by all.

## Shugborough, Staffordshire

'For picturesque grounds and garden furnishings few houses in England can compete with Shugborough'; no small praise from Sir Nikolaus Pevsner himself in *Buildings of England: Staffordshire* – most especially for our purposes, if one of those 'garden furnishings' is a monument to a cat. There are two wildly different theories as to the identity of this nobly elevated creature on the 18th-century monument. One is that it circumnavigated the world with Admiral George Anson on board the flagship *Centurion*, when in 1740 he led a squadron of six war ships and two supply ships on his almost four-year long journey. Britain and Spain were at war and Anson's mission was to capture Spanish ships and possessions in the Pacific. A mission made particularly perilous as at the time the 500 regular infantry that were to be used as a landing force had to be replaced. Thus Anson was forced to take on various recruits, including pensioners from the Chelsea Hospital, most of them 'worn out and crippled' invalids – in fact not all of them managed to make the march to Portsmouth and some actually had to be carried on board. Many of them subsequently deserted and none of the pensioners were to survive the journey. And what a journey it was: returning by way of China to England in 1744, the *Centurion* had circumnavigated the globe.

The journey was a triumph – and Admiral Anson was hailed as a hero on his return, with 32 waggons of his captured treasure being paraded through the cheering crowd-packed streets of London. However, it had been gained at a great and horrific loss of life – as well as killed in battle, the sailors were struck down with typhus, dysentery, malaria and scurvy, not forgetting simple starvation. Around 1,500 men went on the journey and not 200 returned – though one of the survivors was the ship's cat, and it has been said

that this monument is Admiral Anson's tribute to this feline.

The second theory about the cat is that it was the last of the Persian cats – although it has a smooth coat and enormous almond shaped, rather than round, eyes – that were kept as pets at Shugborough by the admiral's brother Thomas, who owned Shugborough; eventually these cats were decimated by distemper. This theory about the monument is supported by a letter from Admiral Anson's wife to her brother-in-law in 1749. Admiring a stone quarry, she writes of 'the engine for turning the stone vases ... the largest and most magnificent of which ... are indeed stupendous ... but six pounds a pair ... if you had fixed upon a Design you might have had Kouli Kan's monument made here ... an experiment of no great cost'. The cat had certainly been given a Persian name – Kouli Khan was the emperor known as the 'Persian Napoleon', who was assassinated in 1747 and was one of the doomed owners of the Koh-i-Noor diamond.

The cat monument sits in grounds picturesquely peopled with 18th-century garden buildings – there is a little white Chinese House of 1747 that was inspired by drawings made of real Chinese buildings seen on Admiral Anson's travels. There is a Tower of the Winds of 1765, as well as some picturesque ruins and a Doric temple. Strangest of all is the 'Shepherd's Monument' on which is incised an enigmatic inscription. This was seen as a coded message and it has beaten the sleuthery of Charles Darwin, Josiah Wedgwood and Charles Dickens. More recently it has been suggested that it gave a clue to the whereabouts of the Holy Grail, and even the code breakers from the National Codes Centre at Bletchley Park have studied it. It hit the headlines, playing a key role in *The Holy Blood and the Holy Grail* published in 1982. This

monument – commissioned by Thomas Anson and paid for by the admiral – was decorated with relief carvings by the Flemish sculptor Peter Scheemakers.

Here is a host of artistic and architectural heroes: the 17th-century house was enlarged in the late 18th century by James 'Athenian' Stuart, then later given a giant portico by Samuel Wyatt. Then there is the Lantern of Diogenes of 1764–71 also by Stuart, as well as the Arch of Hadrian, a whopping great baroque affair commissioned by Thomas Anson to celebrate his brother's triumph. This again was designed by Stuart and carved by Scheemakers. The cat monument was carved by Daniel Pincot and designed by Thomas Wright, another of their illustrious number. An architect, garden designer, instrument maker, antiquary and mathematician, Wright was also an astronomer of note.

## Ilford, Essex

In the newly restored People's Dispensary for Sick Animals' (PDSA) cemetery in Ilford there are many memorials to the animal heroes of various wars. None was more famed in their day than Simon, the ship's cat of HMS *Amethyst*, who was smuggled on board at Stonecutter's Island, Hong Kong, by Ordinary Seaman George Hickinbottom. This was the cat that was once cheered by the nation – he was credited for keeping the crew alive during their 100 days of captivity on the Yangtse River in 1949. Civil war in China had broken out and the opposing forces of Chiang Kai-shek's nationalists and Mao Tse-tung communists were encamped on either side of the river. HMS *Amethyst* had been dispatched to relieve another destroyer stationed on the Yangtse to protect the British at Nanking but then, despite flying the White Ensign and hanging Union Jacks over the side of the ship, the

Right: The tombstone honouring Simon, the ship's cat
from HMS Amethyst, can be found at the PDSA cemetery
in Ilford, Essex.

*Amethyst* was attacked at point-blank range. Many were killed and wounded, including Simon the cat who had his whiskers and eyebrows burnt off and his body gashed through by shrapnel.

The Chinese demanded that the British admit to firing first; the British refused to do so and stalemate set in, with the *Amethyst* stranded in a rat-infested hell. Forced out by the explosions, the rodents had become rampant, eating the fast-depleting stores, as well as, literally, the crew's toes. It had been arranged to get the badly wounded ashore but the sick bay was still full. So who better to deal with all these troubles than Simon the cat? His average rodent cull was at least one a day and when he killed a particularly large and vicious rat – nicknamed Mao Tse-tung by the crew – he was hailed as a hero and promoted to Able Seacat Simon. The thieving from the ship's stores was stayed, the spirits of the bored seamen lifted and the sick seamen soothed – all by Simon the cat.

Eventually the *Amethyst* escaped, in the dark, while under fire; a 'daring exploit...', telegraphed George VI. 'The courage, skill and determination shown by all on board have my highest commendation. Splice the mainbrace.' A special presentation was made on deck to all those who had survived the Yangtse Incident and, as the officers and men stood to attention, Simon, held by a boy seaman, was read the citation to 'Able Seaman Simon for distinguished and meritorious service ... you did rid HMS *Amethyst* of pestilence and vermin with unrelenting faithfulness'. Simon was also presented with the *Amethyst* campaign ribbon.

The cat's role though had been so pivotal that he was straightaway recommended for the Dickin Medal, awarded to animals for acts of bravery while with the police, the civil defence or the armed services. So famous did Simon become throughout the world that a special 'Cat Officer' had to be employed to deal with the fan mail.

The *Amethyst* returned to Portsmouth to a tumultuous welcome, but as all Simon's old pals marched home, he was borne off to the quarantine quarters. There is a sad newsreel of him left alone on the ship, blinking his farewells at the departing men. Sadder still, within a month he was dead – some say from a broken heart at no longer being with his companions. Mourned nationwide, flowers, cards and letters of sympathy were sent by the truckload to the quarantine kennels; his death was even recorded in *Time* magazine and his photograph was on the cover of *Picture Post*. He was posthumously awarded both the Blue Cross Medal of the Dumb Friends League, as well as the Dickin Medal; out of the 63 awarded, as of March 2010 his has been the only Dickin Medal given to a cat. Simon's funeral at the PDSA cemetery was attended by hundreds, including all the survivors from HMS *Amethyst*. With the service conducted by Father Henry Ross of nearby St Augustine's Church, the cat was buried wrapped in cotton wool in a tiny coffin draped with the Union flag. He was given full naval honours.

This anonymous poem was one of the many sent to Simon after the Yangtse Incident:

SAILOR

There was knocking at the Pearly Gates
And when St Peter hurried there
To view the new arrival,
He could only stand and stare.
For waiting in the Outer Court
There stood a small, black cat:
White fur gaiters on his feet
And a smart, white sailor hat.
'Why, bless my soul,' St Peter cried;
'The door for YOU is there:
Just up that marble staircase,
Close by the golden chair.'

The small cat's whiskers quivered;
He neither moved nor spoke a word.
Then good St Peter raised his voice —
He thought he'd not been heard.
'Now off you go to milk and fish
And cushions soft as down.
This door is only VIPs,'
He ended, with a frown.

The small, black cat just looked at him,
His topaz eyes aflame:
'I think I should explain myself –
I thought you'd know my name.
I don't need downy cushions;
I'm not like other cats;
I've won my spurs in battle
And killed off all the rats.
Please won't you let me enter?
The crew's expecting that.
VIP doors will open
To Simon, the Amethyst cat.'

'Come in, most gallant sailor!'
The good St Peter cried.
'Ask ANY favour of us here;
It will not be denied.'
Said Simon, 'I am grateful
For the goodness of the Lord;
I see great Nelson on his ship —
Please pipe me, sir, aboard
St Peter stroked the small, black cat
And fondled his whiskers and fur
'Nelson's needing a sailor like you;
Now go and join him there.'
So with tail erect, and whiskers trim,
Simon walks the decks with him.

The PDSA cemetery in Ilford first opened its doors – or rather its lychgate under which you pass beneath the words 'They are Forever in our Hearts. Love never Dies' – in 1949. It marked another great milestone in the history of this worthwhile and wonderful organisation founded 32 years before by Maria Elizabeth Dickin. However, by the millennium it was in

a sorry state of disrepair and the final resting-place of so many animal heroes was in danger of disappearing. The PDSA applied for and got a grant of lottery money specifically for the restoration of their graves and a grand 're-opening' took place on 18 December 2007. There, joy of joys, among the crowds, was Lieutenant Commander Stewart Hett – the very man made 'Cat Officer' in charge of the avalanche of mail sent to Simon after news of the Yangtse Incident had reached Britain. Over half a century later, this distinguished uniformed figure had come to Ilford, in his naval regalia, to lay a wreath on the ship's cat's grave.

Today over 3,000 animals are buried here including '"TORTY" PET OF THE FAMILY', as well as 12 recipients of the famous Dickin medal.

## Fairford, Gloucestershire

Amidst 17th- and 18th-century tombs in the graveyard of St Mary the Virgin at Fairford, there sits a small stone cat – the memorial to Tiddles who lived in St Mary's, winter and summer, for 15 years. When she was two years old and hating the company of a Labrador at home, she set off to the church where she stayed – welcoming visitors and sitting on the congregation's knees during services – until she died in 1980. The verger, Sidney Jacques, looked after her – 'She ruled you', insisted his wife – and it was he who arranged that the church tabby cat be memorialised. He commissioned Peter Juggins to carve her likeness, convinced that as 'she spent more time in the churchyard than anyone else, she deserved a plot of her own'.

At Morwentstow in Cornwall it was the parson himself, the Reverend Stephen Hawker, who went ever further with his extravagant welcome of cats into the church. Every Sunday, according to his biographer, the Reverend Sabine Baring-Gould,

[h]e was usually followed to church by nine or ten cats, which entered the chancel with him, and careered about it during service. Whilst saying prayers, Mr Hawker would pat his cats or scratch them under their chins. Originally ten cats accompanied him to church, but one, having caught, killed, and eaten a mouse on a Sunday, was excommunicated, and from that day was not allowed again into the sanctuary.

Not only cats were welcomed:

A friend tells me that on attending Morwenstow church one Sunday morning, nothing amazed him more than to see a little dog sitting upon the altar-step behind the celebrant, in the position which in many churches is occupied by a deacon or a server. He afterwards spoke to Mr Hawker on the subject, and asked him why he did not turn the dog out of the chancel and church. 'Turn the dog out of the ark!' he exclaimed, 'all animals, clean and unclean, should find there a refuge.'

*Left: A small memorial to a cat amongst the graves of St Mary the Virgin at Fairford, Gloucestershire.*

*Below: An 18th-century tombstone to 'Poor Tipler' at Dunham Massey in Cheshire.*

11'. 'ALAS! POOR TIPLER, 1762' is with 'POOR TURPIN DIED 17 JULY 1783' and 'POOR CATO DIED 20 APRIL 1786'. 'LYON D.1778' lies with 'POOR BIJOUX D.1783'. FOP (poor Fop!), 'POOR FAITHFUL CLOE' and 'POOR BEAUX' are together, all having died in the 1790s. 'POOR OLD DASH', who died in 1798, was buried alone. There they all lie, with their names finely inscribed in stone.

As if these memorials were not enough of a claim for canine immortality, Old Virtue, the first to die, was also painted in 1697 by Leonard Knyff, a Dutch draughtsman, engraver and painter who was famed for his views of country houses and gardens. Diverging from his usual and precise path of streaking

All this – picture the scene – with the parson poet Hawker dressed in a long claret-coloured tail coat, a blue fisherman's jersey (proclaiming him, as Piers Brendan writes, to be a 'fisher of men' amidst his 'mixed multitude of smugglers, wreckers and dissenters of various hues') knitted with a red cross to mark the entrance of the centurion's spear, hessian boots up to his knees and either a 'Wide-awake-Beaver' or a pink fez on his head. 'I don't want to make myself look like a waiter out-of-place, or an unemployed undertaker.' With his long grey hair flowing, he would process up the aisle – always ankle deep in herbs – followed by his cats.

## Dunham Massey, Cheshire

Rather than hidden away in a dank rhododendron-darkened corner, the dogs' tombs at Dunham Massey lie in pride of place on the lawn by the house. Old Virtue, who died in 1702, is under the same stone as Pugg as well as Old Towzer, who died on 'JULY 15TH 1754, AGED

perspectives, Knyff painted vividly from life, showing a fat – very fat – brindled Dutch mastiff, stomach to the fore, sitting in front of the old domed Tudor house of the day. The painting was commissioned by Henry Booth, the recently ennobled 1st Earl of Warrington, who, through his friendship with the Duke of Monmouth, had escaped death by a whisker when tried for treason in 1686. A special court had assembled, with the infamous Judge Jeffreys at the helm. Warrington's entry in the *DNB* tells us that despite one of the jury – the Earl of Peterbrough, 'groom of the stole' – whispering that Booth was 'Guilty by God', and despite the accused having earlier denounced Jeffreys as behaving 'more like a Jack-Pudding, than with that gravity that beseems a Judge', Booth was freed. He was eventually made Chancellor of the Exchequer by William of Orange. Since he had seen fit to commemorate his old dog with a painting by an artist of renown, heaven alone knows what stone memorial he would have devised for Old Virtue. In the end the old mastiff outlived his master by three years. It was left to George Booth, 2nd Earl of Warrington, to bury him in 1702, establishing the family tradition of commissioning finely carved stones for their dogs. Obviously sensible to matters aesthetic, it was Booth who rebuilt the Tudor Dunham Massey between 1732 and 1740.

The Booth dogs went on being commemorated into the 19th century with memorials to Gipsey, who died in 1806 aged 11, as well as to 'POOR OLD LYON D.1818' and 'POOR OLD LION D.1825'. 'POOR LION', who died on 2 November 1836, was given the extra honour of a verse:

> NOW POOR LION IS DEAD AND GONE
> THOUGHT BY JOSEPH THOUGHT MUCH ON.
> AND THE SERVANTS ONE AND ALL
> DO REGRET POOR LION'S FALL.

## Orchardleigh, Somerset

It is as rare as it is wonderful to come upon the island church of St Mary at Orchardleigh: a tiny 13th-century building, surrounded by water, which has a fine 18th-century memorial to a dog in pride of place in its graveyard. Near the church and elevated on a grassy knoll is this swagged stone urn carved with canine skulls. It is the most prominent and the most beautiful monument in the graveyard – yet it commemorates a hound. Hurray! Three cheers that the diocesan board should have allowed it; that a special dispensation should have been granted; that, most importantly, it should have been applied for. It is a stirring saga that began in the 1790s and reached its triumphant conclusion in 1989.

It is a historic, literary and fantastical mix – part 18th- and 19th-century 'tradition' and part spirited 20th-century action; it is also a tale drawn from scholarship, eye-witness account, hearsay, elaboration and also pure invention. Most importantly of all, it is thanks to the writer Sir Henry Newbolt for having gathered all the strands together for his poem *Fidele's Grassy Tomb* of 1887. From all this you discover a most endearing story.

One version of the story tell us that Sir Thomas Swymmer Champneys, son of Sir Thomas Champneys, had a beloved dog called Azor, a German water pudelhund that had been given to him by the King of Prussia in 1790. When Azor died he commissioned a stone urn to be inscribed to 'his truest friend' – hurting Champneys' wife's feelings so much that she went alone to Wells for six weeks to recover – which was to stand on the edge of the churchyard.

However, there is a variation to this tale, recounted in Newbolt's poem. Newbolt was an exemplary Victorian figure: a lawyer, editor, novelist, playwright and poet. Above all he promoted patriotism – his words

of *Vitai Lampada* of 1897, 'Play up! play up! and play the game!', became common currency in the English language. In 1889 he married Margaret Duckworth whose father owned Orchardleigh and, after hearing of the local legend of a hound who had been buried with his master in the church, resolved to write it in verse. The story went that when Sir Thomas Champneys, the then owner of the Orchardleigh estate, was dying in 1821, he decreed that his hound Fidele, who had once saved him from drowning, be buried at his feet.

> The last that his heart could understand
> Was the touch of the tongue that licked his hand
> 'Bury the hound at my feet' he said,
> And his voice dropped and the Squire was dead.

The dog was laid to rest with his master, to the approval of one and all, until it came to the ears of the bishop:

> Bishop of Bath and Wells was he,
> Lords of the Lords of Orchardleigh;
> And he wrote the Parson the strongest screed
> That Bishop may write or parson read.

> The sum of it was that a soulless hound
> Was known to be buried in hallowed ground:
> From scandal sore the church to save
> They must take the dog from his master's grave.

The dog was exhumed and reburied, and the great urn designed to stand over his remains in the park – or so it was thought. In 1878, when George Gilbert Scott Junior was restoring the church, the skeleton and skull of a large hound were found to be still buried at Champneys' feet. The bishop had been disobeyed and the monument had been designed as a blind. Whatever the truth, this elegant memorial was unquestionably designed to commemorate a dog.

Left: The island church of St Mary, with the dog monument
in pride of place.

Below: A 19th-century tombstone for a dog at
Wynyard Park, County Durham.

When the last squire, Arthur Duckworth, died in
1987, the Orchardleigh estate – including the 'Dog
Monument' – was up for sale. Fortunately, a hero hove
into view – historian Michael McGarvie – who wrote
passionately to the papers of its literary and historical
importance. The monument was withdrawn from the
sale by the Duckworth family who decided to restore
it in honour of the last squire. Thus it was that on
15 August 1989 – the centenary of Henry Newbolt's
wedding to Margaret Duckworth in St Mary's Church –
a plaque was put up on the wall of the porch giving
thanks for the life of Arthur Duckworth and
commemorating 'Azor's devotion to his master, whose
death and burial in the family vault here is said to have
shared, inspired Sir Henry Newbolt's ballad Fidele's
Grassy Tomb.' McGarvie obtained a faculty to allow the
monument to stand in the graveyard. So it is that a fine
18th-century memorial to a hound stands in place of
honour in an English country churchyard. At long last
the monument has been united with the dog's bones.

## Wynyard Park, County Durham

This is one of the memorials to dogs that are scattered
among trees in the wild garden of Wynyard Park
established in the 1800s by Frances Anne, Marchioness
of Londonderry. She was a woman of extreme passions,
in marriage becoming the grandest hostess in all
England and in widowhood becoming a tyrannical force
who single-handedly managed her vast estates as well
as her coal mining and shipping empire. Sailing
through society bedecked in an ever-increasing quantity
of jewels, she was the butt of mirth of many – her
husband was ambassador in Vienna and Martha
Wilmot, the wife of the embassy chaplain, wrote that
'decked out like the Queen of Golconda (Donizetti's
extravagant heroine) she receives you with freezing

pomp'. When he died in 1854 she took charge of the
Londonderry's industrial legacy, living a life in Durham,
when she was described by Disraeli as 'surrounded by
her collieries and her blast furnaces and her railroads
and the unceasing telegraphs ... I remember her five
and twenty years ago a mere fine lady, nay the finest in
London! But one must find excitement if one has
brains.' We read of this in Diane Urquhart's *The Ladies
of Londonderry*, and of how, while spending the social
season in the south, Lady Londonderry would be
planning such sprees as a dinner for 3,000 pitmen and
colliery employees in the north. Hell bent on enjoying
the feast of 32 sheep, 8 cows and 500 round plum
puddings, as well as 60 barrels of beer, they would be
addressed by Lady Londonderry in rousing and
compassionate terms: 'It makes my blood run cold to
dwell on these fearful risks, and I think that any great
calamity among you would break my heart.' Nearby
Seaham Harbour, with its port hewn out of solid rock,
had come into being to serve the Londonderry's empire
and Lady Londonderry in turn, by building several
churches and schools, as well as the town hall and a
hotel, was to serve it well. She also inaugurated a library

and a reading room, as well as temperance and clothing societies. All this work was conducted from Wynyard Park, the whopping great house based on the unexecuted proposals for Waterloo Palace for the Duke of Wellington at Stratfield Saye. The schemes were by Benjamin Dean Wyatt and their realisation by his brother Philip. Disraeli once wrote that never in his life had he anticipated such happiness as when arriving at Wynyard. His friend the duchess was forever and relentlessly improving the estate with such schemes as the dog cemetery. One undated gravestone recalls:

TYDEUS WAS SMALL IN STATURE, BUT WE FIND

HIS LITTLE BODY HELD A MIND

AND TINY CASKETS OFT ENCLOSE A GEM

OF LUSTRE MEET FOR SULTAN'S DIADEM

THE STRANGER THOU THAT VISITEST THIS SPOT

WHERE TINY'S ASHES SLUMBER SCORN IT NOT

BUT IF THE VIRTUES THAT LIE BURIED HERE

LOVE, TRUTH, FIDELITY TO THEE ARE DEAR

GIVE ALL FOND MEMORY ASKS A SINGLE TEAR.

The final dog to be buried, in a bower of beeches, was owned by the last Lord Londonderry to live here. A pianist and musical scholar, he wrote this verse for the memorial slab of his bulldog Butch:

LAID TO REST AT LAST OLD SON

BENEATH THE BULLDOG SHRINE

YOU'VE FINALLY JOINED OUR SARA

YOUR WOULD-BE CONCUBINE.

I'LL MISS YOUR SHORT STACCATO BARKS

AND AWKWARD BLUNDERING GAIT,

YOUR EAR, ALAS THAT COULD NOT HEAR

THOSE SOUNDS I DID CREATE

FAREWELL OLD SON WHOM I WILL LOVE

WHILST BREATH I STILL RETAIN

FOR YOU ALONE MOST CONSTANTLY

RELIEVED ME FROM MY PAIN.

In 1987 the estate was sold to Sir John Hall, creator of the MetroCentre. Time has now marched into the 21st century: today the house is called Wynyard Hall Country House Hotel and is established, according to the website, as a 'premier venue for weddings, events, conferences, accommodation and fine dining'. The Wynyard Park housing estate has been built in the park and is lived in by big-shot footballers; 'Wynyard Park' has been established nearby, described in today's tempting website terms as 'Wow factor offices with wonderful terms' and a '700 acre mixed use development' that 'provides businesses ... with a fantastic opportunity to establish themselves within a prestigious development that is designed to balance Lifestyle, Living and Businesses perfectly'. Light years away from the Marchioness of Londonderry creating Elysian Fields for her dogs, whilst sailing through high society in the 'Family Fender' as she called her enormous tiara.

## Newstead, Nottinghamshire

'Boatswain is dead!' lamented Lord Byron in a letter to his friend Francis Hodgson on 18 November 1808 (recorded by his biographer Thomas Moore). 'He expired in a state of madness ... after suffering much, yet retaining all the gentleness of his nature to the last, never attempting to do the least injury to any one near him. I have now lost everything... .' Boatswain was Byron's beloved Newfoundland dog, who, having followed the postboy to Mansfield, was bitten by a rabid dog and struck down by the disease. His master was distraught and according to Moore, in his *Letters and*

*Journals of Lord Byron*, 'so little aware was Lord Byron of the nature of the malady, that he more than once, with his bare hand, wiped away the slaver from the dog's lips during the paroxysms'.

Byron had inherited Newstead Abbey – originally in fact a 12th-century priory granted to his ancestor by Henry VIII in 1539 – when he was only 10 years old. He then also became the 6th Baron Byron of Rochdale. The house was leased out until he was 20, when he started to live in it for the first time. Boatswain had died soon after and Byron, no doubt also stirred by his great inheritance, determined to bury the dog on what he thought was the site of the high altar of the priory church that had been reduced to ruins by his ancestors. The elegant urned plinth was designed in the dog's

honour to stand above three vaults – one for Boatswain, another for Byron himself and the third for his manservant Joe Murray. Murray, however, would have none of it, saying that although he did not object to lying with Byron, he most certainly did mind lying alone with a dog. This would indeed have been his fate as when Byron died in 1824, Newstead had already been sold and he had to be buried at St Mary's Church in nearby Hucknell. Incidentally, it was years before there was a suitable memorial to the poet; his friends commissioned a statue by Bertel Thorvaldsen but Byron was considered an unacceptable addition to either Westminster Abbey or St Paul's Cathedral. It was a scandal; in 1950 even the American Robert Ripley, of *Ripley's Believe it or Not!,* published a cartoon of

Boatswain's memorial, with the caption: 'Lord Byron's dog has a magnificent tomb while Lord Byron himself has none.' Incredibly, it was not until 1969 that Poets' Corner in Westminster Abbey agreed to commemorate him with a stone slab; Thorvaldsen's statue ended up at Trinity College, Cambridge. Boatswain had not been Byron's only animal at Newstead – there were two other Newfoundland dogs with whom he enjoyed a good swim. Thanks today to the website Crede Byron we can delight in the story of a tenant farmer at Newstead watching the poet 'get into the boat with his two noble Newfoundland dogs, row into the middle of the lake, then dropping the oars tumble over into the middle of the water. The faithful animals would immediately follow, seize him by the coat collar, one on each side, and bear him away to land.' Then of course, there was the bear. Having been told at university that no dogs were allowed, he flouted no rules by instead keeping a bear in his rooms. It came with him to Newstead – which always unnerved the Newfoundland dogs.

During the Byron family's three centuries of building and rebuilding at Newstead, Boatswain's monument was the poet's only contribution. The opening verse of the epitaph carved on Boatswain's monument has recently been discovered to be by his old university friend John Cam Hobhouse; Byron himself of course wrote the verse that follows:

NEAR THIS SPOT
ARE DEPOSITED THE REMAINS OF ONE
WHO POSSESSED BEAUTY WITHOUT VANITY,
STRENGTH WITHOUT INSOLENCE,
COURAGE WITHOUT FEROSITY,
AND ALL THE VIRTUES OF MAN WITHOUT HIS VICES.
THIS PRAISE, WHICH WOULD BE UNMEANING FLATTERY
IF INSCRIBED OVER HUMAN ASHES,

IS BUT A JUST TRIBUTE TO THE MEMORY OF
BOATSWAIN, A DOG,
WHO WAS BORN IN NEWFOUNDLAND MAY 1803
AND DIED AT NEWSTEAD, NOV. 18TH 1808.

WHEN SOME PROUD SON OF MAN RETURNS TO EARTH,
UNKNOWN TO GLORY, BUT UPHELD BY BIRTH,
THE SCULPTOR'S ART EXAUSTS THE POMP OF WOE,
AND STORIED URNS RECORD WHO RESTS BELOW:
WHEN ALL IS DONE, UPON THE TOMB IS SEEN,
NOT WHAT HE WAS, BUT WHAT HE SHOULD HAVE BEEN:
BUT THE POOR DOG, IN LIFE THE FIRMEST FRIEND,
THE FIRST TO WELCOME, FOREMOST TO DEFEND,
WHOSE HONEST HEART IS STILL HIS MASTER'S OWN,
WHO LABOURS, FIGHTS, LIVES, BREATHES FOR HIM ALONE,
UNHONOUR'D FALLS, UNNOTIC'D ALL HIS WORTH,
DENY'D IN HEAVEN THE SOUL HE HELD ON EARTH:
WHILE MAN, VAIN INSECT! HOPES TO BE FORGIVEN,
AND CLAIMS HIMSELF A SOLE EXCLUSIVE HEAVEN.
OH MAN! THOU FEEBLE TENANT OF AN HOUR,
DEBAS'D BY SLAVERY, OR CORRUPT BY POWER,
WHO KNOWS THEE WELL, MUST QUIT THEE WITH DISGUST,
DEGRADED MASS OF ANIMATED DUST!
THY LOVE IS LUST, THY FRIENDSHIP ALL A CHEAT,
THY TONGUES HYPOCRISY, THY HEART DECEIT!
BY NATURE VILE, ENNOBLED BUT BY NAME,
EACH KINDRED BRUTE MIGHT BID THE BLUSH FOR SHAME.
YE! WHO BEHOLD PERCHANCE THIS SIMPLE URN,
PASS ON, IT HONOURS NONE YOU WISH TO MOURN,
TO MARK A FRIEND'S REMAINS THESE STONES ARISE;
I NEVER KNEW BUT ONE – AND HERE HE LIES.

In 2008, on the 200th anniversary of Boatswain's death, a large assembly of dogs and their owners from the Northern Newfoundland Club of Great Britain gathered together at Newstead to put 'a posy' of flowers on the monument. A record of this day can be seen on the club's website, including a photograph of 14 Newfoundland dogs and their owners, along with the words of David Pugsley: 'A fitting tribute to one of the most famous Newfies in our history.'

## Brodsworth, South Yorkshire

The superbly restored 1860s exterior of Brodsworth Hall is somewhat sternly Italianate, while its 1860s interior is a preserved frenzy of Victorian flamboyance. It had a series of 19th-century gardens dating from the 1860s to the 1890s, which have been full whack recreated in their 15-acre entirety, and in their midst is a dog cemetery. Here the Victorian dogs Coup, Dash, Snap and Nell lie buried, while their portraits in oils hang inside the house. There are stones inscribed to the 'keen sportsman' Tatters and his mother Rita, Spot, Roy, Bob and Cuddie. 'Faithful Butty', 'Good Boy' Peter, Charley and Pippey are also remembered, while the dachshunds Max, Wanda, Eldest and Bobby are buried in the same grave. Here they all lie alongside Polly Parrot. Curious enough to make my flesh tingle is to have actually known Polly's owner, as well as one of the inhabitants of this cemetery – a King Charles Spaniel called Binkie, who belonged to Brodsworth's last inhabitant before English Heritage's takeover and triumphant restoration of the house and gardens between 1990 and 1995.

At that time Brodsworth had become a teetering wreck, welcoming you at the front door with the column capitals of the porte cochère worn away to the size of a wasp's waist. I had been commissioned to photograph the house from top to toe and was to spend many days with the frail and funny – although fading as the house was fading with her – chatelaine Sylvia Grant-Dalton. Binkie, I fear, was in fact its least appealing aspect.

Brodsworth was built with the proceeds of a celebrated will made in 1796 by a Swiss banker called Peter Thellusson. He left some £100,000 to his wife and six children, stipulating that the bulk of his fortune – roughly £700,000 – was to accumulate at compound interest during the lives of his four sons and their sons. Mark Girouard, who unravelled the complexities of the will when writing about Brodsworth in his seminal *The Victorian Country House* of 1971, writes that '[o]n the death of the last survivor, the estate was to be divided equally among "the eldest male lineal descendants of his three sons then living"'. It caused a sensation. Over the years so many hundreds of thousands of pounds were spent by the family contesting the will, that, by 1858 when the House of Lords pronounced in favour of the two great-grandsons, there was only about the same amount left between the two of them as was put into the original trust.

Charles Sabine Augustus Thellusson was our man, inheriting the Brodsworth estate with enough money to be able to demolish the large Georgian house and commission the architect Philip Wilkinson to build a fully furnished Victorian showpiece. This was to remain more or less untouched by any modernising hand for the next 129 years. With internal columned 'courtyards' filled with statuary and a cloister-like arcaded corridor with mirrored walls multiplying the parade of marble figures 10,000 times over, here is rich fare. Space flows into space with Minton tiles and matching Axminster carpets underfoot stretching off in every direction. 'It was built to impress', said Sylvia, who by then had lived there for 57 years, 'with its size, the length of its drive, how many pineapples there were on the roof or something like that; it was such a dotty way to judge people; I do think that they were really rather horrid sometimes.' She had married

Charles Grant-Dalton (the grandson of Charles Sabine Augustus Thellusson) in 1916 when only 17 years old. She always jokingly claimed that '[h]e had made up his mind to marry me when I was 12 and he was almost 30!', remembering his odd behaviour of peering through the nursery windows to catch a glimpse of her. 'He was always in the nursery, making such a botheration of himself, which made Nanny and then my governess get in a rage "Why can't he have tea in the drawing room like everybody else?"'

Charles died in 1952 and in 1959 Sylvia married his cousin Eustace Foster Grant-Dalton – 'Dear old Eustace, he was such a brave man, he got into all the wars he could; Queen Victoria signed his first commission for the Boer War and he fought in the Kaiser's War and the last war. When he died he left me the house to look after and I haven't left it for a single day.' She grew fond of Brodsworth although never loved it, instead preferring Georgian architecture – 'I don't care for the sentimentality of Victorian times ... the statues, which I call "poor cold ladies" to the children, are not quite my gusto, I'm afraid.' She begged me to take away as many I could carry – woe to my virtuous honesty! Woe too to my honesty in the attics, where dozens of quite beautiful Gothic chairs were on hidden parade!

Never will I forget the magic of being in those great
dusty rooms alone; of the icy temperature throughout
the house and of the boiling oven-like heat of the lone
room which Sylvia used. It was here, when we were
making a BBC film of Brodsworth, that she cried out to
the gardener to bring his shears for her 'scaggy nail'.
I remember us sitting together in the great dark dining
room as a very old maid tottered round, breaking
several glasses as she went, whilst loudly complaining
that if Sylvia had not asked her to come in that day, she
would never have broken them – 'would I now?'!

How sad it was, photographing those rooms –
capturing the glow of the gilded hand-blocked
wallpaper or the shine, despite dust, dirt and decay, of
the original damask covering the furniture and walls –
and feeling that I was recording the house before it
might vanish forever. It certainly did seem as if
Brodsworth was doomed as, thanks to mining
subsidence, poverty and neglect, it was in a parlous
state. Walking through its peeling and crumbling
rooms, along its cold dark corridors, the future looked
bleak – how could there be anything but disaster
ahead? Who could save such a wreck, and if someone
was found, it would surely be robbed of life: at best
stripped clean by the sterile hand of scholarship, at
worst drained of all atmosphere by becoming either a
country house hotel, a conference centre or a country
club. What did the future hold?

One winter's evening I actually stayed at the house.
Having had dinner with Sylvia, I had set off into the
falling snow only to find that my car would not start.
Worse, I had been locked out by Brodsworth's alarming
19th-century security system by which leaden weighted
ropes, when pulled, send iron shutters crashing to the
ground. All the downstairs windows were fitted with
these alarming contraptions and there was therefore no
way of rousing the cook who was stone deaf and,
incidentally, had only one leg. Eventually, after banging
on her window for a good half-hour she let me in.
Upstairs, in a boiling bedroom Sylvia welcomed me
with open arms. Most of the pictures were hanging
skew-whiff by one wire on the walls and the ceiling had
fallen into my bath, filling it to the brim with rubble. It
was to be a sleepless night, as Sylvia, who was also
deaf, was tuned into the World Service at ear-splitting
volume. With a sense of the surreal, I was to find
myself listening to the last hours of the execution of
President Bhutto of Pakistan resounding through those
great empty rooms.

Having spent such strange times at Brodsworth, it
was of course with the greatest apprehension that I
returned years later after English Heritage's restoration
– dreading the lack of the life that I had so loved. A
step through the door though and I was straightaway
engulfed by the old spirit of the place, of that very
particular atmosphere of a house having marched
through time. It is seldom, if ever, that you can with
personal experience say that a house has retained its
romance after its owner has died and it has been
restored and open to the public. This though has
undoubtedly been the case with Brodsworth – with a
restoration that has retained the all-powerful sense of
its past with the shadows of its history still flitting
within its walls – even, I fear, Binkie's, as despite
revolutionary methods of deep-freeze carpet cleaning
she has left a legacy in the air.

If all of this seems too wild a deviation from the pet
cemetery, it is because Sylvia was integral to
Brodsworth's remarkable survival. She dutifully hung
onto the house and gardens for so many years, living
there alone save for her dogs, many of whom are
buried in this cemetery. When she told me where her

old parrot and canine companions were buried, I had to battle through the rampant undergrowth to find them with her quavering voice still ringing in my ears: 'Give my love to my poor old Poll.'

In those dark days I wrote in *An Album of Curious Houses* that the house was in grave peril, that should Sylvia's daughter not want to live there, 'this extraordinary survival of a c.19th country house will have been lost to us forever'; I had not reckoned with English Heritage.

## Glandford, Norfolk

The village of Glandford in Norfolk is an exemplary architectural exercise that was built or rebuilt in its entirety between 1899 and 1906 by Sir Alfred Jodrell in memory of his mother. Nothing has been left to chance. It is picturesque perfection – yet ebullient with colourful variety and good cheer. Flint Flemish gables march forth, edged and detailed with brick, all

beautifully designed and built with forms so lively that they seem to be saluting the passer-by. One tiny little gabled building of the same brilliant hues is the Shell Museum, with its collection of many thousands of shells, fossils, birds' eggs, local archaeological finds and such 'wonders of the world' as the Lord's Prayer carved into an oyster shell.

The scene is now set – such is the village of Glandford. Looming overall from high ground is the church of St Martin's; originally dating from the 13th–15th century, it was described as ruinous in 1730. And in ruins it was to remain for another 170 years until, in 1899, Sir Alfred decided to rebuild it, along with the whole village of Glandford. Messrs Hicks and Charlewood Architects were called in to rebuild St Martin's and be as faithful to the original as possible, while saving whatever old fabric could be built into the body of the new building – the 15th-century arcade stands here to this day. Other than the stained-glass

*Far left: Polly Parrot's tombstone at Brodsworth Hall, South Yorkshire.*

*Near left: Brodsworth's former owner Sylvia Grant-Dalton with one of her canine companions.*

*Below: A pew end at St Martin's Church in Glandford, Norfolk, is carved with a copy of Sir Edwin Landseer's The Old Shepherd's Chief Mourner.*

windows by Kempe and Bryans, it was the woodwork that was to be St Martin's particular strength, with richly worked screen, choir stall and canopies all made of local oak and cedar. Angels stand in niches with shields that are bearing the instruments of the passion. They stand too on high in the nave roof, as well as on the hammer beams over the chancel where they hold musical instruments. Walter Thompson and Frank McGinnity were the carvers and their names – along with the entire force of men who rebuilt the church, from the bricklayers and stone masons to the 'helpers' – are all proudly recorded on a monument. As for the two heroes of the hour, Thompson and McGinnity, they were to carve each other's likenesses and their fine profiles peep past leaves proudly surveying their handiwork to this day. Rarest of all is the Jodrell pew end carved with the image of Sir Edwin Landseer's famed painting *The Old Shepherd's Chief Mourner* of 1837; a mournful scene that has been copied in its every detail. The sheepdog lays his head on his master's plaid and blanket-draped coffin in a modest room with wooden planks for walls – all clearly to be seen in the carving, along with the open wooden door. The shepherd's old wooden chair has been faithfully represented as has his cupboard on the wall. His bed looms in the background. Both representations have a large book – no doubt the Bible – on a little wooden table. Whereas in the painting the shepherd's hat is lying on the floor, in the carving this has been transformed into a wreath, alongside the letters R I P. As with Landseer's painting, the scene on the pew end is revealed past an old threadbare curtain. Little carved Gothic arches on high give a suitably ecclesiastical sense of place, and the whole scene is richly writhed around with ivy carved in deep and detailed relief.

Although Sir Alfred Jodrell decreed that there were to be no monuments in the church except for the one that honours the men who created St Martin's, there is another of a marble angel to his mother and, of course, there is this carving at the end of the pew in which she would sit with her son. After all, the whole church – indeed the whole village – is her memorial.

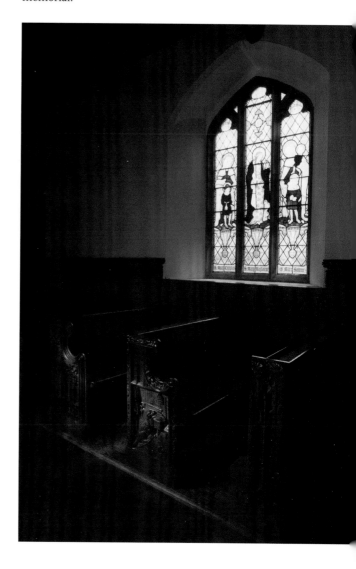

*Right: A white marble memorial stone to an otter hound amidst the picturesque surroundings of Rousham in Oxfordshire.*

## Rousham, Oxfordshire

When the Romantic movement swept through England's gardens, creating compositions that were more akin to the artist's canvas than to the hand of the horticulturalist, it was William Kent – artist, architect and landscape supremo – who was at the helm of this gentle revolution. Having spent 10 years in Rome – where he was known as 'Il Kentino' – he returned to England with the architect Lord Burlington, and together they were to set the new tone. The garden at Rousham is one of the earliest and least altered embodiments of the Picturesque movement to survive, and in the midst of these 25 acres of planned 'natural' beauty, is a memorial stone to an otter hound.

It is to be found in 'Venus Vale', a long and gentle valley framed by trees, down which courses water – through ponds and through two arched and rusticated cascades – to the river. A lead Venus stands atop one of the arches and beneath her is a white marble plaque inscribed to 'RINGWOOD, AN OTTER HOUND OF EXTRAORDINARY SAGACITY'. The inscription continues:

TYRANT OF THE CHERWELL'S FLOOD
COME NOT NEAR THIS SACRED GLOOM
NOR, WITH THY INSULTING BROOD,
DARE POLLUTE MY RINGWOOD'S TOMB.

Another memorial, this time to a cow – more likely than not, the only one in the world – stands near Kent's bovine building designed to house the famous herd of Longhorn cattle (*see* pp 102–3):

FAUSTINA GWYNNE
A COW
DIED 1882. AGED 22.

Faustina was a shorthorn brought to Rousham from Northamptonshire in 1873; she is still a proud feature

Left: A tombstone to a cow at Rousham, Oxfordshire.

Right: This temple-like monument honours a pet Pekinese at Woburn Abbey, Bedfordshire.

## Woburn, Bedfordshire

Alone in a copse in the park at Woburn Abbey there stands a Corinthian-columned temple honouring a pet Pekinese, which was built in 1916 by Mary du Caurroy Russell, 11th Duchess of Bedford. The Pekinese breed had been brought to Europe in 1860 by French and British soldiers who had found them in the Summer Palace after the raid on Peking. As imperial dogs they were the emperor's bodyguards, two to the fore barking his approach, two behind with the hem of the royal robe in their mouths. They had been objects of worship in China for centuries.

The memorial is no mean monument to a Peke. It has a stepped circular base, and six Corinthian columns – carved with decorative bands and linked by benches supported by lions' feet – encircle the tomb. A stone frieze of bows, fruit and flowers carries the dome of wrought-iron work. A bronze effigy of the dog by P V de Kerckhovey lies atop a stone plinth on which are inscribed both his dynastic and familiar names: Che Foo and Wuzzy. We read that he was born in 1904 and died in 1916. On her dog's demise, the duchess had made a desolate entry in her diary: 'My little Che Foo died. He has been my constant companion for over eleven years and a more faithful and devoted one I shall never have.' A memory somewhat clouded by grief as Wuzzy always resolutely refused to be trained to do tricks. The duchess, who relished her rapport with animals, was able to persuade her quantity of Persian or Siamese cats to be photographed as if playing the violin and croquet; Wuzzy, on the other hand, would only go as far as riding on Viking the Shetland pony's back, as well as allowing himself to be pulled along in a tiny carriage drawn by the pony. He was, though, particularly bad tempered. In *The High-Flying Duchess* by Meriel Buxton, the duchess's son Hastings tells all:

of the place, thanks to a painting of her hanging in the house. A huge and handsome brilliant chestnut with white speckles and a table-flat back, she was, though, the terror of local life; a cow who would actually chase anyone that she could down the village street.

Having known this memorial stone for years, it was with shrieks of Eureka! that I discovered her pedigree in the Reverend William Holt Beever's book of the leading shorthorn 'tribes' of her day. Faustina's mother was Flora Gwynne and her father was May Duke. Her grandmother was Fanny Gwynne. Faustina's daughter was called Florence Gwynne and her granddaughter – with the best name of all – was called Fluffy Gwynne. 'The Gwynne Family', wrote Beever, 'having been very prolific of females, it were obviously beyond the limits of my undertaking, to ... trace ... their genealogical tree. Those branches only which I find of celebrity do I include....' Little did the good reverend know of the extent of Faustina's celebrity. Her horns are still at Rousham, where beautiful Longhorn cattle are still bred.

He was the most crotchety aggressive little brute, and even members of the household were not immune from attack ... he made a practice of assaulting me whenever I kissed my mother good-night and also went for the footman when he removed the cloth from the table ... All visitors were anathema to him and on first arrival were attacked with fury. Mr Findlay, an old Indian friend of my parents ... used to be much amused by Che Foo's ferocity ... There is a quaint Chinese description of the principal attributes desirable in a Pekinese ... One ... is that 'he should never fail to bite the foreign devil' ... 'Ah, little man,' Mr Findlay would say to Che Foo, 'you never fail to bite the foreign devil, do you?' – and Che Foo, turning a baleful eye upon him, would growl an emphatic assent.

Such is the stuff for smiles – but the Duchess of Bedford should be judged with serious admiration. Born Mary du Caurroy Tribe, daughter of the Archdeacon of Lahore, she met and married Lord Herbrand Russell when he was Aide de Camp to the Viceroy of India. The dukedom and Woburn were inherited unexpectedly and, with pink-velvet clad footmen behind every chair, she sprang forth into the world becoming a renowned ornithologist and mountaineer. She was also one of the best shots in the country and known as the 'Annie Oakley of Britain'. Nor was that the end of it, because she was a canoeist, ice skater, skilled mechanic, artist and photographer and, most importantly of all, the founder of two hospitals, one in a house at Woburn, the other built from scratch nearby. Having taught herself radiology and radiotherapy, she ran the X-ray department as well as acting as theatre sister during operations, sometimes even performing minor operations herself.

Then, aged 61 years old, she started to fly and thereafter became known as the 'Flying Duchess' thanks to her daredevil and record-breaking flights to India and South Africa. She died aged 71 when attempting to clock up 200 hours of solo flying time; having misread her compass in a snowstorm, she flew out to sea in her Gypsy Moth over Norfolk and was never seen again. Thus was life led by the 'premier aviatrix' who built this temple to her dog.

## Stanway, Gloucestershire

TO THE FRAGRANT MEMORY OF

OLD SMELLY

DIED 1980 AGED 16

A DOG

ALTHOUGH BY ITS FIERCE BLOOD EASILY SMELLY

YET BY ITS OWN SMELLINESS

WAS IT SMELLIER THAN ITS TRIBE

THIS MONUMENT SUCH AS IT IS

JAMES NEIDPATH MASTER

AND HER GREAT-GRAND-DAUGHTER

LITTLE SMELLY

AND THE SCULPTOR RORY YOUNG

HERE THEREFORE IN PIETY CAUSED TO BE ERECTED

IN THE YEAR OF DOGKIND'S SALVATION

MCMLXXXIV

In 1984 James Neidpath commissioned the sculptor Rory Young to carve this memorial to Smelly, his golden Labrador. She stands *en couchant* on either side of the Latin inscription, beneath a tin of PAD ('Prolongs Active Death') being borne aloft by angels' wings. The stone is Hornton blue mudstone from nearby Edgehill. The oval is of blue Welsh slate. Smelly's death mask looks out below.

Below: Our dog Obadiah – 'Ob' – ponders mortality beside
the obelisk to fellow lurcher Flint in the garden at Hedgerley
in Buckinghamshire.

*Below: Our dog Obadiah – 'Ob' – ponders mortality beside the obelisk to fellow lurcher Flint in the garden at Hedgerley in Buckinghamshire.*

## Hedgerley, Buckinghamshire

Flint was a grey-brindle, rough-haired, whiskered
lurcher who died when he was only two years old after
a much too short but happy life. He was killed at the
streaking gallop while chasing a muntjac after being
pierced straight through his lungs by a long thin spear
of a stick which left barely a mark. He did not die
immediately and we found him walking with an odd
gait through the woods. No human could have had
better medical treatment – few as good. Having
survived an operation lasting several hours, his heart
gave out and the ambulance, purring at the door to
whisk him to a waiting veterinary team in London, was
told that it was over – all this paid for by the insurance.
Woe betide not being insured.

I was making a film about memorials to animals at
the time; what could have been a more soothing salve
or more spot-on suitable tribute than to commission a
monument to Flint? Who, though, could possibly pay
for it? I am in constant touch with Harriet Frazer
whose excellent organisation, Memorials by Artists, was
founded to put the bereaved in touch with the most
suitable local craftsmen for their loved one's memorial.
It is thanks to her advice and tireless slogging through
diocesan boards and local councils in pursuit of
planning permission that there are now many
hundreds of contemporary memorials beautifying
Britain today. What joy it is to once again have one's
spirits sent soaring by commemorative art.

Eureka! She was undoubtedly the one to go to for
advice. She told me of Martin Cook, local fourth
generation master mason, whose father, grandfather
and great-grandfather before him were responsible for
what, in my view, are some of the finest sepulchral
artistic works in England at Kensal Green Cemetery in
London. He had just finished a Falklands War

memorial for High Wycombe and had some stone left over, which he would be delighted to make into an obelisk, for a song, for Flint and the film. So it came to be that a handsome monument was created, on which he plied his craft, incising the letters FLINT from top to bottom of the stone. It stands at the bottom of the garden of the 1846 Gothic and diaper-brick Old Rectory, at Hedgerley, where I have lived for many years. As always when a dog died, we had a small funeral ceremony – as always reading the lines of Ecclesiates, 3:19: 'For that which befalleth the sons of men befalleth beasts; even one thing befalleth them: as the one dieth, so dieth the other; yea, they have all one breath; so that a man hath no pre-eminence above a beast: for all is vanity.'

The misery of missing Flint remained raw. Weeks later when working in the Caribbean with Auberon Waugh – his last job before he died and we had been together on his first job 40 years before – that king of cynics, without a shade of that renowned cynicism, knowing that we were mourning for a dog sympathised in a quiet voice: 'I know, I am so sorry, bereavement is sheer hell.'

We were in good company – in 1881 Matthew Arnold wrote the 20-verse poem *Geist's Grave* on his grief at his dachshund's death; a few verses are reproduced here:

Four years! – and didst thou stay above
The ground, which hides thee now, but four?
And all that life, and all that love,
Were crowded, Geist! into no more?

Only four years those winning ways,
Which make me for thy presence yearn,
Call'd us to pet thee or to praise,
Dear little friend! at every turn?

...

That liquid, melancholy eye,
From whose pathetic, soul-fed springs
Seem'd urging the Virgilian cry,
The sense of tears in mortal things –

...

We stroke thy broad brown paws again
We bid thee to thy vacant chair,
We greet thee by the window-pane,
We hear thy scuffle on the stair.

We see the flaps of thy large ears
Quick rais'd to ask which way we go;
Crossing the frozen lake, appears
Thy small black figure on the snow!

...

Yet, fondly zealous for thy fame,
Even to a date beyond our own
We strive to carry down thy name,
By mounded turf, and graven stone.

We lay thee, close within our reach,
Here, where the grass is smooth and warm,
Between the holly and the beech,
Where oft we watch'd thy couchant form,

Asleep, yet lending half an ear
To travellers on the Portsmouth road; –
There build we thee, O guardian dear,
Mark'd with a stone, thy last abode!

Then some, who through this garden pass,
When we too, like thyself, are clay,
Shall see thy grave upon the grass,
And stop before the stone, and say:

*People who lived here long ago*
*Did by this stone, it seems, intend*
*To name for future times to know*
*The dachs-hound, Geist, their little friend.*

## Hedgerley, Buckinghamshire

This design is for a monument to Prickle, our beloved dog who died, aged 16, on 13 December 1984. It is planned that one day it will stand at the bottom of the garden of the Old Rectory in Hedgerley, Buckinghamshire, where she lived for the last years of her life. The monument will be 9½ft high, 4ft wide and 2ft deep and made of reconstituted Bath stone. Along with the crockets and pinnacles – in sympathy with her name – there will be four gargoyles of canine weepers cast in bronze finished resin. Prickle herself, also cast in bronze resin, will sit on a tasselled cushion, prepared to meet her master on Judgement Day. So says my friend Alan Dodd, who designed the monument (inspired by the tomb of St Peter Martyr at St Eustorgio in Milan), and so, plaintively, say I. With the drawing framed and on proud display indoors, this, maybe, is how it will have to stay – after all, many an important architectural scheme has suffered the same fate.

Prickle was bought in 1968 in Shepherd's Bush Market for 10 shillings, and never was any money better spent. She was only six weeks old and we had no idea where she came from, but it must have been from circus stock for every day, many times a day, she would 'canter' round in a circus-size circle, stopping to pirouette on her hind legs at four opposite points of the 'ring'. Who was the ringmaster whose ghost was still cracking his whip over Prickle?

Prickle is already honoured in the house, leading the roll-call of departed dogs on a wooden tablet surrounded by a 10ft-high Gothic wooden frame emblazoned with a palm-bearing gilded angel. Under the gilded words 'JOYFULLY BARKING IN THE HEAVENLY CHORUS' are all their names: Clover and Thistle, Violet and Florence, Hops and Flint. Prickle and Thistle are also commemorated over the door with their names on a painted banner stating: 'HE WHO SOWS THISTLES SHALL REAP PRICKLES'. Violet and Florence, both dachshunds, have their coat of arms painted on the wall – quartered with rabbits, paw-prints, bones and a rampant dachshund, like everything else all gloomily gilded. All their paw-prints are embedded and named, Hollywood-style, in the floor.

# BIBLIOGRAPHY

Adam, W 1811 *Vitruvius Scoticus; Being a Collection of Plans, Elevations and Sections of Public Buildings, Noblemen's and Gentlemen's Houses in Scotland*. Edinburgh: A Black

Adlam, D 2002 *The Enigmatic Fifth Duke of Portland*. Welbeck: The Pineapple Press for the Harley Foundation

Allan, G 1776 *A Sketch of the Life & Character of Richard Trevor...Bishop of Durham. With a Particular Account of His Last Illness...*. Darlington: Darnton & Smith

Anon 1896 'Deeds that won the Empire'. *Evening Post* (Putanga, New Zealand)

Anon 1914 'Small country buildings of to-day. The stables at Manderston'. *Country Life* (4 Jul, supplement), 9

Anson, E 'Letters, Nov 1749' *Mainly Elizabeth, Lady Anson to Thomas Anson* (Staffordshire Record Office, D615/P(S)/1/3/10a)

Archer, M 2006 'Rossetti's wombat: In the March 1965 issue, Michael Archer wrote about the menagerie that Dante Gabriel Rossetti kept at his house in Cheyne Walk. It included a wombat, which inspired numerous stories'. *Apollo* (Apr)

Ashmole, E 1927 *The Diary and Will of Elias Ashmole*. Oxford: Old Ashmolean Reprints

Aslet, C 1982 *The Last Country Houses*. New Haven and London: Yale University Press

Aslet, C 1986 'Lodge Park, Gloucestershire'. *Country Life* (13 Mar), 630–3

Ball, F E 1903 *A History of the County of Dublin: The People, Parishes and Antiquities from the Earliest Times to the Close of the Eighteenth Century*, Vol 2 (6 vols, 1902–20). Dublin: Alex Thom & Co

Baring-Gould, S 1876 *The Vicar of Morwenstow: A Life of Robert Stephen Hawker*. London: Henry S King

Baring-Gould, S 1908 *Devonshire Characters and Strange Events*. London: John Lane

Bechstein, J M 1845 *The Natural History of Cage Birds: Their Management, Habits, Food, Diseases, Treatment, Breeding, and the Methods of Catching Them*. London: W S Orr and Co

Beever, W H 1881 *An Alphabetical Arrangement of the Leading Shorthorn Tribes*. London: J Thornton

Blome, R 1686 *Gentleman's Recreation*, 2 pts. Longon: S Rotcroft

Blunt, W 1976 *The Ark in the Park: The Zoo in the Nineteenth Century*. London: Hamilton

Boswell, J 1950 *Boswell's London Journal 1762–1763* (with an introduction and notes by F A Pottle). London: Heinemann

Bradford, E 2008 *Headingley: 'This Pleasant Rural Village': Clues to the Past*. Huddersfield: Northern Heritage Publications

Brendon, P 1975 *Hawker of Morwenstow: Portrait of a Victorian Eccentric*. London: J Cape

Briggs, M S 1953 *The English Farmhouse*. London: B T Batsford

Brisby, C 1998–99 'Louisa, Marchioness of Waterford: A feminist intervention in the perception of art?'. *Woman's Art Journal* **19** no 2 (Autumn 1998–Winter 1999), 17–23

Burritt, E 1864 *A Walk from London to John O'Groats*, London: Sampson Low, Son & Marston

Burritt, E 1865 *A Walk from London to Land's End and Back*. London: Sampson Low, Son & Marston

Burritt, E 1879 *Elihu Burritt; A Memorial Volume Containing a Sketch of His Life and Labors, with Selections from His Writings and Lectures, and Extracts from His Private Journals in Europe and America*. New York: D Appleton & Co

Burton, I A 1893 *The Life of Captain Sir Richard F Burton*, Vol 1. London: Chapman & Hall

Butler, C 1609 *The Feminine Monarchie*. Oxford: Joseph Barnes

Buxton, M 2008 *The High-Flying Duchess: Mary du Caurroy Bedford, 1865–1937*. Woodperry Books

Buzas, S 1994 *Sir John Soane's Museum, London*. Tübingen: Wasmuth

Calvert, F and West, W 1830 *Picturesque Views and Descriptions of Cities, Towns, Castles, Mansions, and Other Objects of Interesting Feature, in Staffordshire*. Birmingham: William Emans

Cavendish-Bentinck, W (6th Duke of Portland) 1937 *Men, Women and Things: Memories of the Duke of Portland*. London: Faber and Faber

Chambers, W 1757 *Designs for Chinese Buildings, Furniture, Dresses, Machines and Utensils*. London: W Chambers

Childe-Pemberton, W S 1925 *The Earl Bishop: The Life of Frederick Hervey, Bishop of Derry, Earl of Bristol*, 2 vols. London: Hurst & Blackett

Clifford, C 1585 *The Schoole of Horsemanship*. London

Climenson, E J (ed) 1899 *Passages from the Diaries of Mrs Philip Lybbe Powys of Hardwick House, Oxon. AD 1756 to 1808*. London: Longmans, Green & Co

Cobbett, W 1885 *Rural Rides*. London: Reeves & Turner

Collins, G E 1902 *History of the Brocklesby Hounds, 1700–1901*. London: Sampson Low & Co

Compton, W B (6th Marquis of Northampton) 1930 *History of the Comptons of Compton Wynyates*. London: Bodley Head

Conner, P 1979 *Oriental Architecture in the West*. London: Thames and Hudson

Constable, J 1964 *John Constable's Correspondence, II: Early Friends and Maria Bicknell (Mrs Constable)* (ed with an introduction and notes by R B Beckett). Ipswich: Suffolk Records Society

Cooke, A O 1920 *A Book of Dovecotes*. London and Edinburgh: Foulis

Cooper, J 1983 *Animals in War*. London: Heinemann

Cooper, N, *Simon of the Amethyst, 1999–2001*, http://www.nickcooper.org.uk/moggies/simon/simon/htm

Crane, E 1999 *The World History of Beekeeping and Honey Hunting*. London: Duckworth

Crook, J M and Port, M H 1973 *The History of the King's Works, Vol 6: 1782–1851*. London: HMSO

Dale, T F 1899 *The History of the Belvoir Hunt*. London: Archibald Constable & Co

Darley, G 2006 *John Evelyn: Living for Ingenuity*. New Haven and London: Yale University Press

Dixon, E S 1851 *The Dovecote and the Aviary: Being Sketches of the Natural History of Pigeons and Other Domestic Birds in a Captive State: With Hints for Their Management*. London: John Murray

*DNB: Oxford Dictionary of National Biography* (online)

Drummond, C (16th Baroness Strange) n.d. *The Gardens of Megginch Castle*. Privately published pamphlet (mid-20th century)

Duncan, M 1995 'Saints' blood and pale ice pink'. *Frieze Magazine* 21 (Mar–Apr)

Du Prey, P 1978 'Je n'oublieray jamais': John Soane and Downhill'. *Quarterly Bulletin of the Irish Georgian Society* XXI, nos 3 & 4 (Jul & Dec)

Edgcumbe, R (ed) 1913 *The Diary of Frances Lady Shelley 1787–1817*. London: John Murray

Eller, I 1841 *The History of Belvoir Castle, From the Norman Conquest to the Nineteenth Century*. London: R Tyas

Evelyn, H 1915 *The History of the Evelyn Family: With a Special Memoir of William John Evelyn*. London: Eveleigh Nash

Evelyn, J 1901 *The Diary of John Evelyn*, 2 vols (ed from the original manuscript by W Bray). London: M Walter Dunne

Fernand, D 2007 'The truth about the man with no face'. *The Sunday Times*, 25 Feb (http://entertainment.timesonline.co.uk/tol/arts_and_entertainment/visual_arts/article1417261.ece)

Fisher, R 1763 *Heart of Oak, the British Bulwark. Shewing Reasons for Paying Greater Attention to the Propagation of Oak Timber*. London: J Johnson

Forbes, A 1894 'The Duke of Wellington's Charger "Copenhagen"'. *Tuapeka Times*, (Putanga, New Zealand; Aug–Sep 1894)

Fowler, J K 1892 *Echoes of Old Country Life: Being Recollections of Sports, Politics, and Farming in the Good Old Times*. London: E Arnold

Fowler, J K 1894 *Recollections of Old Country Life, Social, Political, Sporting & Agricultural*. London: Longmans & Co

Furnivall, F J (ed) 1890 *Robert Laneham's Letter*. London: New Shakespeare Society

Gandy, J 1805 *The Rural Architect: Consisting of Various Designs for Country Buildings, Accompanied with Ground Plans, Estimates and Descriptions*. London: John Harding

Gaunt, W 1943 *The Pre-Raphaelite Dream*. London: The Reprint Society

Gayford, M 2007 'Looking down on design'. *Apollo* (Mar), 86–7

Gillespie, R 1879 *Round About Falkirk*. Glasgow: Dunn & Wright

Girouard, M 1963 'Arcadian retreats for the chase: Tudor and Stuart hunting lodges'. *Country Life* (26 Sep), 736–9

Girouard, M 1971 *The Victorian Country House*. Oxford: Clarendon Press

Girouard, M 1981 *The Return to Camelot: Chivalry and the English Gentleman*. New Haven and London: Yale University Press

Girouard, M 2008 *Rushton Triangular Lodge*. London: English Heritage

Gower, R (Lord) 1884 *My Reminiscences*, 3 edn. London: Kegan Paul

Greville, C 1938 *The Greville Memoirs, 1814–1860*, Vol 2 (Strachey, L and Fulford, R, eds). London: Macmillan & Co

Grisone, F 1550 *Gli Ordini di Cavalcare*. Naples

Guinness, D and Ryan, W 1971 *Irish Houses & Castles*. London: Thames and Hudson

Hamilton-Williams, D 1993 *Waterloo, New Perspectives, the Great Battle Reappraised*. London: Arms & Armour

Hare, A J C 1900 *The Story of My Life*, Vol 5. London: George Allen

Harper-Bill, C, Rawcliffe, C and Wilson, R G (eds) 2002 *East Anglia's History: Studies in Honour of Norman Scarfe*. Woodbridge: Boydell Press in association with the Centre of East Anglian Studies, University of East Anglia

Harris, E 1990 *British Architectural Books and Writers*. Cambridge: Cambridge University Press

Harris, E 2006 'No Fishy Tale. Kedleston Fishing Room'. *Apollo* (Apr), 23–6

Harris, E 2007 *The Country Houses of Robert Adam: From the archives of Country Life*. London: Aurum Press

Haslam, R 1979 *The Buildings of Wales: Powys (Montgomeryshire, Radnorshire, Breconshire)*. Harmondsworth: Penguin and Cardiff: University of Wales Press

Hibbert, C 1998 *Waterloo: Napoleon's Last Campaign*. Ware: Wordsworth Editions Ltd

Hissey, J J 1891 *Across England in a Dog-Cart from London to St Davids and Back*. London: Bentley & Son

Hobhouse, H 1983 *Prince Albert: His Life and Work*. London: Hamilton

Hunt, J D and Willis, P 1988 *The Genius of the Place: The English Landscape Garden 1620–1820*. Cambridge, MA: MIT Press

Hussey, C 1956 'Belvoir Castle, Leicestershire'. *Country Life* (13 Dec, 1,402–5; 20 Dec, 1,456–9; 27 Dec, 1,500–3)

Hussey, C 1961 'Milton, Northamptonshire'. *Country Life* (18 May, 1,148; 25 May, 1,210; 1 Jun, 1,270)

Hussey, C 1966 'Biddick Hall, Durham'. *Country Life* (28 Apr, 1,016; 5 May, 1,082)

Hutchinson, W 1794 *The History of the County of Cumberland, and Some Places Adjacent etc*. Carlisle: F Jollie

Jeffery, R 2007 *Discovering Tong: Its History, Myths and Curiosities*. Tong, Shifnal: Robert Jeffery

Jekyll, G 1918 *Garden Ornament*. London: Country Life

Jones, B 1953 *Follies and Grottoes*. London: Constable & Co

Jones, J and Jones, M 2002 *Wentworth Woodhouse Gardens: An Illustrated History*. Rotherham: Garden Tree Publications

Kipling, R 1934 *Collected Dog Stories*. London: Macmillan & Co

Kisling, N K (ed) 2000 *Zoo and Aquarium History. Ancient Animal Collections to Zoological Gardens*. Boca Raton and London: CRC Press

Lambton, L 1985 *Beastly Buildings: The National Trust Book of Architecture for Animals*. London: Jonathan Cape Ltd

Lambton, L 1988 *An Album of Curious Houses*. London: Chatto & Windus

*The Landmark Trust Handbook*, 23 edn. (The handbook can also be accessed at http://www.landmarktrust.org.uk/handbook/.)

Langstroth, L L 2004 *Langstroth's Hive and Honey-Bee: The Classic Beekeeper's Manual* (First pub as *A Practical Treatise on the Hive and the Honey-Bee*, Philadelphia). Mineola, NY: Dover

Lightoler, T 1762 *The Gentleman and Farmer's Architect*. London: Robert Sayer

Llanover, Lady (ed) 1861 *The Autobiography and Correspondence of Mary Granville, Mrs. Delany*, Vol 2. London: Richard Bentley

Lonsdale, H 1872 *The Worthies of Cumberland: The Howards*. London: George Routledge

Loudon, J C 1833 *An Encyclopaedia of Cottage, Farm and Villa Architecture and Furniture*. London: Longman

Lugar, R 1811 *Plans and Views of Buildings, Executed in England and Scotland, in the Castellated and Other Styles*. London: For J Taylor at the Architectural Library

Lyell, J 1887 *Fancy Pigeons: Containing Full Directions for the Breeding and Management of Fancy Pigeons, with Descriptions of Every Known Variety*, 3 edn. London: L Upcott Gill

Macaulay, J 1975 *The Gothic Revival: 1745–1845*. Glasgow: Blackie

Mackenzie, E 1825 *An Historical, Topographical and Descriptive View of the County of Northumberland*, 2 vols. Newcastle upon Tyne

Markham, G 1607 *Cavelarice, or the English Horseman: Contayning all the Arte of Horsemanship...*. London: Printed for Edward White

Miers, M 2000 'Lodge Park, Gloucestershire'. *Country Life* (18 May), 82–5

Montgomery-Massingberd, H and Sykes, C S 1994 *Great Houses of England and Wales*. London: Laurence King

Moore, D L 1974 *Lord Byron: Accounts Rendered*. London: J Murray

Moore, T 1830 *Letters and Journals of Lord Bryon: With Notices of His Life*, 2 vols. London

Moore, T 1832 *The Works of Lord Byron: With His Letters and Journals and His Life*, Vol 7. London: John Murray

Moss, M 2002 *The 'Magnificent Castle' of Culzean and the Kennedy Family*. Edinburgh: Edinburgh University Press

Nares, G 1956 'Dropmore, Buckinghamshire: The home of Viscount Kemsley'. *Country Life* (11 Oct, 772–5; 18 Oct, 834–7)

Nash, J 1820–6 *The Royal Pavilion at Brighton*. London: John Nash

Nash, J 1991 *Views of the Royal Pavilion* (introduction and commentary by G Jackson-Stops). London: Pavilion

National Trust 1995 *Ham House, Surrey*. London: National Trust

National Trust 2002 *Lodge Park, Gloucestershire*. London: National Trust

Nichols, J 1815 *Literary Anecdotes of the 18th Century*, Vol 9. London: Nichols, Son and Bentley

Nichols, J 1823 *The Progresses and Public Processions of Queen Elizabeth*, 3 vols. London: J Nichols & Son

Nunn, P G 1981–2 'Ruskin's patronage of women artists'. *Woman's Art Journal* **2** no 2 (Autumn 1981–Winter 1982), 8–13

Paine, T 1791 *Rights of Man*. London: J S Jordan

Paston, G (compiler) 1900 *Mrs Delany (Mary Granville): A Memoir 1700–1788.* New York: E P Dutton and London: Grant Richards

Peck, F 1740 *Memoirs of the Life and Actions of Oliver Cromwell.* London

Pedrick, G 1964 *Life with Rossetti, or No Peacocks Allowed: A Biographical Study of Henry Treffry Dunn and Dante Gabriel Rossetti.* London: Macdonald

Pevsner, N *The Buildings of England* series

Pevsner, N 1959 *The Buildings of England: North Somerset and Bristol* (reprinted 1990). London: Penguin

Pevsner, N 1974 *The Buildings of England: Staffordshire* (reprinted 1990). London: Penguin

Pevsner, N 1986 *The Buildings of England: Derbyshire* (revd by E Williamson, reprinted 1993). London: Penguin

Pevsner, N 1992 *The Buildings of England: Leicestershire and Rutland* (revd by E Williamson and G K Brandwood). London: Penguin

Pevsner, N and Hubbard, E 1971 *The Buildings of England: Cheshire* (reprinted 1990). London: Penguin

Pevsner, N, Williamson, E and Brandwood, G K 1994 *The Buildings of England: Buckinghamshire.* London: Penguin

Sherwood, J and Pevsner, N 1974 *The Buildings of England: Oxfordshire* (reprinted 1979). Harmondsworth: Penguin

Pillement, J 1762 *The Ladies Amusement; or Whole Art of Japanning Made Easy* (facsim edn Ceramic Book Co 1966)

Pindar, P 1816 *The Works of Peter Pindar*, Vol 3. London: Walker & Edwards

Plaw, J 1795 *Ferme Ornée; or Rural Improvements. A Series of Domestic and Ornamental Designs.* London: I & J Taylor

Pliny the Elder 1850 *The Natural History of Pliny*, Vol 3 (trans by J Bostock and H T Riley). London: Henry G Bohn

Powers, A 2000 'The Twentieth Century Society comes of age'. *Context* **66** (Jun), 25–6

Priestley, J B 1969 *The Prince of Pleasure and His Regency, 1811–20.* London: Heinemann

Pückler-Muskau, H 1832 *Tour in England, Ireland and France: In the Years 1826, 1827, 1828 and 1829*, 4 vols. London: E Wilson

Pückler-Muskau, H 1957 *A Regency Visitor: The English Tour of Prince Pückler-Muskau Described in his Letters 1826–1828* (edited with an introduction by E M Butler). London: Collins

Ransome, H 1937 *The Sacred Bee in Ancient Times and Folklore.* London: G Allen & Unwin

Repton, H 1808 *Designs for the Pavillion at Brighton.* London: Printed for J C Stadley

Rhodes, J K and Stanford, A 2004 *Beaufort Court – Zero Emissions Building* (Ovaltine Egg Farm restoration) http://www.2004ewec.info/files/23_1400_juliarhodes_01.pdf

Robinson, J M 1983 *Georgian Model Farms: A Study of Decorative and Model Farm Buildings in the Age of Improvement, 1700–1846.* Oxford: Clarendon Press

Rossetti, D G 1895 *Dante Gabriel Rossetti. His Family-Letters With a Memoir by William Michael Rossetti*, 2 vols. London: Ellis and Elvey

Routh, M J (ed) 1823 *Bishop Burnet's History of His Own Time*, Vol 1. Oxford: Clarendon Press

Russell, M 1829 *Life of Oliver Cromwell* (from *Constable's Miscellany*, vols 47 and 48). Edinburgh: Constable & Co

Russell, M 1968 *The Flying Duchess: The Diaries and Letters of Mary, Duchess of Bedford* (edited and with an introduction by John, Duke of Bedford). London: Macdonald & Co

Rybot, D 1972 *It Began Before Noah.* London: Michael Joseph

Scott, W 1894 *Redgauntlet.* London: John C Nimmo

Sitwell, E 1971 *English Eccentrics.* Harmondsworth: Penguin

Smith, D 1931 *Pigeon Cotes and Dove Houses of Essex.* London: Simpkin Marshall

Soane, J 1778 *Designs in Architecture; Consisting of Plans, Elevations, and Sections, for Temples, Baths, Cassines, Pavilions, Garden-Seats, Obelisks, and Other Buildings.* London: Printed for I Taylor

Soane, Sir J 1835 *Description of the House and Museum on the North Side of Lincoln's Inn Fields, the Residence of Sir John Soane.* London: Privately printed

Stamp, G 2007 'Surreal recall.' *Apollo* (Jul–Aug), 80–1

Staughton, O and Upton, J 1981 *Latimer: A History of Our Village*, revd edn. Price Waterhouse Cooper (sold in aid of Latimer Church)

Stroud, Dorothy 1961 *The Architecture of Sir John Soane. With an Introduction by Professor Henry-Russell Hitchcock.* London: The Studio

Summerson, J 1980 *The Life and Works of John Nash Architect.* London: Allen & Unwin

Switzer, S 1715 *The Nobleman, Gentleman, and Gardener's Recreation.* London: B Barker

Symes M 2005 'Flintwork, freedom and fantasy: The landscape at West Wycombe Park, Buckinghamshire'. *Garden History* **33** no 1 (Summer), 1–30

Tait, A A 1968 'William Adam at Chatelherault'. *The Burlington Magazine* **111** no 783, 316–25

Taylor, D 1986 'West Riding Amusement Parks and Gardens'. *Yorkshire Archaeological Journal* **58**, 179–94

Thomas, K 1983 *Man and the Natural World: Changing Attitudes in England 1500–1800.* London: Allan Lane

Timpson, T 'Abolition's "unexpected hero", *BBC News online*, 23 Mar 2007, http://news.bbc.co.uk/1/hi/uk/6317479.stm

Toplady, A 1837 *The Works of Augustus Toplady. Printed Verbatim From the First Edition of his Works 1794.* London

Toynbee, P (ed) 1927–8 'Horace Walpole's journals of visits to country seats &c'. *Walpole Society* **16**, 9–80

Trumble, A 2003 'Rossetti's Wombat: A Pre-Raphaelite obsession in Victorian England'. (Lecture at the National Library of Australia, Canberra, 16 Apr 2003; http://www.nla.gov.au/grants/haroldwhite/papers/atrumble.html)

Turberville, A S 1939 *A History of Welbeck Abbey and its Owners, Vol 2: 1755–1879*. London: Faber

Turner, E S 1964 *All Heaven in a Rage*. London: Michael Joseph

Urquhart, D 2007 *The Ladies of Londonderry: Women and Political Patronage* London: I B Tauris

Varro, M T 1912 *Varro on Farming* (*Rerum Rusticarum*, trans by Lloyd Storr-Best). London: G Bell

Wallace, C 1967 *West Wycombe Park, Buckinghamshire*, rev edn. London: Country Life Ltd for the National Trust

Wallace, R 1893 *The Canary Book: Containing Full Directions for the Breeding, Rearing and Management of Canaries and Canary Mules, Cage Making, Etc.*, 3 edn. London: L Upcott Gill

Walpole, H 1903 'To Horace Mann, August 2, 1750'. *The Letters of Horace Walpole, Fourth Earl of Orford*, Vol III (ed with notes and indices by P Toynbee). Oxford: Clarendon Press

Walpole, H 1904 'To George Montagu, June 11, 1770'. *The Letters of Horace Walpole, Fourth Earl of Orford*, Vol VII (ed with notes and indices by P Toynbee). Oxford: Clarendon Press

Walton, I and Cotton, C 1897 *The Compleat Angler* (ed with an introduction by R le Gallienne). London: John Lane

Watkin, D 1982 *The English Vision: The Picturesque in Architecture, Landscape, and Garden Design*. London: J Murray

Wessex Archaeology 2007 *Swallowfield Park, Berkshire: Landscape and Building Study*. (Online report, July 2007, http://www.scribd.com/doc/17775804/Swallow-Field-Park-Berkshire)

Wilmot, M 1935 *More Letters from Martha Wilmot: Impressions of Vienna* (ed with an introduction and notes by the Marchioness of Londonderry and H M Hyde). London: Macmillan

Wood, A à 1691–2 *Athenae Oxonienses*. London: Thomas Bennett

Wood, J G 1874 *Man and Beast Here and Hereafter*, 2 vols. London: Daldy, Isbister & Co

Woolrych, H W 1827 *Memoirs of the Life of Judge Jeffreys Sometime Lord Chancellor of England*. London: Colburn

Worsley, G 2004 *The British Stable*. New Haven and London: Yale University Press

Wraxall, N W 1836 *Posthumous Memoirs of His Own Time*, 3 vols. London: Richard Bentley

Wright, T 1755–8 *Arbours and Grottos, With a Catalogue of Wright's Works in Architecture and Garden Design by Eileen Harris* (facsim edn Scolar Press 1979)

Wright, T 1911 *The Lives of the British Hymn Writers. Vol 2: Augustus M Toplady and Contemporary Hymn Writers*. London: Farncombe and Sons

Young, A 1770 *A Six Months' Tour Through the North of England*. London: W Strahan

## Websites consulted

www.archive.org (consultation of archive and out-of-copyright books)

www.bbc.co.uk/ww2peopleswar/stories/11/a4252411.shtml (Ovaltine Egg Farm)

www.beaufortcourt.com/about-beaufort-court/history.aspx (Ovaltine Egg Farm)

www.berkshirehistory.com/ (David Nash Ford's Royal Berkshire History)

www.english-heritage.org.uk/upload/pdf/brodsworth_gardens.pdf (Information for teachers on Brodsworth)

http://flyboy18.tripod.com/early.html (*Early History 1799–1816. Extracts from the Naval Chronicle*)

www.follies.org.uk (Folly Fellowship e-Bulletin, Issue 15, July 2008 (Horton))

www.fountainsabbey.org.uk (Fountains Abbey)

www.hortonpark.org.uk/2.html (Horton Park Conservation Group)

www.jstor.org (JSTOR 'Trusted archives for scholarship')

www.mybrightonandhove.org.uk (Archive photographs of Brighton)

www.nationaltrust.org.uk/seatondelavalhall (Seaton Delaval)

www.netherbyestate.co.uk (Netherby)

www.northernnewfoundlandclub.org.uk/boatswain.html (Lord Byron's dog, Newstead Abbey)

www.pdsa.org.uk (History of the PDSA)

www.penicuikhouse.co.uk (The Penicuik House Project)

www.pigeoncote.com (Fancy pigeons)

www.praxis.co.uk/credebyron (Crede Byron)

www.purr-n-fur.org.uk (Cats)

www.Questia.com (Online library)

www.readytogoebooks.com/LB-dog-P63.html (Lord Byron's dog, Newstead Abbey)

www.silvermerehaven.co.uk (Silvermere Haven pet cemetery)

www.turtlebunbury.com (Turtle Bunbury, writer and historian on Ireland)

www.waddesdon.org.uk/aviary/aviary_history.html (Waddesdon aviary)

www.willingtonvillage.co.uk/Pages/history.asp (Willington dovecote and stables)

www.wynyardhall.co.uk (Wynyard Hall Country House Hotel)

# INDEX

Page references in **bold** refer to illustrations.

IN MEMORY OF MY FATHER

*This photograph shows the dog kennel in his house,
the Villa Cetinale, near Siena, Italy, where he lived
for most of the last years of his life.*